EARTH SCIENCE MADE SIMPLE

Edward F. Albin, Ph.D.
Assistant Professor of Astronomy
Agnes Scott College
and
Astronomer/Planetary Geologist
Fernbank Science Center
with
Frances Chamberlain

Illustrated by Scott Nurkin

BOOKS

A Made Simple Book
Broadway Books
New York

Produced by The Philip Lief Group, Inc.

PRINTED IN THE UNITED STATES OF AMERICA.

Produced by The Philip Lief Group, Inc.
Managing Editors: Judy Linden, Jill Korot.
Design: Annie Jeon.

Library of Congress Cataloging-in-Publication Data
Albin, Edward F.
    Earth science made simple: a clear introduction to the science of our planet / by Edward
F. Albin with Frances Chamberlain: produced by The Philip Lief Group, Inc.
        p. cm. — (Made simple)
    Includes index.
    ISBN 0-7679-1703-0
    1. Earth sciences. I. Chamberlain, Frances. II. Philip Lief Group. III. Title. IV. Made
simple (Broadway books)

QE28.A38 2004
550—dc22
                                                         2004054438

10 9 8 7 6 5 4 3 2 1

For Nancie & Lauren

ACKNOWLEDGMENTS

Earth Science is a broad field of endeavor—covering many distinct disciplines within the realm of science. To be sure, writing a popular book on the subject is not an easy task. Without the assistance of my colleagues and thoughtful editors this project would not have been possible. Over the past year, as this work came to completion, many people have helped—lending their time and kind suggestions. In particular, I'd like to thank my colleagues at Agnes Scott College and Fernbank Science Center for their encouragement and patient assistance. Over a generation of students, at both institutions, has served as a valuable resource that has guided me toward more effective teaching/writing techniques.

Frances Chamberlain is to be highly commended for taking the initial drafts of the text and then molding them into a readable style—conforming my writing into the popular "Made Simple" format. Jill Korot, of the Philip Lief Group, was particularly helpful in coordinating the editing and final layout of the manuscript. Scott Nurkin created all of the illustrations that assist the reader in following my descriptions of everything—from volcanoes to asteroids. Finally, I'd like to thank my immediate family, my wife Nancie and daughter Lauren, who were always there, graciously giving me the necessary time for research in order to put my thoughts into words.

CONTENTS

Introduction   1

PART I   **GEOLOGY**

Chapter 1   **Minerals**   5

What Is a Mineral?

    Chemistry Primer

    Elements of the Earth's Crust

    Crystal Structure

    Crystal Systems

Mineral Groups

    Seven Groups of Minerals

    Physical Properties of Minerals

Economic Value of Minerals

Summary

Chapter 2   **Rocks**   14

What Is a Rock?

    Igneous Rocks

    Metamorphic Rocks

    Sedimentary Rocks

Summary

Chapter 3   **Plate Tectonics**   21

Continental Drift Theory

    How Earth Moves

    Earth's Interior

    Earthquakes and Seismic Energy

    Seismic Waves

    Richter Scale

    Divergent Plate Boundaries

    Convergent Plate Boundaries

    Transform Plate Boundaries and Seamount Chains

Summary

Chapter 4   **Geologic Processes**   30
Surface-Modifying Processes
Volcanism
Fluvial or Water-Modifying Forces
Aeolian Processes
Glacial Processes
Mass Wasting or Gravitational Processes
Summary

Chapter 5   **Geologic Time**   43
How Old Is Earth?
Relative Age Dating
Absolute Age Dating
Geologic Time Scale
Summary

PART II   **OCEANOGRAPHY**

Chapter 6   **Ocean Composition and Layering**   53
Origins of the Ocean
A Brief History of Oceanography
The World's Oceans
Earth's Seas and Lakes
Properties and Composition of Seawater
Layered Structure of Oceans
Oceanic Resources
Ocean Pollution
Summary

Chapter 7   **Seafloor**   65
The Submarine Landscape
Continental Margins
Basin Floor
Mid-Oceanic Ridges
Oceanic Trenches
Seamounts
Seafloor Sediments
Summary

Chapter 8   **Shoreline**   73
              Shoreline Features
                  Sand and the Beach
              Shoreline Environments
              Shoreline Erosion
              Submergent and Emergent Coasts
              Summary

Chapter 9   **Currents**   82
              The Motions of the Oceans
                  Surface Circulation Patterns
                  Deep Circulation Patterns
              Summary

Chapter 10   **Waves and Tides**   90
              Behavior of Waves
                  Parts of a Wave
              Types of Waves
                  Wind-Generated Waves
                  Seismic Sea Waves
              Consequences of Waves
                  Waves and the Shoreline
                  Wave Erosion and Refraction
                  Tides Generated by the Moon and Sun
                  Tidal Currents
              Summary

PART III   **METEOROLOGY**

Chapter 11   **Atmospheric Composition and Layering**   101
              The Sky
                  Origin of the Atmosphere
                  Composition of the Atmosphere
                  Structure of the Atmosphere
              Summary

Chapter 12   **Clouds**   110
    Clouds and Weather
        Water Vapor and Humidity
        Condensation and Cloud Formation
        Types of Clouds
        Precipitation
    Summary

Chapter 13   **Winds**   119
    Circulation of Air
        Air Pressure
        Cyclones and Anticyclones
        Global Circulation
    Summary

Chapter 14   **Storms**   128
    Weather Events
        Air Masses and Fronts
        Thunderstorms
        Tornadoes
        Hurricanes
    Summary

PART IV   **PLANETARY SCIENCE**

Chapter 15   **Introduction to Planetary Science**   141
    Applying Earth Science to Other Planets
        Terrestrial and Jovian Planets
        Impact Cratering as a Geologic Process
    Planetary Exploration Strategy
        Tools of Planetary Exploration
    Summary

Chapter 16   **The Terrestrial Planets**   146
               The Inner Planets
                   Mercury
                   Venus
                   Earth's Moon
                   Mars
               Summary

Chapter 17   **The Jovian Planets**   158
               The Giant Planets
                   Jupiter
                   Saturn
                   Uranus and Neptune
               Pluto
                   Pluto's Moon, Charon
               Summary

Chapter 18   **Asteroids, Comets, and Meteorites**   170
               Geology of Space Rocks
                   Asteroids
                   Comets
                   Meteorites
               Summary

Glossary   178

Index   199

INTRODUCTION

It may seem hard to believe that one book can cover all of earth science in a simple way. Earth is full of mysteries, from fascinating rocks and minerals to the unexplored regions of the ocean floor and deep forests. Humans have slowly but surely explored, studied, and gained an understanding of this planet. We have been on Earth for thousands of years, and it's only in the past couple of centuries that we've explored much of its land surface, and only in recent decades have we learned about the depths of the oceans and the far reaches of outer space.

We still have a long way to go, and earth science is a huge discipline to study. It covers the formation of the planet Earth, plate tectonics, geology, meteorology, oceanography, and finally, outer space. What we have done in *Earth Science Made Simple* is break this complex scientific discipline into four major sections: geology, oceanography, meteorology, and planetary science.

The first section, geology, provides a basic understanding of minerals, rocks, plate tectonics (how our continents attained the shapes they now have), geologic processes, and geologic time. We begin to understand how the study of rocks and minerals, the structure of Earth, and the surface modifying factors like wind and water have contributed to shaping the planet that we live on today.

Three-quarters of our planet is covered by ocean water, and it is essential that we understand the connection between land and sea: the impact of the ocean on our coastlines and the rich resources that the ocean offers to us. Currents, waves, and tides all contribute to our weather patterns, our storms, and Earth's ecology. The second section of this book, oceanography, provides a fundamental examination of the ocean's processes, structures, and resources. Knowing how one thing impacts another and what this could mean in your lifetime, or that of your children, is critical to the continued health of our planet and the maintenance of important resources.

The third section of this book is devoted to meteorology—the science that identifies, tracks, and predicts the behaviors of great storms, blizzards, tornadoes, clouds, and winds. From the simple but deep appreciation of a beautiful, cloud-filled sky to the desperate need to know how the weather patterns might affect agricultural ventures, building projects, fishing enterprises, and many other human activities, the weather impacts us daily in a number of ways. We may not notice the slow degradation of a hillside as wind and rain wash away topsoil or as a dune is created near the beach, but we all take notice when tornadoes rip apart residential neighborhoods in the midwest, or when blizzards hammer the northeast, or when torrential rains cause devastating landslides on the west coast. Meteorology gives us a chance, not necessarily to predict weather (let's leave that to the meteorologists and their technical equipment), but to understand why things are happening and what the consequences might be to our environment.

The fourth section of this book is a survey of planetary science. This may seem irrelevant to life on Earth, but how do you think we got here? This section provides a basic understanding of how the Earth was formed from the solar nebula, why planets orbit the Sun, and how other, foreign planets are made of some of the same rocks and minerals as Earth. The solar neighborhood in which we live is composed of a variety of planets, moons, asteroids, and comets. There is much that we can learn about the structure of Earth by understanding the structures of other worlds in the Solar System.

Putting it all together is important. By studying the geologic history of our planet, its oceanography, its meteorology, and finally its parallels to other worlds, you get a more comprehensive view of the world than you may have had before reading this book.

As careful stewards of this planet, we are wise to understand as much as possible about the world, and Solar System, in which we live. Earth science can be an incredibly complex subject. Many scientists invest their careers in studying one specific area—such as geology, oceanography, meteorology, or planetary science. They may focus on rocks or minerals, volcanoes, tornadoes, weather systems, currents, the deep ocean, marine ecosystems, or a particular planet. The possibilities are endless.

Earth Science Made Simple is intended to provide a manageable overview of the major components of this broad area of study. It is important that you see how all the pieces fit together, like a giant puzzle. Then, if you choose to further your study in one particular area, you will have a foundation of knowledge and a perspective of that discipline within a greater context.

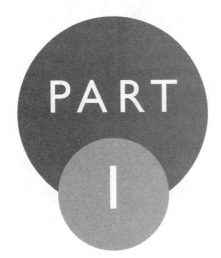

PART

I

GEOLOGY

MINERALS

Every one of us has probably—at some
point—sat on the ground with a stick, a
spoon, or a sharp piece of stone and dug,
just to see what we would find. You can
probably remember chipping away at sandstone, finding a piece of mica that came
apart in glittery slices, playing with wet clay
in a riverbed, or simply wondering what
made hills and mountains. Our fascination
with the natural world dates back to the
Greeks, to our earliest record of human study.

WHAT IS A MINERAL?

The average person may stumble over the
definition of a mineral. Perhaps it is best to
keep in mind that *minerals* are all around
us, all the time. Knowledge of some basic
chemistry will help you understand that a
mineral is a naturally occurring, inorganic,
solid substance with a specific composition
and arrangement of atoms. Ordinary table
salt and an ice cube are good examples of
minerals. Silver and copper are also minerals.

The study of mineralogy is particularly
fascinating because there are more than
3000 identified minerals, and new ones
are discovered every year.

Remember, a mineral possesses certain
qualities. It is

- Naturally occurring
- Inorganic
- Solid
- Composed of a specific arrangement of atoms

Chemistry Primer

Minerals are groups of atoms that are bonded
together, and individual chemical elements are
all composed of similar atoms. These elements
are organized on a chart called the *periodic
table*, something most of us remember from
high school chemistry. There are more than
100 elements arranged on this table. (See
Figure 1.2 on page 6.)

The element, again, is a collection of atoms
of the same type. Each atom contains three
fundamental particles—a proton, a neutron,
and an electron. The protons and neutrons
are in the center, or nucleus, of the atom.
Protons have a positive charge, while neutrons
have no electric charge.

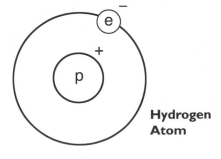

Figure 1.1—An Atom

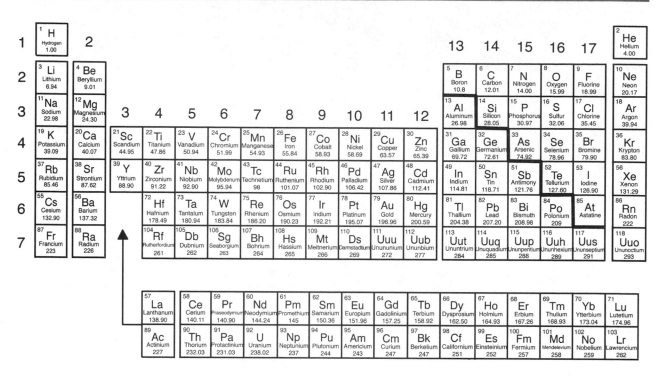

Figure 1.2—Periodic Table

The electrons have a negative charge and orbit about the nucleus at a specific distance. Most atoms have an equivalent number of protons and neutrons. However, in some cases, the number of neutrons can vary within a given atom, forming variations of an element known as an *isotope*.

The number of protons within the atom's nucleus determines the element's atomic number and its place on the periodic table. An element with only one proton is known as hydrogen (Figure 1.1). Iron has 26 protons in its nucleus. Gold contains 79 protons and uranium has 92. All this is easily determined by looking at the periodic table (Figure 1.2).

Common table salt is a good example of how a mineral is formed. An atom tends to be electronically stable (not to have any charge). An atom that gains electrons is negatively charged (it has more electrons than protons)

and an atom that loses electrons is positively charged. Atoms with an unequal charge due to a gain or loss of electrons are called *ions*. Oppositely charged ions attract one another and produce a neutral chemical bond, such as when sodium (Na) and chlorine (Cl) combine to produce sodium chloride (NaCl). They are attracted to each other, creating a charge balance. An *ionic bond* occurs when two ions of opposite charge are attached. In common table salt, the sodium atom has a positive charge and the chlorine atom has a negative charge. Together, they form a balanced and stable molecule.

A mineral begins when an atomic charge imbalance causes an inequity in the ratio of electrons to protons. The ionic bond occurs when *cations* (positively charged atoms) are drawn to *anions* (negatively charged atoms). The balance can be tipped in either direction, depending on this ratio of electrons to protons.

Another example of how this works is water. In this case, two atoms of hydrogen share electrons with an atom of oxygen (Figure 1.3). This is a *covalent bond*, where atoms with similar charges share electrons in order to be stable.

Both ionic and covalent bonds can be found within a single mineral, and these bonds build minerals and give them their physical properties.

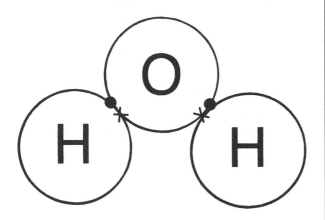

Figure 1.3—H₂O Molecule

Elements of Earth's Crust

Eight elements are most commonly found in Earth's crust. These elements control the type and number of minerals that occur on our planet. The eight most common are silicon, oxygen, aluminum, iron, calcium, magnesium, potassium, and sodium. Most minerals are composed of these elements— particularly silicon and oxygen.

Eight elements commonly found in Earth's crust:

• Silicon (Si)	• Calcium (Ca)
• Oxygen (O)	• Magnesium (Mg)
• Aluminum (Al)	• Potassium (K)
• Iron (Fe)	• Sodium (Na)

The elements of Earth's crust control the type and number of minerals on our planet, and the form that they take often results in a particular kind of crystal structure. Taking a look at how crystals form provides a clearer picture of how certain elements create minerals.

Crystal Structure

Look in a shoebox that holds a child's rock collection and you're sure to find a sample of a crystal. *Crystallography* is one branch of the formal study of minerals. The smooth, flat planes, the sharp peaks, and the shiny surface make the crystal an appealing and satisfying find for any mineral collector.

A *crystal* is a form of mineral that has grown in an orderly and symmetrical manner; when broken, it naturally divides into a common shape, based on its crystal structure. Crystals are the result of the atomic arrangement of atoms, as they grow in a shape that can be duplicated many times. Crystals are made up of molecules that fit neatly together in an orderly way. All crystals of the same material have the same shape.

Crystals take shape only when they are allowed to grow in an undisturbed environment. When certain liquids and gases cool and lose water, crystals form. Precipitation from water produces many minerals, or crystals, such as halite, calcite, and gypsum. Minerals also crystallize from molten rock, or *magma*. This slower-cooling rock has larger crystals, which accumulate at the bottom of the magma chamber and cause the composition of the molten rock to change with time.

In both cases, the minerals are produced from a liquid in which a regular crystal pattern is reproduced and duplicated by a specific arrangement of atoms. The atoms make what is called a *unit cell*, a regular pattern that is repeated throughout a mineral. This repetition of the unit cell creates the crystal face.

**EXPLORATION 1.1
GROW A CRYSTAL IN THE SUN**

Dissolve a tablespoon of Epsom salt (found in your neighborhood pharmacy) in a quarter cup of warm water. Prepare a tin pie pan by placing a piece of black construction paper on the interior bottom, cut to fit the shape of the pan. Set the pan outside in a sunny place. Pour the salty mixture into the pan and let the water evaporate over a period of several days. Enjoy your spikes of new crystals that extend across the black paper!

Crystal Systems

Although there are many possible crystal styles known in nature, it isn't so hard to learn about the six crystal systems into which they all fit (Figure 1.4). These are defined by the *orientation* (direction) and length of the crystallographic axes (lines) that pass through the center of the crystal.

1. *Isometric crystals* typically have faces that are square or triangular; the three axes intersect at 90° angles and have equivalent lengths.

2. *Tetragonal crystals* are usually of a prism shape; the axes intersect at 90° angles, but only two axes are of equal lengths.

3. *Orthorhombic crystals* have a pyramid shape; the axes intersect at 90° angles and are all of unequal lengths.

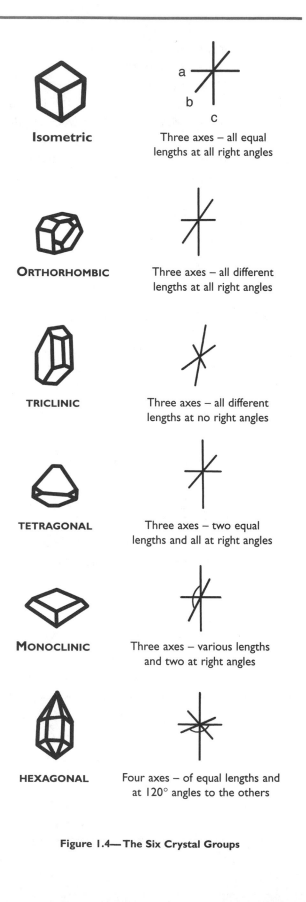

Isometric — Three axes – all equal lengths at all right angles

ORTHORHOMBIC — Three axes – all different lengths at all right angles

TRICLINIC — Three axes – all different lengths at no right angles

TETRAGONAL — Three axes – two equal lengths and all at right angles

MONOCLINIC — Three axes – various lengths and two at right angles

HEXAGONAL — Four axes – of equal lengths and at 120° angles to the others

Figure 1.4—The Six Crystal Groups

4. *Monoclinic crystals* are prisms, domes, and pyramids; they have axes of unequal length and only two axes are perpendicular to each other.

5. *Triclinic crystals* have a pinacoid form; they have three unequal crystallographic axes that occur at oblique angles to each other.

6. *Hexagonal crystals* have four crystallographic axes of equal length at angles of 120° to each other.

Understanding crystal systems is important because the chemistry and resulting crystal structure ultimately control the physical properties of all minerals.

MINERAL GROUPS

Minerals are divided into major groups based on their composition and crystal structure. These seven groups—native elements, silicates, carbonates, halides, oxides, sulfides, and sulfates—allow us to classify minerals.

Remember that the eight most common elements of Earth's crust are silicon, oxygen, aluminum, iron, calcium, magnesium, potassium, and sodium. Most minerals are composed of these elements. Classifying minerals becomes easier when you recognize the eight common elements and the six major crystal structures.

Seven Groups of Minerals

When a single type of atom occurs alone or does not bond with other atoms it is called a *native element*. It is the simplest type of mineral; examples include sulfur, copper, and gold.

Silicates are the most abundant mineral group because of their structures. The configuration is four oxygen ions surrounding a silicon ion, or SiO_4. The primary building block of the silicate is known as a *silicon tetrahedron*. It has a net charge of -4, allowing it to bond with positive ions (or cations) to make different silicate minerals. As mentioned earlier, minerals are formed when groups of atoms are bonded together. The atom strives to be electronically stable. To achieve this, the positively and negatively charged ions are attracted to each other, creating an ionic bond.

Subgroups of silicates are produced depending on how the tetrahedra bond to the different cations. Single tetrahedra form one subgroup, and produce a common mineral called pyroxene. In this case, iron or magnesium is bonded to the silica tetrahedron and is called *neosilicate*. If two silica tetrahedra bond together, *sorosilicate* is formed. The mineral epidote is an example of this.

Silica tetrahedra that are linked in a ring-like structure are called *cyclosilicates*. An example is the gemstone mineral called *tourmaline*. Chains of silica tetrahedra make a class called *inosilicates*. They are important soil-forming minerals. When the chains of silica tetrahedra are linked in sheets, *phyllosilicates* are formed. They often form important clay minerals such as pyrophyllite.

The final subgroup of silicate mineral is *tectosilicate*. In this case, all the oxygen atoms of the silica tetrahedron are shared. Significant tectosilicates include the minerals feldspar and quartz.

Carbonates are a group of minerals that have the carbonate ion (CO_3) bound with a cation.

The most common carbonate mineral is calcium carbonate ($CaCO_3$), or calcite.

Halides incorporate gaseous elements (halogens like chlorine and fluorine) with other elements. For instance, a common halide is halite, which is produced from a combination of sodium and chlorine.

When metallic elements are combined with oxygen ions, *oxides* are produced. The most common oxides are magnetite and hematite.

Sulfides are formed when sulfur bonds to one or more metallic elements. Pyrite, or fool's gold, is probably the best known of the sulfide minerals. However, more important sulfides are ore deposits such as minerals that have copper, lead, and zinc in their structures. *Ore* is a metal-bearing mineral or rock, or a source of some nonmetallic substance such as sulfur.

Sulfates are minerals constructed of a sulfate anion (SO_4) combined with other elements. Gypsum ($CaSO_4$) is a common sulfate mineral used in building construction.

**EXPLORATION 1.2
MINERAL REACTION TO DILUTE ACID**

Some minerals fizz or effervesce when exposed to a drop of dilute hydrochloric acid, available from www.postapplescientific.com. This is an effective test for carbonate minerals. Try it on a piece of calcite (limestone or chalk). Watch how the bubbles form immediately when exposed to the acid. Be sure to thoroughly rinse off the specimen after the test.

Physical Properties of Minerals

Now that we've learned what minerals are and what they are made of, how do you tell them apart? Both professional mineralogists and amateur collectors can tell one mineral from another in only a few seconds. The key is to understand the physical properties—crystal habit, hardness, color, cleavage, and luster.

Crystal Habit

The shape of a mineral is sometimes called its *crystal habit*. It is rare, however, for perfect crystals to develop in nature, and the faces that form on a crystal depend on the environment in which it develops. Although crystals may develop certain forms more commonly than others, the symmetry may not be easy to identify. Using crystallographic forms to identify minerals may prove too challenging for the novice collector.

Hardness

Some minerals are more difficult to scratch or break than others, giving them the physical property of *hardness*. We've all heard that the hardest substance on Earth is the diamond, and it has become one of the best-known minerals. This hardness, or robustness, partly accounts for its value, both aesthetically and industrially. In addition to being used in wedding bands, diamonds are often used to make tough abrasives for grinding purposes.

On the other end of the spectrum is the softest mineral on Earth, talc, which is used to make talcum powder.

Mineralogists define mineral hardness on a scale with diamonds at one end and talc at the other. There are eight variations of hardness in between. This scale is formally known as *Mohs' Hardness Scale* (Figure 1.5), which was created by the German mineralogist Friedrich Mohs in 1812.

HARDNESS OF COMMON ITEMS

Talc is the softest mineral and is easily scratched by a fingernail. Talc actually feels soft and greasy and is considered "Hardness 1" on Mohs' Scale. Gypsum, of "Hardness 2," can also be scratched by a fingernail, but isn't soft and greasy.

When you reach "Hardness 3" (calcite, for example), a fingernail can't scratch the sample, but the sharp edge of a copper penny could. "Hardness 4" is something that can be scratched by a knife, but not necessarily by a penny. Fluorite, or fluorspar, is an example of a "Hardness 4" mineral.

Apatite is an example of "Hardness 5," and although it might barely scratch ordinary glass, it also is too hard to be scratched by a knife. Feldspar, with "Hardness 6," cannot be scratched by a knife, but it can scratch ordinary glass if you press hard enough. Quartz, at "Hardness 7," can scratch glass easily and is harder than many other minerals that you will come across.

Topaz, which can easily scratch quartz, is "Hardness 8." Finally, anything that can scratch topaz, like corundum, is "Hardness 9," and the diamond, the hardest known substance, is at the top of the scale at "Hardness 10."

Color

Color is another important identifying characteristic of a mineral. Some minerals always have the same color, but it can be a difficult property to determine. Sulfur, with its distinctive yellow hue, is easy to recognize, but others are not so straightforward. Many minerals can display a wide range of colors, and a large number of minerals actually share the same color. Quartz can have many colors, from clear to yellow to gray to purple; however, both plagioclase and barite are solid white.

10	Diamond
9	Corundum
8	Topaz
7	Quartz
6	Feldspar
5	Apatite
4	Fluorspar
3	Calcite
2	Gypsum
1	Talc

Figure 1.5—Mohs' Hardness Scale

Color is often only determined after a mineral is scratched across an unglazed porcelain surface known as a *streak plate*. The backside of an ordinary bathroom tile makes a good streak plate. To determine color, a mineral is ground until a fine powder is seen on the plate. Against this stark, white surface it is now possible to see the true color of the mineral.

Sometimes the mineral color is different from the streak, but the color of the streak powder is always consistent. When a mineral is powdered, its color is consistent because it eliminates larger reflective and rough surface differences that can sometimes give misleading color information.

EXPLORATION 1.3— THE TRUE COLOR OF MINERALS

Acquire small pieces of the minerals magnetite and hematite. These are very common minerals that should be available at any natural history or science museum gift shop. Observe the specimens and describe their apparent color. Use the back of a piece of ceramic tile for your streak plate. You can buy the tile at any hardware store. Scratch the magnetite across the backside of the tile. Note its color. Scratch the hematite across the plate and note its color. How do they differ? Are the colors different from what you saw when you looked at the solid minerals?

Cleavage

Cleavage is another useful property in identifying minerals. It is created by the mineral's internal arrangement of atoms, which causes a mineral to break in a specific direction along smooth planes. The tenacity at which a mineral resists breakage is due to the strength of chemical bonds between atoms and the crystal structure.

If the bond is strong, it is more difficult to break the mineral. Cleavage will have a natural tendency to occur across the weakest bonds in a structure. Minerals can display cleavage along one or more planes. A mineral like mica has a cleavage in one direction and breaks across a single plane, producing very flat sheets of the mineral. In other cases, minerals like fluorite can have four planes of cleavage. This characteristic produces perfect octahedral mineral fragments that are easy to identify. Octahedral mineral fragments look like little diamonds and break along cleavage planes that are related to their crystal structure. When minerals have small differences in the strength of chemical bonds from one part of the mineral to another, they will break along rough surfaces in a manner described as *fracture*.

Luster

The final property used to identify minerals is *luster*, which is the way a surface reflects light. Minerals can have a metallic luster, not unlike light shining on a piece of broken metal. More often, however, minerals have a nonmetallic luster. These minerals can be described in several ways. If the mineral looks like a piece of broken glass, it is said to have a *vitreous luster*. Some minerals have the appearance of pearls and are said to have a *pearly luster*. Should the surface look like silk, it is said to have a *silky luster*. Minerals that look like a broken brick or dry soil are referred to as having a dull or *earthy luster*.

Understanding these properties assists amateur collectors and mineralogists alike in identifying minerals.

ECONOMIC VALUE OF MINERALS

Minerals are fascinating to collectors and scientists, but they also have great economic value to our society. More than 100 different minerals are mined from the Earth on a regular basis.

EXPLORATION 1.4
BUILDING A MINERAL COLLECTION

If you're interested in minerals, it can be fun to put together your own collection for handy reference. Although lots of pictures are available in books and on the Internet, nothing compares to having the actual mineral to look at and hold. You can purchase minerals from any natural history or science museum, or order them from a scientific company like Wards (www.wardsci.com).

The most important minerals to have are those that are commonly found in rocks. These rock-forming minerals can be organized into groups, depending on their composition and crystal structure, as we mentioned earlier in this chapter. (See Seven Groups of Minerals.)

One way to get started on a collection is to attend a rock and mineral show in your area. Larger cities often have several shows that are sponsored by local mineral or geology clubs. Beginners may want to assemble a collection of small minerals called micromounts or thumbnails. These specimens are easily accessible and cost only a few dollars each. The advanced collector will eventually develop a taste for larger and more visually pleasing minerals.

For example, minerals are useful construction materials. Quartz is melted and fused into plate glass. Calcite or limestone is used to produce cement, which is used for everything from paving roads to building skyscrapers. The mineral wollastonite is a major component in the production of automotive parts and electrical panels. Copper is used in a variety of ways, including electrical wiring. Halite is used for food, medicines, and road salt. Any mineral used for decorative objects, jewelry, or art is also considered quite valuable. A *gemstone* is defined as any of various minerals highly prized for beauty, durability, and rarity. A few noncrystalline materials of organic origin (e.g., pearl, red coral, and amber) are also classified as gemstones, although they are not classified as minerals.

SUMMARY

A mineral is a naturally occurring, inorganic, solid substance that has a specific composition and arrangement of atoms. We already know of more than 3000 different minerals, and new ones are being discovered all the time. Mineralogy is the scientific study of minerals.

Because minerals are made up of an arrangement of atoms, an understanding of basic chemistry helps the scientist to understand the composition of each mineral. Each element on the periodic table is a collection of atoms of the same type, and each atom contains a proton, a neutron, and an electron.

The protons (with a positive charge) and the neutrons (with no electric charge) are in the nucleus of the atom. The electrons (with a negative charge) orbit about the nucleus at specific distances. Most atoms have an equivalent number of protons and neutrons, although in some cases, the number of neutrons can vary, forming an isotope.

Minerals are composed of groups of atoms that are bonded together. The inequity in the ratio of electrons relative to protons creates an imbalance. The imbalance creates atoms called ions—positively charged ions are cations and negatively charged ions are anions.

Positively and negatively charged ions are attracted to each other, and the atoms come together and are bonded, either through an ionic bond (opposites are attached) or through covalent bonds (atoms share electrons in order to be stable). These bonds are responsible for building minerals and for giving them their physical properties.

The internal arrangement of atoms causes minerals to grow in an orderly and symmetrical manner. This leads to crystal structures called unit cells, which are regular patterns repeated throughout the mineral. There are six basic crystal systems that can be identified in minerals.

Seven mineral groups can be found in nature: native elements, silicates, carbonates, sulfates, sulfides, halides, and oxides. Minerals can be identified by several different physical properties including hardness, color, shape or crystal habit, luster, and cleavage or the way a mineral breaks.

Minerals are fun to collect and study, but they also have great economic value and are used in a variety of ways from jewelry and decorative objects to construction materials.

ROCKS

KEY TERMS

igneous rock, metamorphic rock, sedimentary rock, porphyritic, phaneritic, pegmatitic, aphanitic, vesicular, felsic, mafic, intermediate, ultramafic, clastic sedimentary rocks, nonclastic sedimentary rocks

WHAT IS A ROCK?

A rock is essentially a collection of minerals, but the composition of those minerals and the way in which the rock is formed help us to distinguish various types of rocks. The three major rock types that occur in nature—igneous, metamorphic, and sedimentary—are each formed in a specific environment.

Igneous rocks are produced from the crystallization of an assemblage of minerals from magma, or hot liquid rock. Fresh magma is white hot, and as it cools, it turns yellow, then red, and eventually cools enough to form an igneous rock. Granite and basalt are the two most common igneous rocks. As the magma cools, elements such as silica, iron, sodium, and potassium chemically combine into rock-forming minerals.

The mineralogy and texture of preexisting rocks are changed when they are subjected to extreme pressures and temperatures. The objects that result from this process are called *metamorphic rocks*. The word *metamorphic* comes from the Greek words—*meta*, which means to change, and *morph*, which means to form. Therefore,

a metamorphic rock is one that has changed its original form.

The metamorphic rock can start out as either igneous or sedimentary rock, but when exposed to great heat and pressure inside Earth, it is changed into something else. For instance, limestone can be changed to marble, sandstone can be changed to quartzite, and shale can be changed to slate. Metamorphic rocks can be thought of as recycled rocks.

Sedimentary rocks are formed by a process that we could actually see, if we could stay still long enough to watch it happen. Wind and water flowing across Earth's surface can weather both igneous and metamorphic rocks. This process breaks these rocks into small pieces known as *sediment*. As sediment accumulates and compacts into a solid mass, a sedimentary rock is formed. Again, if the sedimentary rock is subjected to extreme heat and pressure, it can be converted into igneous or metamorphic rocks. All three rock types are linked through this continuous process known as the *rock cycle*. (See Figure 2.1.)

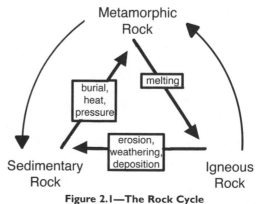

Figure 2.1—The Rock Cycle

Igneous Rocks

The word *igneous*—which comes from the Latin word *igneus*, meaning fire—means fire-formed. Igneous rocks originate deep within Earth as magma pushes its way toward the surface. Molten rock is not as dense as the encasing rock and therefore buoyantly rises upward. If the magma should cool and solidify prior to reaching the surface of Earth, it will crystallize into masses that are referred to as *intrusive* or *plutonic* igneous rocks.

The texture of the igneous rock is controlled by the rate of cooling. Slow cooling produces large grain size, while quick cooling produces fine grains. Sometimes magma can begin to cool slowly, producing larger crystals, but is then cooled suddenly when it reaches the surface of Earth. This mixed cooling history produces a unique igneous texture known as *porphyritic*. Large crystals, called phenocrysts, in a matrix or ground mass of smaller crystals characterize such a texture.

Some igneous rocks cool very slowly because they are insulated by the encasing rock, and thus allow for the growth of large mineral crystals. The size of the grains of minerals will depend on just how much time the rock has to cool. The grain size of crystals is usually between 1 and 10 millimeters (mm). Rocks having crystals large enough to discern with the naked eye have a *phaneritic* texture. If cooling takes an exceptionally long time, very large mineral grains—some exceeding 2 centimeters (cm) in diameter—can occur. This coarse grained texture is called *pegmatitic*.

Extrusive igneous rocks, unlike the igneous rocks encased by other rock, are produced when magma works its way up to Earth's surface and erupts to form lava flows and volcanoes. Such molten material does not have an insulating layer of rock around it, so it cools rapidly upon exposure to the atmosphere or to seawater. Quick cooling does not allow for the growth of large mineral crystals. The crystals are too small to be seen with the naked eye and produce an *aphanitic* igneous rock texture. Individual mineral grains are typically less than one millimeter across. In some cases, extrusive rock is cooled so rapidly that a volcanic glass called obsidian is formed.

There are two other interesting igneous rock textures. One is known as vesicular texture and refers to rocks that are filled with holes, or vesicles. These form when gases escape or bubble out of the once-molten rocks. Another interesting texture in igneous rocks is *pyroclastic* texture, which happens when volcanic rock fragments and ash are welded together from intense heat.

Chemical Composition

Both texture (discussed in the previous section) and chemical composition are the basis for the classification of igneous rocks. There are four major classes of igneous rock:

- Felsic

- Mafic

- Intermediate

- Ultramafic

Felsic rocks tend to be light in color and are composed chiefly of minerals enriched in the elements silicon and aluminum. They are associated with thick and slow-moving (*viscous*) magmas or lava flows. Felsic rocks occur primarily on continental landmasses.

Granite is a prime example of a felsic rock with a phaneritic texture, or large crystals. If the texture is fine-grained or aphanitic, then the felsic rock is called rhyolite. Both granite and rhyolite are composed chiefly of the minerals quartz, potassium feldspar, and plagioclase feldspar.

In contrast, *mafic* igneous rocks are gray to black in color and are made up of mostly silicate minerals with magnesium and iron. Mafic magmas and lavas have a low *viscosity* (resistance to flow). They occur in association with oceanic crust and have calcium plagioclase and pyroxene as their primary minerals. These magmas, in the form of basaltic rock, make up virtually all of Earth's oceanic crust. The rocks are rich in iron and magnesium and thus are denser than continental crust. Basalt is the fine-grained version of a mafic rock. It is one of the most common of all igneous rocks found not only on Earth, but also within the entire solar system. The coarse-grained variety of basalt is known as gabbro.

Another type of igneous rock, *intermediate*, is in the spectrum of compositions between felsic and mafic. These intermediate species form two common rock types: diorite, if the texture is phaneritic, and andesite, if the texture is aphanitic. The dominant minerals in intermediate rock are calcium and sodium plagioclase feldspars and amphibole.

Rocks that have an extreme mafic composition are called *ultramafic*. Peridotite is an ultramafic rock that has an origin deep within the lower crust of our planet. It is composed mainly of the minerals pyroxene and olivine. Peridot, the popular birthstone for August, is a gemstone variety of olivine. (See Figure 2.2.)

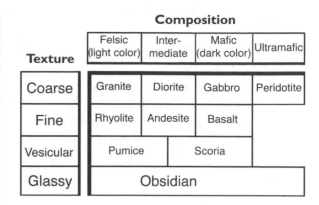

| Texture | Composition | | | |
	Felsic (light color)	Inter-mediate	Mafic (dark color)	Ultramafic
Coarse	Granite	Diorite	Gabbro	Peridotite
Fine	Rhyolite	Andesite	Basalt	
Vesicular	Pumice		Scoria	
Glassy	Obsidian			

Figure 2.2—Igneous Rock Classifications

EXPLORATION 2.1
BOWEN'S REACTION SERIES

A chart known as *Bowen's Reaction Series* can best model the mineralogy of igneous rocks (Figure 2.3). The chart has a Y shape—with ultramafic minerals (olivine, pyroxene, amphibole, and biotite) on the left part of the Y and mafic to intermediate minerals (calcium to sodium-rich plagioclase) on the right section of the Y. The felsic minerals (orthoclase, muscovite, and quartz) are found on the bottom part of the Y. The minerals found on the upper section of the Y crystallize out of the magma at higher temperatures than those near the bottom. For instance, olivine is a high-temperature mineral compared to quartz, which is considered a low-temperature igneous mineral. If you have started a mineral collection and have the right specimens, you can arrange a display that illustrates Bowen's Reaction Series. Many of these specimens are available at a museum shop or through www.wardsci.com.

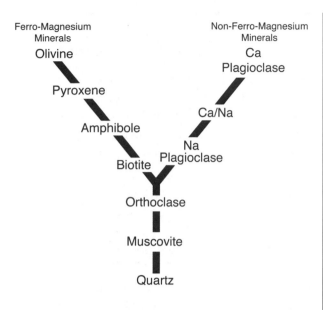

Ferro-Magnesium Minerals
Olivine
Pyroxene
Amphibole
Biotite

Non-Ferro-Magnesium Minerals
Ca Plagioclase
Ca/Na
Na Plagioclase

Orthoclase
Muscovite
Quartz

Figure 2.3—Bowen's Reaction Series

As a magma body works its way toward the surface, its composition evolves through a process called *fractional crystallization*. Deep within Earth, crystallization forms ultramafic and mafic minerals like olivine and pyroxene. The production and settling of these minerals change the overall composition of the magma as it migrates upward. This fractionation process continues, changing the composition of the magma from ultramafic to mafic, then from mafic to intermediate, and finally, from intermediate to felsic. So, as the magma's composition evolves with time, the igneous rocks that solidify from the molten mass change or evolve as well. In this manner, a single magma can deposit rocks with a variety of compositions—from ultramafic peridotite to felsic granite.

Metamorphic Rocks

Metamorphic rocks are produced from the alteration of preexisting rocks by heat and pressure. Temperature within Earth's crust increases with depth, so burial of rock can give rise to higher temperatures. Magma that intrudes into existing rock, or what is called country rock, can also produce temperature increases. The *country rock* actually surrounds the magma or the rock that is being changed. The magma moves toward the surface through cracks or fissures in the crust. It's also more buoyant than the surrounding rock, so some magma can actually "float" toward the surface of Earth.

There can be pressure on a rock from all directions, although it's usually not uniform. This differential stress can cause rounded minerals to become flattened or layered. Metamorphism occurs when temperatures exceed 200°C and pressure is greater than 3000 atmospheres of pressure. Metamorphism is either low- or high-grade, depending on the temperature and pressures imposed on the rock. *Low-grade metamorphic rocks* are formed when temperatures are between 200°C to 300°C and pressures are relatively low. This type of metamorphism involves minerals that have water within their crystal structures. These hydrous minerals include chlorite, serpentine, and clay minerals.

If pressures are high and temperatures are above 300°C, then *high-grade metamorphic rocks* are produced. At these higher pressures and temperatures, water is lost from the crystal structure and the minerals are said to become less- to nonhydrous. Examples of common high-grade metamorphic minerals are garnet; biotite, a black or dark-colored mica; and muscovite, a light-colored mica.

Geologists define four types of metamorphism: cataclastic, burial, contact, and regional. Small-scale deformation—for instance, along a fault boundary—results in *cataclastic metamorphism*. The weight of sediment on rock can create sufficient pressures to cause *burial metamorphism*—

simply defined as rock that is altered by the weight of overlying rock. When country rock is inundated by an igneous magma, rocks are altered by the heat, in a process known as *contact metamorphism. Regional metamorphism* occurs when the rock is shaped by compressional stresses on a large scale.

Foliated and Nonfoliated Rock

Metamorphic rocks are classified as either foliated or nonfoliated. Metamorphism that causes the minerals to combine in one orientation causes the rock to break along parallel sheets. This is known as *foliation* and is aligned perpendicular to the direction of maximum stress inflicted on the rock.

Slate, schist, and gneiss are all characterized by a foliated texture. These rocks, like common mica, tend to break in sheets rather than clumps. Slate is a low-grade metamorphic rock made up of fine-grained chlorite and clay minerals. Its texture is characterized by *slatey cleavage*, or the preferred orientation of minerals at some angle to the original bedding plane. *Preferred orientation* means that the layers of minerals, regardless of type, are all parallel to each other.

A higher grade of metamorphism can produce schist, characterized by the preferred orientation of the mica minerals biotite and muscovite. Foliation of this rock type is known as *schistosity*. Schist might be something like mica-schist, with layers of quartz and mica.

The highest grade of metamorphism gives rise to gneiss. It has dark bands of the minerals pyroxene and hornblende, a black or dark-colored form of amphibole, producing a texture called *gneissic banding*.

**EXPLORATION 2.2
SIMULATING A FOLIATED ROCK**

Mix a tablespoon of dry rice grains in a small quantity of modeling clay. Be sure to roll the dough thoroughly so that grains are evenly distributed throughout the mass. Next, flatten the modeling clay to a thickness of about 1 cm between two pieces of wood. Using a knife, cut the slab in sections and examine the orientation of the rice grains. Are the grains randomly placed or do they show a preferred orientation? Relate your observation to foliated rocks.

Nonfoliated metamorphic rocks are produced from the alteration of certain igneous and sedimentary, or layered, rocks. (Sedimentary rocks will be discussed in the next section.) Low-grade metamorphism of basalts and grabbos forms a new rock type called greenschist. This stone has some evidence of foliation and is dominated by amphibole and chlorite minerals that were derived from olivine, pyroxene, and plagioclase. A higher grade of metamorphism can produce amphibolite or granulite. Here, the foliation is totally lost as the rock is fused, or compressed so tightly.

The mineral calcite, in limestone, grows larger when subjected to high pressures and temperatures. Metamorphism converts limestone to a new rock called marble. This same scenario is also true of sandstone, except it changes into a nonfoliated rock called quartzite.

Sedimentary Rocks

When igneous and metamorphic rocks are broken down by mechanical or chemical processes, they become a new type of rock called sedimentary rock (Figure 2.4). These rocks are composed of a material called *detritus*—sediments that are the small pieces of rocks and minerals formed from erosion by water and wind. These sediments are carried away from their source and are later converted into rock through a process called lithification. *Lithification* occurs when there is the pressure of accumulated layers of sedimentation and minerals are cemented between the grains.

There are two major forms of sedimentary rocks: clastic and nonclastic. *Clastic sedimentation* occurs when particles suspended and transported by water or wind are deposited and the energy source for transport decreases. Rocks produced by this process are known as *clastic sedimentary rocks*. Clastic sedimentation is solely caused by physical forces.

Nonclastic sedimentary rocks are formed by chemical precipitation from water in a process called *chemical sedimentation*. Nonclastic sediments can also be formed by *biogenic sedimentation*, which happens when living organisms take ions from seawater and use them to build shells and bones. When these organisms die, their remains accumulate to form *biogenic sedimentary rock*.

Clastic sedimentary rocks composed of pebbles or larger-sized grains are called *conglomerates*.

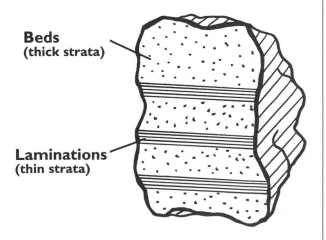

Beds
(thick strata)

Laminations
(thin strata)

Figure 2.4—Sedimentary Rock

EXPLORATION 2.3
THE WENTWORTH SCALE

Clastic rocks are classified by sediment size. A subdivision of grain size is charted on what is known as the *Wentworth Scale.* The finest sediments are called clay, while the coarsest are gravel—which includes pebbles, cobbles, and boulders. To understand how the Wentworth Scale works, sort some clastic rocks, from the smallest to largest, and arrange them in ascending or descending order. For practical purposes, it might be best to locate a boulder (anything greater than 256 mm in diameter) and then place the smaller specimens next to it. A cobble is between 64 and 256 mm, pebbles are 2 to 64 mm, sand is 1/16 to 2 mm, silt is 1/126 to 1/16 mm, and clay is anything 1/256 mm or less. From largest to smallest, they should be organized in this order: boulder, cobble, pebble, sand, silt, and clay. Geologists often distinguish clay from silt by placing a small sample in the mouth. Silt has a gritty feel, while clay is very smooth.

If the dominant grains are sand-sized, then the rock is termed *sandstone*. The mineralogy determines the classification. Sandstone composed mainly of quartz grains is simply called **quartz sandstone**. When quartz is mixed with feldspar mineral grains, the rock is called an **arkose**.

A rock containing a mixture of numerous different minerals and rock fragments is called a *graywacke*. Should quartz be pulverized into very fine silt and then cemented together, the rock is called siltstone. If it remains as loose material, then it is still considered to be sediment. The most abundant of all sedimentary clastic rocks are the *shales*. They are made of very fine-grained clay particles. Their cleavage is typically such that they break into flat sheets along parallel planes.

Nonclastic sediments have grains that are interlocked through a process of crystallization. Limestone is a good example of this, because the grains are produced by the precipitation of calcite from seawater. Some limestones, such as coquina and chalk, have an organic origin and are formed by biogenic sedimentation (the accumulation of shells). Coal is another example of a rock made of organic material. In this case it is composed of lithified, or solidified, plant parts.

Another group of nonclastic sedimentary rock—the evaporites halite and gypsum—is created by the evaporation of seawater within an enclosed basin. *Evaporites* occur when evaporation leaves behind ionic compounds previously dissolved in water.

EXPLORATION 2.4
MAKING A SEQUENCE OF LAYERED SEDIMENTARY ROCK

Sedimentary rocks most often occur in layers and have a stratified appearance. Individual layers, called strata, are based on color and texture. The thickest strata are called beds, while those layers less than about one centimeter in thickness are called laminations. You can simulate a stratified rock sequence with colored sand. Obtain or make at least three different colors of sand. Materials to do this can be purchased in a pet or craft store. In a clear dish, pour a layer of colored sand, spreading it out across the surface. Next, pour a different color of sand on top. Continue to pour sand of various colors. Note the resemblance to a sequence of layered sedimentary rock.

The grain size can decrease from the bottom to the top of a rock, showing graded bedding. Often, layers are inclined at some angle to the horizontal, producing a cross-stratification.

Such a feature indicates that the sediments were shifted by moving wind or water. When layers are separated, features known as *bed forms* are sometimes visible. These include mud cracks, ripples, or raindrop imprints.

SUMMARY

There are three major rock types in nature: igneous, metamorphic, and sedimentary. They are formed in different ways and you can tell them apart by both the structure of the rock and their mineral composition.

Igneous rocks are created by hot magma and whether they cooled slowly or quickly can be determined by the size of mineral grains in the rocks. Igneous rocks can also be vesicular (with holes throughout the rock) or pyroclastic (with volcanic rock fragments and ash welded together).

The four major classes of igneous rocks are felsic, mafic, intermediate, and ultramafic. These classifications refer to both the texture and the chemical composition of the rock.

Metamorphic rocks are altered by heat and pressure. The four processes that make metamorphic rock—contact, regional, burial, and cataclastic—are governed by the amount of heat and pressure applied to the existing rock. Metamorphic rock can also be either foliated or nonfoliated, something that is demonstrated by the way the rock breaks.

Sedimentary rocks are either igneous or metamorphic rocks that are broken down by mechanical and/or chemical processes. The pieces of small rock, either detritus or sediment, are carried away by water and wind and later changed into a new form of rock by lithification.

PLATE TECTONICS

CONTINENTAL DRIFT THEORY

At the turn of the twentieth century, the seeds of the plate tectonics theory were planted. Back then, however, the idea was called *continental drift*. In 1912, a German meteorologist named Alfred Wegener (1880–1930) claimed that the continents were actually moving over Earth's surface, and that sometimes these continents would collide and break into pieces. Other scientists of Wegener's time scoffed at this theory, claiming the surface of Earth couldn't move without massive resistance from friction. It wasn't until the 1960s that the validity of Wegener's theory was proven.

Wegener suggested that 250 million years earlier, Earth's continents had been combined into a single giant landmass, *Pangaea*. His theory suggested that the continents actually moved over the Earth's surface. The idea was first referred to as continental drift, and it was based, in part, on the way the continents seemed to fit together like the parts of a children's puzzle. The distribution of similar fossils on various landmasses was also part of his argument.

Alexander du Toit (1878–1948), another geologist, supported Wegener's continental drift theory, but he believed that there were two supercontinents rather than one. The northern one, *Laurasia* (comprised of what are now known as North America, Europe, and Asia), was separated from the southern one, *Gondwanaland* (comprised of what are now known as Australia, Africa, South America, India, New Zealand, and Madagascar), by a narrow, now-extinct sea called *Tethys*.

Today researchers believe that Pangaea did exist about 250 million years ago and was divided to form Laurasia and Gondwanaland about 50 million years later. About 100 million years ago, Laurasia and Gondwanaland individually began to break apart. By 50 million years ago, the distribution of continents was not much different from what we see today.

EXPLORATION 3.1
PANGAEA PUZZLE

Find a map of the world that shows the distribution of all seven continents. Examples can be found on the Internet and then printed out. Be sure to choose a map that is at least the size of a standard letter size sheet of paper. Cut out each of the major continental landmasses. Now see if you can reassemble them into a single super continent. Assemble the northern landmasses into Laurasia. Then put the rest into the southern giant continent, called Gondwanaland. Do the pieces fit together precisely?

How Earth Moves

Once scientists had accepted the concept that the seafloor and continents moved, the study of plate tectonics developed in the 1960s and 1970s. The surface of the Earth—in particular the *lithosphere*, the rigid plates of Earth's crust—moves in pieces that range from several hundred to thousands of miles wide. The lithosphere is broken into seven large, rigid plates: the African, North American, South American, Eurasian, Australian, Antarctic, and Pacific plates. Several minor plates—the Arabian, Nazca, and Philippines plates—are also part of the lithosphere. The lithosphere, obviously, is not a single shell that envelopes Earth but is fragmented into many pieces, not unlike the broken shell of an egg (Figure 3.1).

Figure 3.1—Plates of the Earth

The lithosphere includes the crust and the upper part of Earth's surface, to a depth of approximately 100 kilometers (km). The crust is divided into two parts based on density: continental and oceanic. *Continental crust* is composed of lighter felsic minerals and rock like granite. *Oceanic crust* is made up of mafic minerals, and rock such as basalt. These two crustal components play a vital role in the theory of plate tectonics.

EXPLORATION 3.2
LAYERS WITHIN THE EARTH AND AN ORANGE

Very simple methods that can help you to understand the interior structure of Earth can be glimpsed by slicing an ordinary orange in half (see Figure 3.2). If an orange is cut right down the middle, its layered structure, like that of Earth, is readily apparent. At the center is a small core. Earth's core is about 1200 km in diameter. Directly above the core of Earth is the outer core, which is approximately 2200 km thick. Above the core of the orange is the largest layer—the pulp, which is comparable to the mantle. Earth's mantle is about 2900 km thick.

Finally, at the top is the thin peel, which is flexible in an orange, representing Earth's rigid mantle. Actually, if Earth were the size of an orange, its crust would be thinner than the orange's peel (more like the zest). The crust varies from 8 to 40 km thick. After your experiment, share your discovery—and a section of your orange—with a friend!

Earth's Interior

In order to understand how the outer crust of Earth moves, it is important to review the layered structure of our planet. These layers are separated according to density. When Earth was formed, its molten state caused heavier elements like nickel and iron to settle deep within, near the core. This central core is solid, but bound by an outer core of molten nickel-iron. The planet's magnetic field is generated from here.

Lighter elements, like silica, floated toward the surface, like froth on a cup of cappuccino. The continents would take their shape from this lighter material floating on top of the

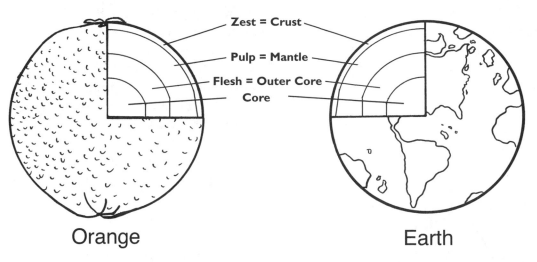

Orange

Earth

Figure 3.2—Parts of an Orange; Layers of Earth (not drawn to scale).

newly formed planet. Between the core and the crust, there is a thick intermediate layer called the *mantle*.

Since plate tectonics concerns the upper mantle and crust, we'll focus more specifically on how the seismic energy of *earthquakes*, vibrations or movements of part of Earth, changes these layers. *Seismic energy* is literally the energy created by the force of the earthquake.

Earthquakes and Seismic Energy

Earthquakes happen when two plates in Earth's crust push against each other, building up pressure and eventually causing movement or vibration. The seismic energy that comes from an earthquake is used to map the distribution of the layers within our planet. When rocks under intense strain move, energy in the form of seismic waves propagate through Earth. This seismic energy can also be produced by volcanic eruption and, more significantly, by slippage along a fault boundary.

The study of the motion and effects of these waves is called *seismology*. The distribution and intensity of the seismic waves is recorded

by a device known as a seismometer. Computer programs allow researchers to construct a *seismograph* showing these properties. Seismic waves are released from a specific point within Earth called the *focus*. This is where elastically strained rocks break and release the energy to produce an earthquake. Above the focus, on Earth's surface, is the *epicenter*—the place where we see the change and damage, and the point from which the earthquake's waves seem to extend. The closer you are to the epicenter, the more intense the shaking caused by the earthquake.

Seismic Waves

It's fairly obvious when an earthquake occurs what the damage is on the surface of Earth—buildings collapse, houses are destroyed, and the landscape is changed. What we don't see, however, is what happens below the ground. The earthquake is not just a surface phenomenon; it's also one that generates energy above and below ground, changing both the surface of Earth and the interior below.

Earthquakes generate two types of seismic waves—body waves and surface waves

(Figure 3.3). *Surface waves*, as the name implies, travel across the surface of the planet away from the epicenter. They generate a characteristic side-to-side as well as an up-and-down motion of the surface.

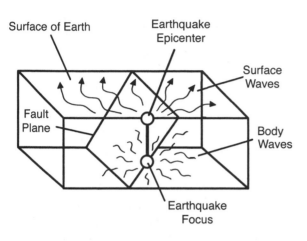

Figure 3.3—Seismic Waves

In contrast, *body waves* originate from the focus and travel in all directions through the interior of Earth—not just across the surface. Two classes of body waves are known: *compressional waves*, or P waves, and *shear waves*, or S waves.

P waves are very much like sound waves in that they travel by the compression and subsequent expansion of the material through which they pass. Their velocity is a function of the rock type. Since rock can vary significantly in its density and rigidity, the velocity of a P wave can vary as it moves through our planet. Even so, P waves are the fastest of all seismic energy and always reach detection centers first. For this reason, P waves are often called primary waves.

S waves also have velocities that are dependent on rock type. These seismic waves propagate by cutting rock in a direction perpendicular to

the motion of the wave itself; however, such motion prevents these waves from moving through liquid or molten rock. Since a shear wave will arrive later than a compressional wave, it is typically referred to as a secondary wave. Both P and S waves reach a seismograph before surface waves.

The travel times for P and S waves are used to determine the exact location of an earthquake event. It is necessary to gather data from at least three seismograph stations to make an assessment, and the interval between the arrival times of these two waves is required for accurate measurement. A series of concentric circles is drawn about each recording station, and where they intersect provides the location of the epicenter.

Timing earthquake waves allows scientists to find out how far away an earthquake is. Measurements from three different stations can be used to pinpoint the epicenter, or the exact spot above the earthquake focus. Unfortunately, although we can measure earthquakes, understand a lot about them, and know where they are likely to take place, it is impossible to predict *when* they may happen.

Richter Scale

The intensity of an earthquake can also be calculated in terms of magnitude on the *Richter scale*, developed by seismologist Charles Richter in 1938. Richter suggested that the intensity of an earthquake could be measured in terms of the height or amplitude of the greatest wave at a set distance from the epicenter. His method of measuring the intensity of earthquakes has been used for about the last 70 years.

TYPES OF FAULTS

A fault is any break, with evidence of displacement, that occurs within a brittle rock unit. The block above the fault is called the hanging wall block, while the block below it is referred to as the footwall block. Four types of faults can be identified by observing the positions and movements of the blocks. They are normal faults, reverse faults, thrust faults, and strike-slip faults. See Figure 3.4.

Normal fault—The hanging wall block is shifted downward on the footwall block and horizontal extensional stress on the rock unit pulls the footwall block apart.

Reverse fault—The hanging wall block is pushed upward, relative to the footwall, and horizontal compressional stress is applied to the rock unit, squeezing the blocks together.

Thrust fault—A reverse fault that occurs when the fault space separating the upper and lower blocks creates an angle of less than 15°.

Strike-slip fault—The motion of the two blocks is horizontal due to the vertical orientation of the actual fault plane.

You can illustrate these faults with a couple of 2x4 blocks of wood, about 6 inches long. Cut one block at a 45° angle. When refitted, the blocks can be used to show normal or reverse faulting. Another block split in half, crosswise, at a 90° angle can be used to illustrate a strike-slip fault.

On the Richter scale, magnitude can range from 1 to more than 8. Each increase in magnitude represents about a 30-times increase in the amount of energy released. The Hiroshima atomic bomb created a

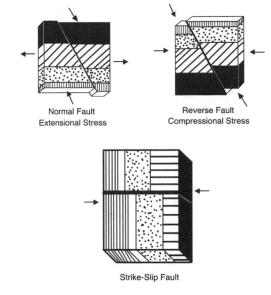

Normal Fault
Extensional Stress

Reverse Fault
Compressional Stress

Strike-Slip Fault

Figure 3.4—Types of Faults

magnitude equivalent to a 5.5 earthquake. The largest earthquake ever recorded registered at 8.6 on the Richter scale in Alaska in 1964. This was significantly more powerful than the atomic bomb at Hiroshima. Earthquakes of a larger magnitude are certainly possible but have not been recorded.

Divergent Plate Boundaries

Scientists have now come to a fairly good understanding of plate boundaries and how they move to create earthquakes, thereby changing Earth's surface. As we'll soon discover, lithospheric plates can collide, move away, and simply rub against each other. Earthquakes, volcanism, and mountain building have their origins at these plate boundaries.

Lithospheric plates, the rigid outer shell of Earth, have their origin at spreading centers found within ocean basins. As new material is formed, it moves away in a direction perpendicular to the area of volcanism, the area of volcanic activity. In this case, the two plates make what is known as a *divergent plate boundary* and they produce an oceanic ridge. This process can happen on land as well as in the ocean. Some well-known examples of divergent boundaries are the East Africa rift in Kenya and Ethiopia, and the Rio Grande rift in New Mexico. The oceanic rift valley is much narrower—only a kilometer or less across— and includes the Mid-Atlantic Ridge and the East Pacific Rise.

The magnetic polarity of the rock curiously alternates with distance away from the spreading center. When magma is in a molten, moving state, the magnetic grains are randomly aligned. At temperatures above 580°C, Earth's magnetic field causes the grains to become aligned, with a distinctive north–south polarity. At this critical temperature point, called the *Curie temperature*, the magnetic grains freeze in place and retain a record of the orientation relative to the magnetic field. It turns out that Earth's magnetic field is not constant with time. Every few hundred thousand years the north–south polarity reverses. Because it is rich in iron, oceanic crust faithfully records these changes in polarity like the needle of a compass. The bands of positive and negative polarity make magnetic "stripes" across the ocean basin.

Oceanic crust ultimately gets destroyed. No portion of the crust is older than about 200 million years. The rate at which oceanic crust is being created varies across ocean basins. Magma upwells from within an area known as the asthenosphere. The *asthenosphere*, a molten or plastic layer, resides at a depth of about 700 km. This basaltic magma causes oceanic crust to be pushed away from the ridge in opposite directions. Oceanic crust is recycled when it encounters a continental landmass or another oceanic plate.

As you move farther away from the oceanic ridge, sediment thickness increases. This happens because the crust was exposed to sediment deposition for a longer period of time. You can calculate the rate of spreading by the age of the sediment and its distance from the ridge.

Spreading rates vary because the ocean crust follows the curvature of Earth and so is not really a flat plate. In addition, lithospheric plates that have the continental crust resting on them will move more slowly than lithospheric plates that consist of only oceanic crust. High spreading rates also indicate voluminous amounts of magma were extruded from the ridge. Since oceanic crust cools as it settles and moves away from the ridge, the depths of the ocean basin increase with distance and age.

Convergent Plate Boundaries

Convergent plate boundaries are created by the crashing or crunching together of different plates. They move so slowly that a collision might occur over millions of years. However, the collision of plates has consequences. The resultant folding and bending of edges of the plates creates earthquakes; it also causes melted rock to rise up through the continental plate, causing more earthquakes and forming volcanic eruptions as the molten rock reaches the surface.

On the west coast of South America, where the oceanic Nazca plate is crashing into the continent of South America, the Andes Mountains have formed, including a long string of volcanoes along the mountain crest and the deep trench off the coast in the Pacific Ocean.

Equilibrium is established between the amount of new oceanic crust formed and the amount of oceanic crust being destroyed. Crust is removed as two plates collide to form a trench. These trenches often represent the deepest portions of an ocean basin. When the two plates encounter each other, one must be pushed, or subducted, beneath the other. The plate that is pushed beneath is ultimately recycled within the asthenosphere. These areas where plates are pushed into the asthenosphere are referred to as *subduction zones*.

Subduction zones are distinguished by lithospheric plates that descend into the mantle beneath another overlying plate. This process marks a seismically active zone. This zone of earthquakes extends from the surface to the asthenosphere. Earthquake focal depths determine that these zones of faults pass from the ocean trenches down more than 600 km into the mantle. These are called Wadati-Benioff Zones, or simply Benioff Zones, after the two seismologists, Kiyoo Wadati and Hugo Benioff, who independently established the pattern of earthquakes.

Convergent plate boundaries come in many forms. One variation consists of an ocean-to-ocean plate convergence. Frictional heating of the subducted crust can produce a chain of volcanoes called an *island arc*. These volcanic chains run parallel to the *oceanic trench*, a linear trench on the seafloor where the most dense oceanic crust is sliding into the asthenosphere. The volcanic chains are on the plate that had not been subducted. The Aleutian Islands, found off the coast of Alaska, are an example of this phenomenon.

Another variation of a convergent plate boundary is when oceanic crust is subducted beneath continental crust. In this case, both an oceanic trench and a volcanic arc are produced; however, the volcanism occurs on the nonsubducted continental crust. An example of this can be seen where the Pacific plate is

pushed beneath the North American plate. In another scenario, a continental-to-continental plate convergence occurs. At the point of contact, the buckled plates create a large mountain range. The tall Himalayan Mountains are the product of such a collision. The once-free, drifting Indian plate came into contact with the Asian plate, resulting in the collision of a small and large continental landmass.

EXPLORATION 3.3
FOLDED AND DEFORMED ROCKS

Rocks along the margins of plate boundaries show signs of deformation since the forces of plates colliding often bend or fold rock. Rocks, on a large scale, are flexible. There are three different types of folds.

Anticline folds show signs of having been bent upward so that two limbs of the fold aim downward away from the hinge of the fold.

Syncline folds occur when the once-horizontal layered rock has been folded and pushed downward with two limbs pointing upward.

In reality, anticlines and synclines are part of a regional fold system—with the limb of an anticline being shared with an adjacent syncline.

Monocline folds occur when the two limbs are still horizontal, and the rock has been pushed upward.

You can create your own folds with a thick stack of paper. Make sure that all pages are aligned and then try bending the stack to form an anticline, a syncline, and a monocline. It is useful to draw a series of straight lines on the sides of the paper in order to observe small-scale deformation effects.

Transform Plate Boundaries and Seamount Chains

Sometimes new crust is neither created nor destroyed. In this case, two plate boundaries glide past one another. These *transform faults* lack the catastrophic consequences of convergent or divergent boundaries; instead, they create linear valleys where rock has been ground up by the sliding. The area between the offset ridges is where the *transform plate boundary* occurs. Due to the nature of the plate contact, earthquakes along transform boundaries have a shallow focus (they're not very deep below Earth's surface). A well-known example of this plate contact type is the San Andreas Fault, which is located along the western edge of California, from Los Angeles to beyond San Francisco.

FUN FACT: The part of California to the west of the fault is slowly moving north relative to the rest of California. Since motion along the fault is sideways and not vertical, Los Angeles will not crack off and fall into the ocean, but it will keep moving toward San Francisco at about 6 cm per year. In about ten million years, the two cities should be side by side.

Clear evidence that plates are in a state of motion is demonstrated by the occurrence of chains of islands distributed across the Pacific plate floor, comprised of volcanoes along the ocean floor known as *seamounts*, or underwater volcanoes. These include the Hawaiian and Marshall-Ellis island chains. They extend from the southeast to the northwest across the central Pacific basin. Only the extreme southeastern sections show evidence of active volcanism, while the rest of the islands farther west are dormant.

Current thinking suggests that these volcanic island chains formed as the Pacific plate moved over a stationary heat source deep beneath the lithosphere. These may be hot areas within Earth's mantle that are stationary relative to the moving lithosphere or crust. Hot spots may originate from melting induced by a high concentration of radioactive elements that liberate heat, and thus, melt rock. Plumes of magma then rise toward the surface above the hot spot. From the location of these hot spots relative to the volcanic chains, it is possible to calculate the absolute velocity of the moving plate. Although the active area of volcanism is centered above the hot spot, it will ultimately move away to become an eroded suboceanic mound or a seamount.

EXPLORATION 3.4
CONVECTION CURRENTS

Mantle convection currents, like currents of heat produced by a pot of boiling liquid, can be simulated on the kitchen stove. Place a pan of water on a flat burner. Set the heat on medium. As the water begins to heat up, watch for the motion. Currents form such that warm water at the base of the pan rises to the surface—only to cool when in contact with the air. This circulation pattern is known as convection. Now place two small sponges on the surface and watch how they move. Do they move apart or stay together? Discuss how the sponges simulate lithospheric plates moving on a convecting asthenosphere.

Like the currents produced by the boiling water, heat gets the semimolten upper mantle moving in slow currents. This exerts dragging forces on the rigid lithospheric plates, causing eventual movement.

SUMMARY

Our view of the world and how its continents were formed has changed dramatically over the centuries. It is only since the 1960s that the concept of plate tectonics has been fully accepted and understood.

Now scientists believe the seafloor and continents move and the lithosphere, consisting of the rigid plates making the outer shell of Earth, is constantly shifting. Earthquakes are the product of the seismic energy that is made as Earth's plates shift around. How Earth's interior is layered can be explained through an understanding of the different kinds of seismic waves and their interactions with rock.

There are three kinds of plate boundaries: divergent plate boundaries, where material moves away from the area of volcanism; convergent plate boundaries, where two plates encounter each other and one is subducted or covered by the other; and transform plate boundaries, where two plates glide past one another.

Seamounts, eroded suboceanic mounds or chains of volcanoes along the ocean floor, help demonstrate that the plates are in constant motion. By measuring the distance between active areas of volcanism and seamounts, calculations of the velocity of the moving plate can be made.

GEOLOGIC PROCESSES

SURFACE-MODIFYING PROCESSES

Consider tectonic plates as the behind-the-scenes work that Earth does. The globe is constantly changing and moving in ways that we are not usually conscious of. What might be more obvious are the ways that Earth's surface is constantly sculpted by a variety of geological processes. Volcanism, tectonism, water, wind, ice, and gravity are all constantly at work on Earth's surface, sometimes changing it dramatically in a short time and at other times making slower, almost imperceptible changes.

Volcanism

As you'll recall from Chapter 3, *tectonism*, or the fracturing and deformation of the planet's crust, is one geological process that contributes to the formation of Earth's surface. Another is *volcanism*. Volcanism is defined as the process that occurs whenever molten rock reaches the surface of Earth. This might result from the slow flow of molten material or the violent eruption of a volcano.

The average person tends to fear the power of a volcano, but in spite of the terrible damage a volcano can do, there are some positive results as well. If you think of them as beginning in holes or cracks in Earth's outer layer, then it is easier to understand how they helped to create the continents that we live on. Many people now live on volcanic islands as well.

In addition to rich volcanic soil, many other natural resources come from volcanic activity. Sand comes from the once-molten rock; granite is used in mortar; gold and tin are formed in molten rock; even electricity can be extracted from the heat of hot volcanic rocks.

We all have mental images of an erupting volcano, but there are several different forms that this eruption might take. There are several types of volcanic flows. *Basaltic lavas* and *mudflows* are very fluid eruptions. *Pyroclastic flows* consist of solid debris that ranges in size from rock- to dust-sized fragments.

Basaltic Lavas and Mudflows

Basaltic lavas and mudflows have earned special names because of their physical characteristics. Basaltic lava comes in three varieties: pahoehoe, aa, and pillow lava. The first two varieties were named by the native Hawaiian people because of the high concentration of active volcanoes in that region. The third variety is named for its visual similarity to a pillow. *Pahoehoe lava* has a smooth surface texture. It might sometimes have a ropy-looking surface, caused when the moving lava bunches together. *Aa lava* has a rough, jagged texture. Its appearance is created when the more-quickly moving lava flows over slower lava. Pillow lava is smooth and bulbous-looking, and it occurs in underwater settings.

When lava erupts from Earth, it surfaces through vents called *fissures*. A curtain of flaming lava, or a *fire fountain*, may mark the site at the time of the event. After the eruption, small beads and strands of glass can be found around the fissures. The native Hawaiians named these Pele's tears and Pele's hair, respectively, for the Hawaiian goddess of the volcano world.

Obviously, something as dramatic as the eruption of a volcano has a lasting effect on Earth. Flowing lava often forms a crust, while the liquid rocks move beneath in a tube. Once drained, these lava tubes remain as empty tunnels beneath the ground. These lava tunnels, a permanent reminder of the volcano's force, are often discovered later. They can run for hundreds of meters and are large enough for people to walk through.

FUN FACT: At Craters of the Moon National Monument in Idaho, there are lava tunnels that are 10 m in diameter and a few hundred meters long. Springs within the tunnel are quite cool—one stays at about 2°C, even when the air temperature is about 25°C. Pools of water in the tunnel have ice on them. A place known as the Bottomless Pit is a natural ice well, and a 3 m pile of snow remains unmelted there throughout the year.

Massive eruptions of lava can form extensive lava flows known as *flood basalts*. An example of this is in the northwestern United States, extending from Washington and Oregon into Idaho, in an area called the Colombian River Flood Lavas.

Another type of fluid flow is called a *lahar*, or mudflow. This is a hybrid product of volcanism that is often produced by the melting of mountainous ice and snow. The heat of the volcano can melt glacial ice, and a mudflow can strike without warning. The smaller but most frequent debris flows that occur at Mount Rainier in Washington state, for example, begin as glacial outburst floods. These are sudden releases of stored water that are unpredictable and travel at speeds of 15 to 30 km per hour.

A mudflow can occur as a result of heavy rainfall or rapid snowmelt. It becomes a river of rock, earth, and other debris. The mudflow can travel several kilometers from its source, growing in size as it picks up trees, cars, and other materials along the way. The consequences of these events can be devastating for the unsuspecting residents on lower ground.

Pyroclastic Flows

Like mudflows, pyroclastic flows do not consist of lava, but of an avalanche of glowing ash and rock fragments. These types of flows come out of the fissures, or vents, of volcanoes, and move downhill, hugging the terrain. Some pyroclastic flows eject hot incandescent ash and gases, creating a fiery cloud known as *nuée ardente*. These volcanoes rush down slope at 160 km per hour, while expanding gases hold up solid particles, carrying them in avalanche fashion. These flows can be catastrophic to the communities lying at the base of the volcano. In 1902, a nuée ardente from Mt. Pelee, a small volcano in the West Indies, destroyed the town of St. Pierre (except for a couple of survivors out of 28,000 people). The whole event took only about five minutes and was described as one great flash of fire.

Pyroclastic flows leave behind debris ranging in fragment size from giant volcanic blocks, to gravel, to pebble-sized *lapilli* (stones no larger than a walnut), to very fine ash. Sometimes gases rapidly escape from the hot rock, forming substances with countless small holes or vesicles such as pumice or *scoria*, the slag or clinkerlike remains of melted rock.

SHIELD VOLCANOES

A volcano produced from layers of lava flows is called a *shield volcano*. Its name comes from the shape of the structure, because it looks like an inverted warrior's shield. Although the flanks have shallow slopes, they can extend for a considerable distance, thus producing very tall volcanoes. In areas where there are many long fissures in the ground, lava flows out of these openings during eruptions. This is the kind of activity that builds a shield volcano.

These volcanic mountains are huge; in fact, some of the largest volcanoes on the planet are classified as shield volcanoes. The largest example of a shield volcano is Mauna Loa, on the island of Hawaii. The volcanoes of the Galapagos Islands are also examples of shield volcanoes.

Volcanoes have *reservoirs*, which are caverns of melted rock deep inside Earth. At the top of this reservoir is a long tube or chimney through which the magma can climb to the surface. As the lava flows out, the reservoir fills up again.

During an eruption, the reservoir is emptied. If no more magma or lava comes up from below, the eruption stops and the ground may collapse into the reservoir, creating a larger crater. A crater that is enlarged by the collapse of the top of the volcano is called a *caldera*.

The reservoirs of volcanoes can be at different depths in Earth. The reservoir of Mount Etna is about 19 km deep, while Vesuvius is only 5 km deep. Kilauea in Hawaii has two reservoirs; one is 3 km deep and the other is 50 km below Earth's surface.

CINDER CONE VOLCANOES

Cinder cones are another volcanic form, created primarily from particles of congealed lava ejected from a single vent. As the lava is pushed into the air, it breaks into small fragments, or cinders, around the vent. These small volcanoes are almost entirely made up of pyroclastic deposits.

As the magma builds up in the volcano, it mixes with gas that was formed when the rock melted. This mixture is light; it rises toward Earth's surface, and finally explodes from the top of the volcano. This type of eruption builds up a cinder cone.

Cinder cones can occur on fissure vents when the style of volcanic eruption changes from a fluid basaltic flow to a pyroclastic event. The slopes of these volcanoes are rubble-laden and steep, and a central pit marks the summit.

Cinder cones are common in western North America. One example is located near Paricutín, Mexico; scientists observed it for nine years as it developed and then eventually destroyed the nearby towns of San Salvador and San Juan.

COMPOSITE CONE VOLCANOES

Volcanoes that consist of a combination of pyroclastic materials and lava are called *composite cones*. Alternating layers of lava or pyroclastic deposits formed as the eruption style changed. These volcanoes have very steep flanks and viscous lavas that erupted violently.

Composite cone volcanoes, like cinder cones, may have a crater at the summit, but they can contain one central vent or a clustered group of vents. Lava flows through breaks in the crater or through fissures. As it solidifies, it forms dikes that strengthen the cone. The volcano is built up by the accumulation of these materials.

Some of the world's most scenic mountains are composite volcanoes, including Mount Fuji, in Japan; Mount Shasta, in California; Mount Hood, in Oregon; and Mount St. Helens and Mount Rainier, in Washington.

EXPLORATION 4.1
BUILD A SHIELD VOLCANO

Make your own shield volcano using paraffin wax. Melt about a pound of wax in a pan on a hot plate. You can color the wax gray by using a chip of coloring agent such as a crayon. This gives the final product a basaltic look. Start by using a small ladle to pour molten wax onto a flat tin or cookie pan. After it solidifies, which may take 30 seconds or so, pour another layer of wax atop the same spot. Continue to do this and watch how the mound grows into a shield volcano. If the wax is carefully poured at the same position each time, then a central crater or caldera will form. Watch how the wax ponds within this depression, only to overflow down the flanks of the ever-growing structure. The molten liquid takes the easiest route down the flanks of the volcano.

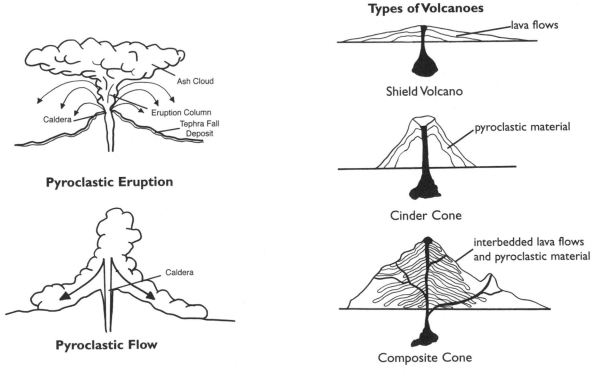

Figure 4.1—Types of Volcanoes and Their Formation

PLUTONS, DIKES, AND SILLS

Some volcanic materials never make it to the surface of Earth. They solidify underground, forming *plutons*, bodies of igneous rock formed beneath Earth's surface. It is only later, through the process of erosion, that these plutons might be exposed. For instance, an extremely weathered volcano may reveal an internal column of rock called a *volcanic neck*. This was once-molten lava that never quite made it to surface.

Other subsurface plutons include dikes and sills, which are differentiated by their orientation to the encasing rock. *Dikes* are plutons that are inclined toward the inclosing rock. Country rock is the deeply embedded rock that doesn't move, while the plutons take shape within it. *Sills* are tabular igneous bodies that intrude parallel to the layer of preexisting rock. Large magma bodies that solidified beneath the surface are called *batholiths*. These are huge chunks of granite that have cooled and hardened underground.

Finally, the eroded remnants of a volcano can leave a column of material called a *stock*, which is actually the neck of the volcano.

Fluvial or Water-Modifying Forces

Of all the ways that Earth's surface might be changed, the most obvious to us is probably the force of water. Everyone has seen a road or path with ruts after a heavy rainstorm, sediment and brush collecting at a turn in the creek, or the more dramatic effects of a flood. Water can change our landscape in the span of just a few hours.

Fluvial forces cause the erosion and transport of sediment by water. This material might be carried from the source of a river to the mouth,

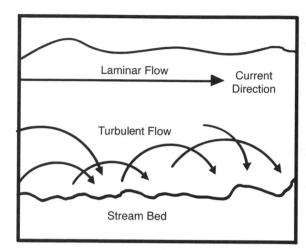

Figure 4.2—Fluvial Forces

where it is eventually discharged into the sea. Scientists measure the normal amount of discharge as being equivalent to the cross-sectional area of the stream channel times the water flow velocity. The faster and harder the water flows, the more sediment will be deposited.

Water can flow in parallel layers and be referred to as *laminar flow*, or it can flow in choppy, uneven layers and be referred to as *turbulent flow*. (See Figure 4.2.) Sediment is transported in two fashions, depending on the type of flow. If it is carried smoothly and evenly across the bottom of the streambed by a laminar flow, it is known as the *bed load*. If it is carried in short spurts, in a bounding manner across the river bottom by a turbulent flow, it is known as *saltation*. In this process, small silt and clay particles can be suspended in the water, and some sediment is so small that it dissolves completely.

Stream channels, the beginning of all rivers, evolve with time. They begin as relatively straight waterways. The stream channel may bubble up out of the earth, beginning as a small spring and eventually flowing into a stream. Stream channels ultimately flow into a river, where they are joined by other streams, and flow into the sea.

The younger rivers will have a deeper channel carved by water flowing at higher velocities. In areas where the water speed decreases, sediment is deposited, forming *sandbars*. As a river ages, its path begins to wander. These meandering channels mirror the subsurface rocks that the river must cut through. When the river encounters a tough rock, it simply works its way around it.

The deeper sections of the channel are found on the outer part of its curve, where water velocity and erosion rates are high. On the inner portion of the channel, where water velocity is low, sediment accumulates to form point bars. Sometimes, channels or meanders can be pinched off by *point bars*; this process results in the formation of isolated lakes that are separated from the main channel. These features are called *oxbow lakes*. Ancient river channels can become choked with sediment and develop a braided appearance, as islands of sediment and oxbow lakes punctuate the course of the river.

Streams have a host of deposits that form along the course of the channel. Natural *levees*, the accumulation of sediment, form banks and confine the river to the channel. When there is a flood, water spills over the levees, forming extensive flat sediment layers or *floodplain deposits*. Beyond the floodplain are *terrace deposits*, sediment that comes from the erosion of the floodplain into other areas.

The fluvial process continues as the river reaches the sea. The streams and rivers reach the mouth of the river where they can flow, more or less unobstructed, into the sea, and the fluvial process—the flow of water, deposits

of sediment, and the changing natural landscape—is even more marked.

Deltas are fan-shaped deposits of sediment that accumulate at the mouths of rivers, where they open to the ocean. Within these deposits are *distributary channels*, which are passages of flowing water that carve their way to the sea. Similarly, there are *alluvial* fans (fan-shaped deposits formed by a stream as it issues from a ravine into a plain) that form at the base of a mountain, where a stream begins to extend upon a flat valley floor.

As a river reaches the ocean, its forward motion is quickly lost, and the sediment that it was carrying may be deposited quickly. This is why you might see sandbars, sediment, and deltas extending outward. The Nile and the Mississippi, two great rivers, have deltas that extend over thousands of square kilometers. New Orleans, for instance, sits on a site that was ocean less than 5000 years ago.

EXPLORATION 4.2
CARVE YOUR OWN RIVER CHANNEL

Pour a bucket of fine play sand (available from most hardware stores) into a large shallow pan. Smooth it over and then sprinkle water over the surface, making it damp so that it will hold together. Next, place the pan at an angle of approximately 20° and allow a steady stream of water to spill over the surface, flowing from the higher to the lower elevation. Watch as a stream channel forms. Place an obstacle, like a rock, in the path of the growing stream channel. How does this affect the flow and shape of the developing channel?

Depending on the environment and the topography, the land and waterways always reflect the history of the fluvial process. For instance, in places where the Mississippi River has flooded its banks in past years, a natural levee has resulted. This is coarse sediment in strips bordering the channel of the river. The gentle slope up to the river makes it difficult for heavy rainwater to flow into the river and a tributary stream may follow the course of the river for as much as 300 km before it finds a way to empty into it. Such natural levees can also help to create what is known as back swamps in areas adjacent to the river.

Streams are typically isolated from one another by topographic highlands called *divides*. The drainage pattern of an individual stream is often controlled by topography and the rock through which the stream cuts. The stream will tend to go around divides or rock structures rather than cut through them. Streams that branch out are called *dendritic*, because they branch out in the same manner as a tree limb. Tributaries also join the main stream at some angle. If you could look at them from the air, they too would look like tree limbs. They form in areas where the slope and rock

type do not change appreciably, allowing the water to flow more freely.

If the tributaries meet the main channel at a 90° angle, the drainage pattern is called a *trellis*. It forms where there is considerable structural control to the subsurface rocks. *Radial drainage* occurs on the flanks of mountains or volcanoes where small channels extend away from the summit.

Just like tectonic or volcanic forces, the flow of water on Earth's surface continues to effect change. All the fluvial processes, from the tiniest stream to the largest river, contribute in some way to sculpting Earth's surface. We might see sudden and dramatic change over a short period of time in the case of a hurricane or flood, but water is always at work—moving sediment, forming sandbars, shaping a natural levee, or carving a new stream through a rain-soaked valley. The impact of a flood is obvious, but the constant flow of a stream or river is always changing the land, sometimes in ways that are imperceptible to the casual observer.

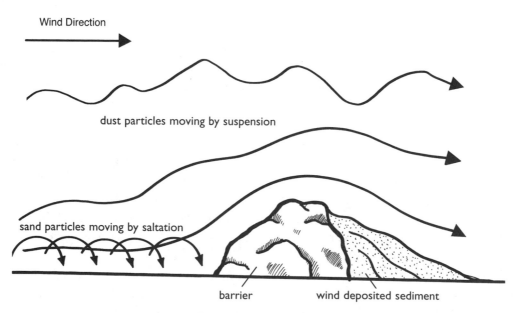

Figure 4.3—Aeolian Processes

Aeolian Processes

An *aeolian process* is one that is mutable, or varying with respect to some property, like the wind, traveling in a different direction. (See Figure 4.3.) Like water, wind can transform the landscape slowly over time or dramatically in a violent storm. Aeolian processes erode, transport, and deposit sediment in a variety of ways. Large particles like sand bounce along the ground, while smaller particles, like dust, silt, and clay are carried through the air by the wind. In either case, the transported sediment is deposited when the wind slows down or encounters an obstacle.

For instance, sediment will accumulate on the side of a boulder that is blocked by the wind. In the area in front of the boulder, the air will actually increase in velocity due to converging air currents. Behind the boulder, air currents diverge, causing a decrease in wind velocity and resultant sediment deposition.

Wind erosion wears down and removes sediment from a surface. Larger pebbles and cobbles are left behind, producing what is called *desert pavement*. Saltating grains of sand, which are carried by the wind, abrade larger rocks that cannot be transported by wind. The surfaces of these rocks become sculpted, creating a rock known as a *ventifact*.

In addition to ventifacts, wind erosion also produces boat-shaped mounds called *yardangs*. These consist of consolidated sand that runs parallel and then tapers in the direction of the wind. The windward face of the yardang has been sandblasted blunt. The sculpting and creation of ventifacts and yardangs demonstrate how powerful a force the wind can be.

FUN FACT: In the Mojave Desert, in southeastern California, metal skirts are placed around the base of telephone poles to prolong their lives. If saltating sand can actually cut down telephone poles, how difficult is it to imagine blowing sand sculpting a rock?

The constant force of the wind can create wind-formed accumulations of sand called *sand dunes*. (See Figure 4.4.) Basically, this is sand pushed into a pile with the shallow slope facing the wind's force and the steeper slope dropping off in the direction that the wind is

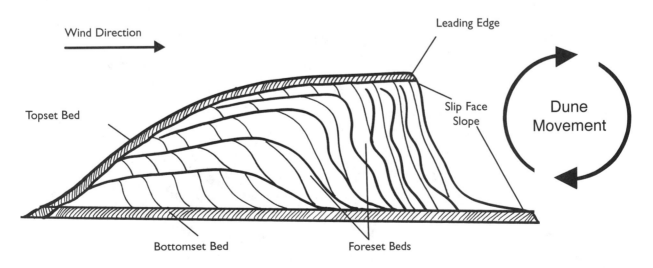

Figure 4.4—Dune Formation

blowing. The shallow slope is called the *topset bed*, and from here the sand saltates up and over the top of the dune, just as if it is dancing in the wind. When sand reaches the *leading edge*, or the top of the steepest slope, it rolls down the steep slope making the *foreset bed*s. This is also known as the *slip face slope*, and it is inclined so that the grains slide down at a rate proportional to that at which they accumulate. A dune migrates by rolling over itself as it moves, so that the topset beds are created by sand moving from the *bottomset beds*.

Dunes are classified by their morphology, or shape, which is a function of the direction of movement relative to the wind. The barchan dune, one of the most common shapes of dunes, is a crescent-shaped pile of sand with horns that are aimed downwind. This should not be confused with the parabolic dune, which is similar in shape, but with the horns of the crescent oriented upwind. In the case of the parabolic dune, vegetation has stabilized the outer portions of the dune so movement is slowed as the central part of the dune overtakes its flanks.

Other dunes are fairly straight in appearance. Transverse dunes are constructed so that the longest axis is perpendicular to the blowing wind. In contrast, linear dunes have their long axis more or less parallel to the prevailing wind direction. They are formed where winds converge from two directions at a slight angle. Star dunes are clumps of ridges with the overall look of a starfish. In this case, variable winds from all directions push sand up into a pointed dune with several arms attached.

The shoreline and its dunes may be cut away by fierce storms, or they may be built up by the continuous blowing of sand. Here, certain hardy plants that thrive on a moist environment may take root. The types of plants may vary from one part of the world to another, but plants and trees adapt to the climate, extending the shoreline, protecting it from storms, and changing the face of Earth.

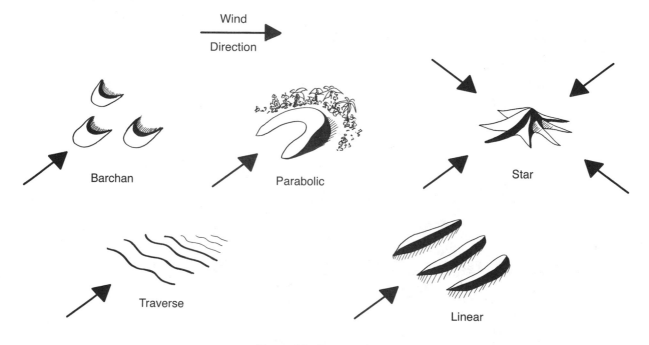

Figure 4.5—Types of Dunes

EXPLORATION 4.3
BUILD A WIND TUNNEL

Wind is a fluid movement of air and debris that can erode sediment or cause it to pile up into mounds. This process can be modeled in a homemade wind tunnel. Construct a linear box that is open on both ends, with a window fan at one end. On the floor of the box, spread out a layer of fine-grained play sand. Turn the fan on the high setting and observe what happens to the sand grains. Do the sand grains bounce or saltate in the direction of the blowing wind? Place an obstacle in the path of the blowing wind. How does it affect the motion of the moving sand? Describe the shape of any sand accumulations or dunes that may develop.

Glacial Processes

We tend to think of glaciers as something that just happened during the Ice Age, but like wind, water, earthquakes, and plate tectonics, glaciers are a daily force at work on our planet. Glaciers are one of the slowest-moving forces that change Earth's surface, but their impact from eons ago is obvious wherever you travel. Some obvious examples might be the Matterhorn in the Swiss Alps and various spots in the Northern Rockies. There are also spectacular fjords, crevasses, cliffs, and other rock formations that are the result of glacial movement. But early glaciers left behind lots of other traces of their passage across the continents. In fact, one of the things glaciers did was to level the landscape, leaving behind rocky pastures in New England, softly rolling farmland in the Midwest, and odd formations like kettle ponds, or *drumlins*, which are streamlined asymmetrical hills (examples of these can be found in upstate New York).

Glaciers can cover mountains or even continents, as they move slowly downslope as a result of the pull of gravity. *Glaciers* are actually blocks of recrystallized snow. The snowflakes have been compacted and all air has been removed. Gradually, the weight of snow and ice squeezes the ice together, creating a solid mass. When snow and ice have developed over time and become more than 20 m deep, the resultant, frozen mass begins to move. It may happen slowly— perhaps between a few centimeters to a couple of meters per day—but when it starts moving, it is no longer an ice field, but transforms into a glacier. Clearly, such heavy masses of ice and snow can have a tremendous impact on shaping Earth's surface.

Glaciers move in one of two ways. They can actually slide along their base, or there can be an internal flow of ice. Imagine magma flowing underneath Earth's surface, bubbling up toward the crater of a volcano. In almost the same way, while the massive glacier is sliding downward, ice is moving within.

Melting ice lubricates the base of a glacier at the same time that the deformation of ice crystals causes the entire structure to move downward. The top of a glacier doesn't move this way though; its surface is very brittle and breaks into large cracks called *crevasses*, which form when the glacier moves across rugged terrain.

Glaciers are dynamic and can change in size as a result of a shift in the delicate balance between the accumulation and melting of snow. Because of the constant cold of the polar regions, glaciers are usually found in these areas and the *snowline*—the altitude at which snow doesn't melt—is actually at sea level. In more temperate latitudes, the snowline is several thousand meters above sea level.

Glaciers are classified based on the surface that they cover. Glaciers that can cover significant portions of continents are called *ice sheet glaciers*. These land-based formations include the most extensive glaciers found on the planet. Some glaciers rest on top of seawater and form what are known as *ice shelves*. These glaciers are found on the coasts of continents in higher latitudes and can be up to 1000 meters thick. The glaciers that blanket the peaks of tall mountains are called *mountain glaciers*. The smaller varieties of mountain glaciers are called *cirques glaciers*, as they occupy only a small section of the mountain. Other mountain glaciers, called *valley glaciers*, can extend over a considerable portion of the mountain. When valley glaciers reach the coastline, deep valleys can be cut, producing *fjord glaciers*. *Piedmont glaciers* extend from the flanks of the mountain onto the surrounding lowlands. Sometimes an entire mountain becomes enveloped by *glaciation* (a thick mass of ice showing signs of former flow), forming an ice cap. The *ice cap* is itself a glacier, but one that is formed on an extensive area of relatively level land flowing outward from its center atop a mountain or plateau.

Glaciers can form in a variety of ways, given the presence of water and extreme cold. All these different types of glaciers, from ice sheet glaciers to ice caps, may cover different areas. They may exist on a mountaintop, in a valley, on the ocean, on the slopes of the mountain, or even, as in the case of an ice cap, cover the entire mountaintop. Wherever they may be, the impact of the glacier is similar. They move slowly, changing the surface of Earth as they slide downslope.

As glaciers move, they cause erosion and produce distinctive landforms, making their own contribution to the sculpting of Earth's surface. Rocks in immediate contact with the moving ice sheet are often polished and covered with long parallel grooves called *striations*. Often, ice sheet glaciers sculpt linear mounds of material, called drumlins, which are unstriated ovals or streamlined, asymmetrical hills of glacial drift.

EXPLORATION 4.4
ICE AS A GEOLOGIC FORCE

When water freezes into ice, it expands its volume by about 9 percent. This is significant, because the expansion can break a rock apart. In an everyday setting, water changing into ice can be a problem as well. For instance, if the water in your car's radiator is not mixed properly with an antifreeze solution, on a cold winter night the radiator will crack due to the freezing and expansion of water. In a geologic context, the freezing and subsequent thawing of ice can tear rocks apart in a process known as frost wedging. This is something those of us in northern regions experience every year as frost heaves create potholes in the roads and cracks in the sidewalks.

Try this experiment to see the power of ice for yourself. Place a plastic bottle of water in your freezer. Be sure that the bottle is filled to the very top, with no air remaining inside. After a day or two has passed, remove the bottle from the freezer and notice how it has been deformed or even broken by the conversion of water into ice!

Much of North America and Europe was covered by glaciers 20,000 years ago. You can see signs of glaciers by finding scratches on bedrock, a big boulder standing all alone, or a river cutting through a valley. Often rocks carried by a glacier are broken into tiny pieces and then eventually ground into what is known as *rock flour*. The impact of glaciers, like those of other Earth-changing forces, can be huge or so tiny that we may never see some of the changes they have made.

Glacial drift refers to sediment deposited by the *glaciation process*—the freezing, melting, and movement of ice, along with accumulated debris. The size of this sediment can vary immensely, from small clay particles to enormous boulders. Glaciers can move rocks of all sizes far from their origins. Once they are deposited, they are called *erratics*. Smaller particles of unsorted sediment are called *till*. Mounds of till are called *glacial moraines*. The rock that is ground too fine to actually distinguish with the human eye ends up as rock flour.

Mass Wasting or Gravitational Processes

An unconsolidated layer of sediment called *regolith* blankets our planet's surface. If regolith resides on a slope, it may slide downward due to gravity. Such a surface-modifying process is called *mass wasting*. This happens when the slope cannot support the weight of water, ice, and regolith all at once.

Regolith often cascades downslope when a hill suddenly collapses, leaving curved scars and depressions on the surface of Earth. Earthquakes and saturation of a steep hillside with rainwater can trigger this type of mass wasting. Rocks can loosen and fall from cliffs, and then they sometimes mix with finer sediments to form a pile of material called a *talus* (an accumulation of rock debris at the bottom of a cliff or at the base of a slope).

Mass wasting can be particularly dramatic in cold climates. As you saw in Exploration 4.4, when water freezes, it expands in volume by approximately 9 percent. We also learned, when we discussed glaciers, that ice can flow, even though it is actually a solid. Sometimes there are pockets within the glacier that move, or the bottom layer might partially thaw, causing sliding of the whole mass. When water-saturated ground freezes, rocks are pushed upward from the soil and then slide downslope upon thawing. Similarly, frozen soil moves downslope during the summer months in a process called *gelifluction*, mass movement of soil material over the permafrost layer. Rocks can be cemented within a matrix of ice that forms rock glaciers.

Although we've talked about the processes of sculpting Earth separately, it sometimes happens that things work in tandem. For instance, Iceland's ice cap, which covers 5000 square km, has an active volcano buried beneath it. The heat melts the ice, forming a reservoir, and every now and then it bursts out from under an edge of the cap. The force of the water will carry huge boulders and blocks of ice, immediately transforming that landscape.

Rarely does one force act upon Earth in isolation. Volcanoes trigger mudflows and earthquakes, which may change the course of a stream or precipitate flooding. All the forces that impact Earth's surface are at work all the time, occasionally combining to cause even more drastic changes. Although we may think of these things as catastrophes, these same processes created our continents, made rich farmland, set the course of rivers, and built up beautiful mountains.

SUMMARY

The forces of volcanism, tectonism, water, wind, ice, and gravity constantly change the surface of Earth. Tectonism, the process of fracturing and deforming the Earth's crust, was discussed in Chapter 3. Volcanism happens when molten rock reaches the Earth's surface. Volcanoes can take different forms and appear as shields, cinder cones, or composite cones.

Fluvial, or water-modifying, forces erode and transport sediment by water. This is a constant and somewhat gradual process, although dramatic changes can be seen in an extreme weather event.

The aeolian process refers to the way that wind transforms the landscape. The wind erodes, transports, and deposits sediment in a variety of ways, depending on the strength of the wind, the type of landscape, and the materials that the wind carries.

Glaciers or ice sheets tend to cover areas of high altitude and then move down slope because of the pull of gravity. Like wind and water, glaciers cause erosion and create distinctive landforms. Glaciers also pick up and carry sediment, including rocks of all sizes, with them to other locations.

The force of gravity is also a major contributing factor in the phenomenon known as mass wasting. Unconsolidated layers of sediment, or regolith, slide downward because of gravity. The presence of water and ice may increase this tendency, causing significant changes in the landscape.

GEOLOGIC TIME

KEY TERMS

uniformitarianism, stratigraphy, relative age
dating, faunal succession, radiometric age dating,
radioactive half-life, carbon-14 dating,
Precambrian, Phanerozoic

HOW OLD IS EARTH?

It wasn't until the 1800s that people began
to have a sense of how old Earth really is.
Before that time, everyone believed that the
world was 6,000 years old. This was based
on a theory proposed by Archbishop James
Ussher of Armagh, Ireland in 1650 (See Figure
5.1.). He claimed that Earth was created at
9 AM. on October 23, 4004 BCE. His theory
was formulated by calculating the ages of all
the great men in the *Bible*.

Figure 5.1—James Ussher

Biblical scholars often dominated popular
theories about Earth's origins, and early
studies suggested that the planet's features
resulted from events that happened over brief
spans of time. For example, it was often stated
that the great Biblical flood of Noah's day
created all sedimentary rocks. People who
followed this theory were called *Neptunists*—
named for the ancient Greek god of the seas.

Others proposed that all rocks were of an
igneous origin, formed of molten magma.
These scholars were called *Plutonists*—named
for Pluto, the ancient Roman god of the
underworld.

These early ideas about Earth's origins began
to change, however, when Sir Charles Lyell
(1797–1875), an English geologist, published
Principles of Geology in 1830. In this work,
Lyell proposed the theory of *uniformitarianism*,
which states that physical forces such as water,
heat, wind, ice, and earthquakes change
Earth's surface over time.

His theory was based, in part, on the belief
that the thickness of the strata and the
number of layers—which take a great deal of
time to form—had to have begun way before
4000 BCE. He went on to write *The Antiquity
of Man*, a book that supported Charles
Darwin's theory of evolution. Darwin had
revolutionized the way humans viewed Earth's
development with his 1859 book, *The Origin
of the Species by Means of Natural Selection*. His
research challenged the religious belief in the

FOSSILS: KEYS TO THE PAST

The remains of plants and animals preserved within sedimentary rocks are called fossils. Fossils most often are composed of the hard parts (bones, teeth, and shells) of organisms. Preservation only happens when burial is quick and there is protection from microorganisms or other animals. Occasionally, soft parts can be preserved by impressions left in fine sediment. In other rare instances, some organisms are completely fossilized in amber, a translucent, yellow, hardened resin of extinct pine trees.

Most major cities have a Museum of Natural History. Fossils are prized museum specimens that are always on display. When you visit one of these sites, look especially for specimens that were found in your part of the country; these will be more popular because of the local interest.

When you tour the museum, keep in mind that there are two major classes of animals—*invertebrates* (organisms with no backbone) and *vertebrates* (those with a backbone).

Many invertebrates are found in the fossil record. These include sponges, corals, jellyfish, shelled organisms, and insects.

Collectors know of several familiar groups. Bryozoans are colonial animals, like sea moss, while Brachiopods are lamp-shelled creatures that are mollusk-like with arms. There are the Arthropods, which include trilobites (an extinct early crustacean), crabs, and insects. The Mollusk groups are made up of ammonites, which are coiled, chambered fossil shells, squid, and snails. Echinoderms are collected as sand dollars, sea urchins, crinoids, seahorses, and starfish. Crinoids are spiny-skinned organisms with a cap or head, numerous radiating arms, and a jointed stem with a root structure that attaches to the ocean bottom.

As these creatures were preserved in sedimentary layers of rocks, their internal structures remained intact, giving us wonderful specimens that illustrated the history of life on Earth.

---

theory of creation and maintained that Earth and all life forms were the result of an evolutionary process.

Relative Age Dating

In the fifteenth century, natural philosopher Nicholas Steno took a close look at how rock layers were formed and at the curious fossils within them. He would lay down the important principles of stratigraphy that have been used to help with relative age dating of rocks. *Stratigraphy* is the study of layered sedimentary rocks. Steno's law of superposition states that older rocks are found beneath younger rocks. This happens because when sediments settle out of a fluid, the youngest layers will be deposited on top of previous layers. According to the principle of original horizontality, these layers will initially be set down in a horizontal fashion. Any change from this orientation occurs at another time when the rocks have been tilted by tectonic forces.

Early detectives of Earth's history used this technique, *relative age dating*, to place rock units into a chronological sequence.

Other principles have been discovered as well. For instance, a principle of *lateral continuity* has been proposed, which states that layered sediments extend in a lateral fashion in all directions from any single point. The importance of this concept is that it allows one to predict the position of stratigraphic layers far from any given locality. For instance, if you discover a particular composition of layers, that composition will extend for some distance, laterally, unless it is interrupted by another natural obstacle.

When a fault or an igneous dike or sill cuts across a layer of rocks, it must be younger than the sediments through which it cuts. This idea is known as the principle of *crosscutting relationships*. Country rock, with igneous rocks and components of sedimentary rocks within, must be older than the igneous rocks which they enclose.

Fossils are used to place sedimentary layers in a relative age sequence. The principle of *faunal succession* indicates that fossils are deposited in a logical order, with new species replacing older species in an order reflected in the geologic record. The word *faunal* refers to animal life, and *succession* refers to chronological sequence. The oldest fossils, therefore, will be found underneath the later ones. The identification of fossils of a similar type at two widely separated localities suggests that the strata (the plural of stratum, or layers) were formed during the same period of Earth history.

Absolute Age Dating

In recent decades, techniques such as relative age dating were used to estimate the ages of fossils and relics found in the earth. These systems served geologists, archaeologists, and paleontologists well over the years, but they have been limited. It is now possible to determine a true age for the formation of igneous, metamorphic, and some sedimentary rocks using a *radioactive* or *radiometric age dating* technique. This process is based on the proportion of original material to decay

UNDERSTANDING UNCONFORMITIES

An important aspect of stratigraphy is how two or more rock units come in contact with each other. If the two rocks lie flat and securely against each other, then there is uniform exposure to the environment. If there are areas that are exposed at different times, or evidence of a gap between the rocks, then there is a break in the depositional history. This is a period of exposure to erosion that results in a contact surface known as an unconformity. These *unconformities*, or breaks in "geologic time," are important because they each tell us a different story about how Earth's surface was formed.

There are three types of unconformities. A *disconformity* is a surface that separates two layers of sedimentary rocks. If the overlying sedimentary layer is at some angle to the layer beneath, then the unconformity is called an *angular unconformity*. An unconformity separating igneous and/or metamorphic rocks from overlying sediments is known as a *nonconformity*. Each type of unconformity helps to tell a different story to the scientist studying Earth's structure.

products present in a rock sample. When these proportions are measured, scientists can perform simple calculations to determine the exact age of the rock sample.

In 1896, French physicist Henri Becquerel (1852–1908) discovered that uranium changed with time through radioactive decay. In 1905, Lord Ernest Rutherford (1871–1937), a British physicist who understood the structure of an atom, was the first to suggest that radioactivity was the key to measuring the ages of rocks.

At the beginning of the twentieth century, radiometric aging allowed scientists to determine realistic ages for some rocks, indicating for the first time that Earth's history could be measured in billions of years. This was even more remarkable since isotopes were still unknown and decay rates could not be accurately determined.

Radiometric dating became very valuable after the 1950s, when technology allowed for more precision and accuracy in the dating of rocks. The invention of the mass spectrometer, after World War I, led to the discovery of 200 isotopes—molecules of the same element that have different atomic mass numbers. This change in atomic mass numbers is caused by the decay of the element over time. Isotopes are actually the result of a series of decays leading from a radioactive element to a stable one.

The absolute ages for rocks are based on the natural radioactive decay of certain elements. When uranium decays, it turns into the element we know as lead. When this happens, the parent atoms of uranium are converted into daughter atoms of lead over a fixed interval of time. This interval is the *decay constant*.

The ratio of parent to daughter atoms changes and is a quantity that can be measured in the laboratory. A value known as the *radioactive half-life*—the amount of time required for one-half of the parent atoms to be converted to daughter atoms—is used to calculate the age of the rock. (See Figure 5.2.) The half-life of the uranium to lead sequence is about 4.5 billion years. The potassium to argon decay is also used in dating. The half-life for this sequence is 1.2 billion years. (See Figure 5.3.) Only five radioactive isotopes are actually

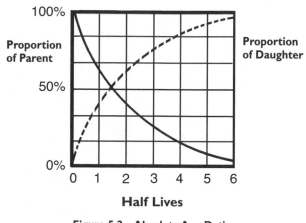

Figure 5.2—Absolute Age Dating

useful in dating rocks. Some are too rare, and some have half-lives that are too short or too long. However, these isotopes can date rocks from 50 thousand to 4.5 billion years in age.

Radioactive isotopes are found predominately within igneous rocks. The clock starts when the molten rock solidifies. Minerals that have sufficient potassium for dating by the potassium-argon method include orthoclase, muscovite, and amphibole. Minerals useful in the uranium lead technique include apatite, zircon, and sphene. A sedimentary mineral called glauconite or greensand is enriched in potassium and is the only mineral useful for dating sedimentary rocks.

Radioactive Parent	Stable Daughter	Half Life
Potassium 40	Argon 40	1.25 billion years
Rubidium 87	Strontium 87	48.8 billion years
Thorium 232	Lead 208	14 billion years
Uranium 235	Lead 207	704 million years
Uranium 238	Lead 206	4.47 billion years
Carbon 14	Nitrogen 14	5730 years

Figure 5.3—Frequently Used Radioactive Isotopes

Carbon-14, or radiocarbon, is used to date more recent rocks or events. This technique—commonly known as *Carbon-14 dating*—works well because all living things have a constant ratio of Carbon-14 to Carbon-12. At death, Carbon-14 exchange ceases and the Carbon-14 begins to decay. The change in the Carbon-14 to Carbon-12 is the basis for dating. With recent innovations in technology, Carbon-14 techniques have become sophisticated enough to date substances as far back as 75,000 years.

FISSION TRACK DATING

There is an entirely different way of dating rocks that contain mica minerals. It is called *fission track dating*. The spontaneous radioactive decay of uranium releases charged particles that leave discernable trails, or fission tracks, within a mineral's crystal lattice, the space between crystal structures that comprise the mineral. The density of tracks in a given area is directly related to the uranium concentration and age of the rock. This is particularly useful in dating micas and natural and synthetic glass.

In addition to dating individual rocks or fossils discovered on the Earth's surface, these modern techniques can actually be used to determine the age of our planet. The age of Earth is derived from radiometric dating of meteorites, or rocks that have fallen to our planet's surface from space. Some of these stones are thought to be very close in age to the time when the solar system formed. By considering Earth to be part of an evolving system of planets revolving about the Sun, scientists have determined the age of our planet to be 4.6 billion years old.

Geologic Time Scale

Much of the meaning of the geologic time scale has to do with the evolution of life on our planet. Evidence for this is found in the fossil record. Because fossils can help to indicate time, they are one of the most useful methods of finding rocks of similar ages in different regions. Fossils range from simple to complex and tell us a lot about the history of our planet and the progression of life. They are also important environmental indicators, telling us much about a particular region's history. Fossils of clamshells imbedded in limestone, for instance, might indicate that a region was once covered by a shallow sea.

Geologists employ two methods of considering or classifying layers of rock in the field. The first method, *rock stratigraphy*, examines the makeup of rocks, while the second technique, *time stratigraphy*, considers the time at which the layers of rock were deposited. The key unit of measure in rock stratigraphy is called the *formation*. The key unit of measure in time stratigraphy is called a *period*.

Formations might indicate previous geologic events—earthquakes, glaciers, volcanoes, or floods. Time stratigraphy helps the geologist to understand when rock was deposited.

EXPLORATION 5.1
AGE OF ROCKS

Acquire a geologic map of the United States from the United States Geological Survey (www.mapping.usgs.gov/). The map is color-coded based on the type and age of rocks exposed at the surface. Find your position on the map. Determine the age of the sediment or rocks beneath your house. How old, in millions of years, is the property on which you live? During what period of geologic history were these rocks formed?

EARTH HISTORY COMPRESSED INTO A YEAR

It is difficult to fathom the immense periods of time separating you from early Earth history. One way to make this span of 4600 million years more comprehensible is to compress the entire history of our planet into a single year.

January 1–Earth was formed.

February 20–The heavy fall of meteoroids onto our planet's surface, as Earth sweeps up debris left over from planetary formation, comes to an end.

March 1–The oldest dated rocks were formed.

March 25–Life appears.

September 12–Oxygen starts to accumulate within our atmosphere from the photosynthesis of marine plants.

November 7–The first multicellular organisms appeared.

November 10– The first organisms with shells appeared.

November 20–Vertebrates are found.

November 22–The first fish swam the oceans.

November 28–Plants and animals began to colonize the land.

December 2–Amphibians appeared.

December 3–The first insects thrived.

December 7–Reptiles appeared.

December 13–Dinosaurs roamed Earth.

December 14–Mammals were found.

December 26–Dinosaurs became extinct.

December 31–At 3:00 PM, the first hominids, human-like creatures, occurred.

—At 11:00 PM, Homo sapiens appeared!

EONS AND ERAS

We now know that Earth is very old, and its history has been sectioned into many groups of time. For simplicity, two very long segments of time, or *eons*, have been labeled—the Precambrian, which extends from the formation of the planet to 570 million years ago—and the Phanerozoic, which covers the period of time from 570 million years ago to the present.

The geologic calendar does not contain many details until the first period of the Phanerozoic eon. The 4 billion years before that are simply referred to as *Precambrian*—a time about which we know very little. What we do know is that primitive organisms, such as algae, bacteria, fungi, worms, and sponges populated the Precambrian eon.

About 600 million years ago, more complex organisms evolved and began to proliferate. This eon is called *Phanerozoic*, meaning "of visible life." An eon is further subdivided into sections called *eras*. There are three eras in the Phanerozoic eon: Paleozoic (570 to 245 million years ago), Mesozoic (245 to 66 million years ago), and Cenozoic (66 million years ago to the present time).

To further organize the history of the planet, the eras are broken into distinct segments of time called *periods*. The Cenozoic era is sectioned into two periods. These additional subdivisions allow us to conveniently discuss specific blocks of time.

The diversity of life prior to the Cambrian period is very sketchy due to the lack of fossil preservation. Insects and algae got a foothold on the land during the *Ordovician* period. Vertebrate sea animals resembling jawless fish originated during this time as well. With the onset of the *Silurian* and *Devonian* periods, vertebrates called amphibians took to land. While these creatures had to return to the seas to lay eggs, they spent the majority of their time on land.

Great coal swamp forests are known from the *Mississippian* period, and the reptiles appeared in the *Pennsylvanian* period. At the beginning of the Mesozoic era, during the *Triassic* period, the first mammals are recorded.

The super-continent Pangaea begins to come apart at about this time as well. Dinosaurs began to flourish in the *Jurassic* period, only to become extinct—perhaps by the impact of an asteroid—at the end of the *Cretaceous* period. Other theories concerning the extinction of dinosaurs—one of the most intriguing questions about Earth's history—revolve around global climactic change, increased volcanism (which could have triggered climactic changes), and major changes in plate tectonics (which, of necessity, would be tied to volcanism). Fossil records are incomplete or confusing, making it difficult to determine exactly what happened, but climactic changes, caused by shifting continents and regression of the sea, are possible factors, as is the impact of an asteroid.

Eons: Precambrian and Phanerozoic

Eras of the Precambrian Eon: Hadean, Archean, and Proterozoic

Eras of the Phanerozoic Eon: Paleozoic, Mesozoic, and Cenozoic

Periods of the Paleozoic Era: Permian, Pennsylvanian, Mississippian, Devonian, Silurian, Ordovician, Cambrian

Periods of the Mesozoic Era: Cretaceous, Jurassic, Triassic

Periods of the Cenozoic Era: Tertiary, Quaternary

The first flowering plants took hold in the Cretaceous period of the Mesozoic era. It wasn't until the Cenozoic era that mammals diversified and ruled the surface of the planet. Primates first appeared during the *Tertiary* period of that era.

SUMMARY

Our concept of geologic time used to be based on the works of Biblical scholars. Archbishop James Ussher, in 1650, announced the time of Earth's creation based on the ages of all the great men in the *Bible*. This belief that Earth was only about 6,000 years old persisted until the 1800s. The idea that much of Earth's formation revolved around major short-term events, like Creation or the Great Flood, was also popular.

Principles of Geology, written by Sir Charles Lyell in 1830, proposed the theory of uniformitarianism. He held that water, heat, ice, wind, earthquakes, and other natural events shaped Earth's surface over time.

Stratigraphy, the study of layered sedimentary rock, was proposed by philosopher Nicholas Steno, and it gave scientists the means to use relative age dating to figure out how old certain rock formations might be.

Once the theory of radiometric dating was proposed—studying the rate of radioactive decay of certain elements—scientists were able to ascertain that Earth was, in fact, billions of years old.

The labeling of the Precambrian eon—extending from the formation of the planet to 570 million years ago—and the Phanerozoic eon—covering the period of time from 570 million years ago to the present—provides a helpful frame of reference. Within these two significant eons, there are eras and periods, which help to further organize the events that comprise the history of Earth.

It is important to remember that we are talking about a huge period of time when we discuss the geologic time scale. Scientists continue to make discoveries that are significant in the way we view these early eons, eras, and periods. Future study will help us to understand more about what Earth was like before humans and how it has changed and evolved since our existence on the planet.

PART

2

OCEANOGRAPHY

OCEAN COMPOSITION AND LAYERING

KEY TERMS

outgassing, photosynthesis, bathythermography, salinity, hydrogen bonding, brines, surface zone, pycnocline zone, thermoclines, haloclines

ORIGINS OF THE OCEAN

The oceans of our planet are a source of unending mystery, and it is only in very recent time that serious scientific study has made knowledge about these huge bodies of water available to us. Oceans actually cover about 70 percent of Earth's surface—about 225 million square kilometers—and have an average depth of about 3 km. In fact, the water on Earth totals 480 million cubic kilometers. The impact of these enormous bodies of water on our planet is significant in many ways. We'll begin by exploring how the oceans might have formed, and then delve deeper into *oceanography*—the study of the chemical, physical, biological, and geological aspects of the oceanic world.

Scientists believe that water now exists beneath Europa and Ganymede, moons of the planet Jupiter, and within the polar ice caps and subsurface permafrost of Mars. It is also a widely held belief that the earliest life forms developed in Earth's oceans, as well.

The first water on our planet is believed to have been the result of a process that took millions of years. *Outgassing* is the process by which gases, including water vapor, are released from the mantle and vented out from beneath Earth's surface through volcanoes. The early atmosphere created by outgassing contained no oxygen—that would come later with *photosynthesis*, the process by which plants turn carbon dioxide into oxygen. This atmosphere did contain methane, ammonia, and carbon dioxide in vapor form.

At this time, Earth was too hot to allow the vapor to condense to form liquid water. As the planet cooled, gaseous water vapor in the primitive atmosphere condensed and fell as the first rain. Over millions of years Earth cooled enough for this water to collect in the ocean basins.

To put the process of evolution into some perspective in terms of the development of Earth and other life forms, think about this: the galaxies formed 13 billion years ago, and Earth formed 4.6 billion years ago. The oceans began to form about 4.2 billion years ago, the oxygen revolution, or the time at which oxygen became plentiful enough to support life, is dated at about 2 billion years ago, and the ocean and atmosphere reached a steady state at about 0.8 billion years ago. The process obviously took millions of years to be accomplished.

Although volcanic outgassing is usually accepted as an explanation for the formation and development of the oceans, there is also some evidence that ice-rich comets may have

ORIGIN OF THE OCEANS

Have you ever wondered about where the vast oceans of Earth came from? Our oceans were formed billions of years ago. Early in the history of Earth, volcanism was much more active than it is today. Volcanoes released voluminous amounts of the gases that formed the atmosphere, which included nitrogen, carbon dioxide, and water vapor. The water vapor accumulated, and then eventually condensed into rain that fell on the surface of the young Earth. Torrential storms filled the lowlands of the planet, eventually forming the oceans we have today.

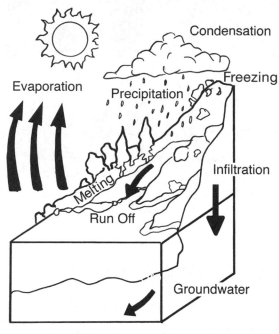

Figure 6.1—Process of Evaporation

hammered Earth, delivering some of the water that now makes up the oceans.

Evaporation is the process of converting a liquid to a vapor, while condensation occurs when water vapor is changed to the liquid state. Figure 6.1 shows the water cycle, which includes freezing, melting, evaporation, and condensation.

A BRIEF HISTORY OF OCEANOGRAPHY

Oceanography, sometimes called marine science, is a complex field of study, which incorporates many characteristics of the ocean. *Marine geology* focuses on the study of Earth's crust and composition (the part covered by water); *physical oceanography* studies the waves, currents, and climates; *marine biology* studies the nature and distribution of marine life; *chemical oceanography* is the study of the gases and solids dissolved in the ocean; and *marine engineering* is the design and construction of structures used in or on the ocean.

If you looked at Earth from space, it is mostly a blue, oceanic world—unlike any other place in our solar system. With so much of our planet covered by water, it is not surprising that the sea has always fascinated humankind. Early knowledge was limited, however, and it is only since the twentieth century that we have acquired significant information about the oceans. Because the deep ocean is dark, cold, and the water pressure is substantial, it wasn't until humans united in international efforts (due to cost) to develop submersibles for exploration, computers for modeling complex ocean processes, and remote sensors, that oceanography made significant progress.

Greek philosophers appreciated the significance of the oceans. In the fourth century BCE, Aristotle (384–322 BCE) suggested that the volume of the oceans did not change. He speculated that the amount of rainfall was about equal to the amount of evaporation across Earth.

In the second century CE, Claudius Ptolemy (87–150 CE) proposed a coordinate system based on a grid of latitude and longitude. It was then possible to accurately map the distribution of the continents and seas. During the Renaissance, myriad explorers would chart the oceans. Even then, however, the cost of sailing a large ship with a crew was prohibitive.

Probably the first true expedition for the sake of science was one funded by the Royal Society of Britain in 1872. The *HMS Challenger* sailed and charted the oceans for four years. It was an interdisciplinary voyage that would set high standards for all following seagoing missions. The crew studied all aspects of the ocean—from temperature to currents and from ocean bottom samples to the organisms living in the water.

Only a few years before this voyage, scientists had assumed that life could not be sustained in the ocean depths. The discoveries made about ocean life, currents, water temperatures, oceanic ridges, and a multitude of other things became the substantive materials of a 50-volume report published almost 25 years after the trip ended. The findings of the scientific explorers aboard the *HMS Challenger* provided rich material for oceanographic study for years to come.

In the United States, the Department of Charts and Instruments was created in 1830. Its mission was to assist with all aspects of shipping, especially formulating charts related to wind and currents. The United States Coast Survey was established in 1807, the United States Weather Bureau in 1870, and the United States Commission of Fish and Fisheries in 1871. These organizations are ancestors of the modern-day National Oceanic and Atmospheric Administration. After the sinking of the *Titanic* in 1912, the International Ice Patrol commission was established. While many of these organizations were created to fulfill a specific need, each, in turn, helped us to learn more and more about the ocean. The necessity of predicting severe weather, managing oceanic resources, charting maps and protecting ships at sea led to the first oceanic research.

WHAT DO THE FIVE FIELDS OF OCEANOGRAPHY STUDY?

Marine geology—The study of the parts of Earth's crust and composition that are covered by water

Physical oceanography—The study of the waves, currents, and climates

Marine biology—The study of the nature and distribution of marine life

Chemical oceanography—The study of the gases and solids dissolved in the ocean

Marine engineering—The study of the design and construction of structures used in or on the ocean

World War II was the catalyst for several oceanographic studies. The field of *bathythermography* was established in order to study the thermal effects on sound waves as they were transmitted through seawater. The investigation was initiated to help track submarines. At the same time, the seafloor was mapped so that submarines could navigate through potential submerged hazards. Amphibious troop landings required detailed knowledge of coastal tidal conditions.

Although the ocean was always open and free to ships of all nations, there have long been regulations governing how close ships could come to another country's shoreline. In 1635, nations agreed to allow this distance to be a narrow, five-nautical-kilometer, territorial zone. This zone was maintained until the Conference on the Law of the Sea, held by the United Nations in 1974, extended the off-limits boundary from 5 to 20 nautical kilometers from shore. In addition, a new concept of an economic exclusive zone, extending 320 km from shore, was established that granted fishing and resource exploration rights to the country bordering the water.

For many centuries, the study of oceanography has focused on war strategy, shipping, fishing, and economic resources. Now, technology allows us to explore the depths of the ocean in a scientific way. Not only can we learn the extent of the ocean's resources, but we can also begin to understand how the oceans impact our lives and ways to protect these resources for the future.

THE WORLD'S OCEANS

A quick look at a globe shows that the oceans and landmasses are not evenly spread across Earth. There is significantly more water within the Southern Hemisphere than the Northern Hemisphere. About 81 percent of the surface of the Southern Hemisphere is beneath water. In contrast, about 61 percent of the surface of the Northern Hemisphere is submerged. Based on this information, it is appropriate to refer to the Southern Hemisphere as the water hemisphere and call the Northern Hemisphere the land hemisphere.

If it were possible to spread the oceans across a smooth and perfectly spherical planet, their depth would be more than 2000 meters. But Earth's surface is rough, with the continents extending above the level of the sea by more than 840 meters.

FUN FACT: The Mariana Trench, located in the Pacific Ocean just east of the 14 Mariana Islands near Japan, is the deepest part of Earth's ocean system—indeed, the deepest location on Earth, at 11,000 meters below sea level. The average depth of the ocean is 3,800 meters.

There are five recognized oceans that cover the current surface of the planet—the Pacific, Atlantic, Indian, Arctic, and Southern oceans. Of these, the Pacific Ocean is by far the largest with the greatest average depth. It holds almost half of all the water on the planet and is as vast as the Atlantic and Indian oceans combined. The Atlantic Ocean extends from the southern polar region to the northern polar region. The Arctic Ocean, the northernmost body of water on Earth, is the smallest of oceans and is confined to the Northern Hemisphere. On average, it is the shallowest of all the oceans. For many years, only four oceans were officially recognized. However, in the spring of 2000, the International Hydrographic Organization recognized the Southern Ocean, which surrounds Antarctica. The Southern Ocean includes all water below 60 degrees south, and some of it, like the Arctic Ocean, is frozen.

We know that about 70 percent of Earth's surface is covered by ocean waters. Although we call the oceans each by individual names, they are, in fact, one body of water, or a global ocean. This global ocean is connected to smaller bodies of water that are partly closed off by land. These are called seas, and they include such bodies of water as the Mediterranean Sea, the Caribbean Sea, the South China Sea, and the Andaman Sea. Other bodies of water that are classified as seas but are not named seas include bays and gulfs, such as the Hudson Bay and the Gulf of Mexico.

THE EARTH'S OCEANS			
Ocean	Area	Average Depth	Deepest Depth
Pacific Ocean	60,060,900 sq mi (155,557,000 sq km)	15,215 ft (4,638 m)	Mariana Trench, 35,827 ft (10,920 m)
Atlantic Ocean	29,638,000 sq mi (76,762,000 sq km)	12,881 ft (3,926 m)	Puerto Rico Trench, 30,246 ft (9,219 m)
Indian Ocean	26,469,600 sq mi (68,555,950 sq km)	13,002 ft (3,963 m)	Java Trench, 24,460 ft (7,455 m)
Southern Ocean	7,848,300 sq mi (20,327,000 sq km)	14,750 ft (4,496 m)	The southern end of the South Sandwich Trench, 23,736 ft (7,235 m)
Arctic Ocean	5,427,100 sq mi (14,056,000 sq km)	3,953 ft. (1,205 m)	Arctic Basin, 18,456 ft (5,625 m)

Salinity is the measure of the saltiness of seawater and it is defined as the amount of material dissolved in 1 kg of seawater. Seawater is usually found to have a salt content of 3.5 percent or more. Ninety-seven percent of all the water on Earth is salt water. Because seas, bays, and gulfs are connected to the oceans, they are all saltwater bodies.

Earth's Seas and Lakes

Out of the remaining 3 percent of water on Earth, 2 percent is locked up in icecaps and glaciers, and 1 percent is left for all our needs such as agricultural, residential, manufacturing, community and personal needs.

Freshwater bodies of water include large inland lakes, such as the Great Lakes on the Canadian-U.S. border, which contain about 25 percent of the world's freshwater and provide 95 percent of the United States' freshwater supply.

FUN FACT: If you took all the water out of the Great Lakes and spread it out, it would submerge the continental United States under about three meters of water.

As magnificent as the resources of the oceans are, lakes are also quite important because they serve as catchment basins for much of our fresh water, supplying drinking water, generating electricity, irrigating fields, and providing recreational areas. Obviously, with the Great Lakes alone providing 25 percent of the world's freshwater, it is clear that lakes are not evenly distributed across the globe. They tend to be located at high altitudes and in mountainous regions. Although it is often assumed that lakes contain fresh water, some are actually quite salty because of a high rate of evaporation and the concentration of inflowing salt. The Caspian Sea in northern Iran, the Dead Sea in Israel, and the Great Salt Lake in the United States are among the world's largest and best-known salt lakes.

MAJOR SEAS OF THE WORLD	
South China Sea	Caribbean Sea
Mediterranean Sea	Bering Sea
Arabian Sea	Sea of Okhotsk
Sea of Japan	East China Sea
Andaman Sea	Black Sea
Red Sea	Gulf of Mexico
Hudson Bay	

FUN FACT: The Gulf of Mexico and Hudson Bay are considered seas, and the Dead Sea is actually a lake.

THE WORLD'S MOST WELL-KNOWN LAKES

Great Lakes

Lake Tahoe

Lake Placid

Lake Okeechobee

The Dead Sea

Lake Baikal, Asia —the largest lake on Earth, containing one fifth of Earth's fresh water, with a maximum depth of 1600 m

Properties and Composition of Seawater

If you've ever been to the beach, gone swimming in the ocean, and gotten a mouthful of ocean water, you know how salty it is. Although the ocean is 96.5 percent water and 3.5 percent salt, that small percentage of salt is quite noticeable when you swallow it! It is actually sodium chloride (NaCl, common table salt), combined with smaller amounts of potassium, magnesium, sulfur, and calcium. (See Figure 6.2.) Most of these elements came with water accumulated over time as a result of the weathering of rocks.

FUN FACT: Since the ocean is about 3.5 percent salt, if it dried up completely, enough salt would be left behind to build a 290-kilometer-tall, 1.5-km-thick wall around the equator. About 90 percent of that salt would be sodium chloride, or ordinary table salt.

Water is a unique substance. Its boiling and freezing points are unusually high, compared to other liquids. These properties are attributed to the way water molecules bond with each other. Two atoms of hydrogen and one atom of oxygen combine to make one water molecule. Polar molecules, such as water molecules, have a weak, partially negative charge near the oxygen atom and a partially positive charge near the hydrogen atoms. So when water molecules are close together, their positive and negative areas are attracted to the oppositely charged areas of nearby molecules. The force of this attraction is called a *hydrogen bond*, and each water molecule is hydrogen-bonded to four others. This allows water to remain as a liquid over a wider range of temperatures than would be found for other molecules of similar size. Further, a large amount of energy is needed to convert liquid water where the molecules are attracted through their hydrogen bonds, to water vapor where they are not.

Water is also one of the few substances that can be readily found as a gas, as a liquid, or as a solid. Seawater can be frozen into ice at low temperatures when water molecules are arranged into six-sided ring structures. Salts are exuded as these structures form. This results in pockets of salty liquids within sea ice known as brines. At higher temperatures, water can exist in a vapor phase or as a gas. Gaseous water consists of water molecules that are totally separated from one another. They are free to move about, not having a specific size or shape.

The major components of seawater are chloride, sodium, sulfate, magnesium, calcium, and potassium. Taken together, they make up 99 percent of the matter dissolved within seawater. The salinity of the oceans has not changed significantly with time. This is because the amount of salt brought into the oceans, derived from the weathering of

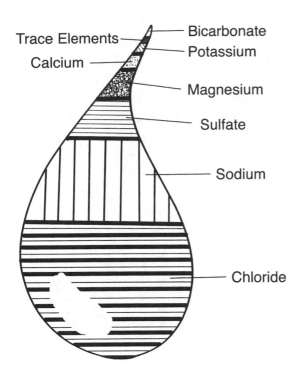

Trace Elements
Calcium
Bicarbonate
Potassium
Magnesium
Sulfate
Sodium
Chloride

Figure 6.2—Composition of Seawater

terrestrial rock, is equal to the amount of salt removed from various seawater reactions and aquatic organisms. About four billion tons of salt is cycled through this steady-state equilibrium every year.

You may wonder how animals ever manage to live in such a salty environment. Saltwater creatures, however, usually keep the salinity inside their bodies at about the same concentration as the water outside. If the animals were put into fresh water, the process of *osmosis*—water flowing from the low-salinity environment into the high-salinity environment to equal out the salt content—would make the creature swell and die. A creature used to a low-salt environment would experience the same fate in the opposite way—all the water in its body would flow out through its skin, and it would shrivel and die.

SALINITY IN WATER

Water in different environments contains different levels of salt. Ocean salinity usually only varies between 32 and 37 parts per thousand (ppt) depending on runoff, ice formation, and evaporation. Freshwater salinity is usually less than 0.5 ppt. If you measure the concentration of salt in water, by parts per million, you can identify classes of water.

• Freshwater—Less than 1000 ppm

• Slightly saline water—From 1000 ppm to 3000 ppm

• Moderately saline water—From 3000 ppm to 10,000 ppm

• Highly saline water—From 10,000 ppm to 35,000 ppm

Ocean water is approximately 35,000 ppm, or 3.5 percent (35,000/1,000,000 = 3.5%).

Atmospheric gases are also dissolved within seawater. These gases include nitrogen, oxygen, and carbon dioxide. They are incorporated within the oceans at the *air-sea interface*, the place where the seawater comes into first contact with the atmosphere. Of these gases, the most important is carbon dioxide, which is a key element in biological processes—including photosynthesis and the production of shells in marine plants and animals.

Once dissolved, carbon dioxide can take the form of a dissolved gas, carbonate, bicarbonate, or carbonic acid. The most interesting of these is carbonate. When carbonate is combined with calcium, as in the production of shelled organisms, carbon dioxide is removed from the oceans. Once shelled organisms die, their shells accumulate on the sea bottom to form thick deposits of calcium carbonate called limestone.

Bubbles that form on the surface of the seas, due to the action of waves and storms, provide a mechanism for the exchange processes that occur between the air and the ocean. Bursting air bubbles produce water droplets within the atmosphere. The wind can carry the drops of water far from their place of origin. Small salt particles are liberated into the atmosphere as these water droplets evaporate. It is estimated that more than a billion tons of salt are transported in this manner each year. These tiny salt grains are important, because they can serve as nuclei about which snowflakes or raindrops are formed. The salt is eventually returned to the seas as precipitation. Refer back to Figure 6.1, which shows how the evaporation cycle works.

EXPLORATION 6.1
DETERMINING THE SALINITY
OF SEAWATER

You can calculate salinity, or amount of salt found in seawater, very easily. Pour a measured amount of seawater into a pan. Let it evaporate over a period of a few days. After the water has evaporated, notice the gritty salt left in the pan. The weight of this residue relative to the measured amount of seawater originally placed in the pan can be used to calculate the salinity of the original seawater.

Since seawater contains about 35,000 parts per million of salt, you can make simulated seawater by adding about 35 grams of salt to a liter of water. If the water is hot, the salt will dissolve. When the liter of water has evaporated, you should have about 35 grams of salt remaining.

Layered Structure of Oceans

The oceans of the world are vertically layered according to the density of the water they contain (Figure 6.3). Temperature and salinity are the primary controlling factors in determining water density. If the temperature of seawater is decreased, its density increases. If the salinity of seawater is increased, its density increases. These factors work to form thinly stratified layers of water masses in the ocean. The layers are very stable, because a water mass will naturally rise or sink to a comfortable density level, with the heavier, saltier water below and lighter levels of water above that. Oceanographers have defined three major layers within the oceans: the surface zone, the pycnocline zone, and the deep zone.

The upper 100 meters of the ocean make up the *surface zone*. It is the least dense of all oceanic layers. Since this layer is in contact with the atmosphere, storms and solar heating cause substantial mixing. As light can penetrate this upper part of the ocean, photosynthesis is possible; and because of this, all marine foods are derived from this layer, even though it consists of only about 2 percent of all the oceans.

The stable layer of water that resides beneath the surface zone is called the *pycnocline zone*. In this layer, density changes markedly with depth due to changes in either salinity or temperature. Oceanic waters found within the low to mid latitudinal areas have pycnoclines that are controlled by temperature variations with depth. These layers with steep changes in temperatures are called *thermoclines*. In areas of higher latitudes and coastal areas, salinity is often the cause of water mass density variations. Oceanic layers having marked changes in salinity are called *haloclines*.

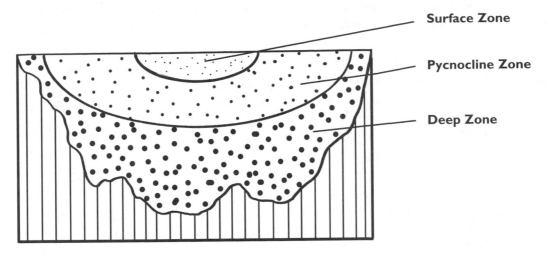

Figure 6.3—Layered Structure of the Oceans

Obviously the deepest ocean waters, what we know as the *deep zone*, the layer below the pycnocline zone, are a dark, cold place. Although great strides have been made in oceanography in the past 100 years, research on the deep ocean has required more advanced technology. The physical properties of water are affected by depth within the oceans. For every 10 meters of depth, the pressure increases by a factor of 1. The deepest areas of ocean basins experience an equivalent of an atmospheric pressure more than 1000 times that at sea level. Increased pressure eases the flow of water molecules. With depth, the viscosity of water (its resistance to flow) decreases. The water pressure alone is not something a human could endure, much less the extreme cold and dark. Small submarines called submersibles now allow people (with cameras, powerful lights, mechanical arms, and other technology) to explore below the surface. Many of the deep-sea fish look like monsters with large eyes, huge mouths, and sharp teeth. The fish themselves are quite small. Food is hard to find and so they might have body lights that flash on and off to attract prey. Animals also cluster around hot spots, where bacteria thriving on chemicals in the hot water are eaten by larger creatures such as fish, crabs, shrimp, clams, and giant red tubeworms up to three meters long.

Oceanic Resources

The oceans are a valuable resource for our species. For millennia, people have harvested food from the seas. But the oceans now provide much more—minerals, fossil fuels, and energy.

Fish as a Resource

Each year, more than 100 million tons of fish are harvested from the planet's seas and oceans. This is estimated to be approximately half the amount of the theoretical maximum yield that could be taken from the oceans. The maximum theoretical yield is the absolute weight of fish that can be pulled from the sea and still allow the population to reproduce to replace the catch. It means that we haven't reached this point, but if we exceed it, the resource will become depleted. About a third of the current catch is processed into fish meal for animal consumption or fertilizer. Fish are an important renewable resource.

Most varieties caught for consumption are taken from the near-shore environment.

It has been found that a fish population reaches its largest when it is in a steady state; that is, when the population does not increase nor decrease. Heavy fishing has the effect of a net reduction of the numbers of fish in competition for food and space. This allows the number of young fish that reach maturity to increase. Fisheries strive to attain what is called a maximum sustainable yield, where the harvest is near 70 percent of the overall catch potential. Limiting the harvest to 70 percent allows the fish, or stock, the capacity to recover. If the population is depleted beyond that percentage, the subsequent yield may not be as good. Another factor that must be considered in addition to the maximum sustainable yield is the growth rate of individual species. For instance, some seagoing life, like whales, mature very slowly, while others, like anchovy, grow rapidly.

A limited effort has been put into the "agriculture" of marine organisms. In an attempt to avoid the vagaries of working with wild stocks of fish, it is possible to gather young marine animals from their spawning grounds and relocate them to a controlled area where they can be groomed and raised for later harvest. The field of aquaculture, or fish farming, has been developed with this idea in mind.

An example might be the gathering of oysters from their natural spawning grounds, and then placing them into a manageable area like a bay for later harvesting. In other instances, it is possible to have a more controlled environment where feeding can be restricted, such as in a fish pen.

Petroleum and Natural Gas Resources

By far, the most valuable resources taken from the seas are petroleum and natural gas. Areas on the continental shelves or shallow marginal ocean basins, such as the Gulf of Mexico, the Arabian Gulf, and the North Sea, have proven to be the best locations for harvesting such resources.

Organic material buried in ocean bottom sediments can change over time into petroleum and natural gas. These deposits are produced only in certain environmental settings. In areas where there is a limited amount of dissolved oxygen and sluggish bottom currents, organic matter, in the form of mostly *phytoplankton* or photosynthetic plants, accumulates on the seafloor. These photosynthetic plants turn carbon dioxide into organic matter with the aid of sunlight. After bacterial breakdown and subsequent heating from tectonic activity, the organic matter is transformed into petroleum and natural gas. With time, the weight of overlying sediments causes the oil to move away from its source, and eventually into a porous rock unit like sandstone. Petroleum then accumulates and is held in place by a nonpermeable cap rock.

Offshore oil and gas wells supply about 17 percent of the world's petroleum. Shallow areas are the easiest place to harvest these resources, but deep-sea drilling techniques may help us to mine petroleum in deeper areas.

Many mineral resources are also mined from the floor of the oceans. Rivers and glaciers continuously transport granular sediments to the sea. These deposits accumulate on the continental shelves, with grain size increasing toward the coast. Gravel and sand are found near shore, while silt and clay sediments occur on the outer continental shelves and slopes. Deposits called placer minerals are also dumped into the seas by rivers. Such minerals, because of their weight, settle very near the coast, and include platinum, tin, titanium oxide, and gold.

Sand and gravel, used primarily for building construction, make up the largest tonnage of any ocean mineral produced, and they are essential for new buildings and developments. The United States uses most offshore sand and gravel for beach renourishment and coastal restoration and protection—a commonly accepted technique for restoring an eroded coastline. Gravel, coarse sand, and finer sand are common on most continental shelves; but while coarser gravel occurs close to the coast, finer materials are found on the outer shelves and slopes.

Other minerals are found in the deep ocean or associated oceanic ridges, where volcanoes produce mineral-rich waters. Minerals associated with volcanic activity, or *hydrothermal deposits*, include zinc, lead, copper, silver, and gold. Hydrothermal deposits are often formed in association with underwater vents of mineral-rich hot water called "smokers." Minerals that form by precipitation from seawater, or *hydrogenetic deposits*, include phosphorite, salt, barite, iron-manganese nodules, and crusts rich in cobalt, platinum, nickel, copper, and rare earth elements.

Ocean Pollution

The oceans remain one of Earth's most valuable resources. However, we have become increasingly aware of the dangers of pollution. We depend on the ocean for so many things—food, energy, building materials, and recreation—and the potential for disastrous consequences exists if we don't safeguard these waters.

When industrial and municipal waste is discharged into the seas, the fragile balance is threatened. Petroleum, chemical spillage, and sewage disposal have had devastating effects on certain areas. We also must pay attention to the effects of insecticides and pesticides on marine fish and birds, the increasing levels of lead in surface waters, and the disposal of hot water from power plants.

Although oceanic resources are plentiful, we know they are not infinite; and more and more concern has been voiced about the impact of human growth and expansion, especially along coastline areas.

SUMMARY

The oceans on our planet took millions of years to form. They probably were created as Earth cooled, and water vapor suspended in the atmosphere fell to fill basins. Another theory is that a battering by ice-rich comets might have resulted in a lot of the water that fills our oceans today.

Oceanography is a fairly new science, since most early explorations were for the purpose of discovering new land, good fishing grounds, or new trade routes. People today understand the vast resources that the oceans offer, as well as the fascinating mysteries, and are willing to invest time, money, and energy into learning more about them.

The oceans, in fact, comprise a significant portion of our earth, covering about 70 percent of the surface. The average depth is about 3800 meters. There are five oceans—the Pacific, Atlantic, Indian, Arctic, and Southern, comprising about 480 million cubic kilometers.

Ocean water is salty, something that is obvious to anyone who tastes it. This distinguishes it clearly from freshwater—mountain streams, inland lakes, and rivers—but the ocean is also much more vast than freshwater bodies and contains rich and varied resources.

The distinctive properties of the oceans, the properties and composition of seawater, and the layered structure of the water, make it even more complex. Oceanic waters are layered, depending on the density of the water. Both temperature and salinity impact the density. Resources vary, according to the depth, salinity, and viscosity of the water.

Fish are one of the ocean's most important resources. More than 100 million tons of fish are harvested each year, and about one-third of that amount is processed into fish meal for animal consumption or fertilizer.

Petroleum and natural gas are also important natural resources. These are found on continental shelves or shallow marginal ocean basins, but new technology may allow us to mine petroleum, natural gas, and sulfur from deeper areas.

Sand and gravel are the largest tonnage of any ocean material harvested. This is used for construction and for replenishment of coastal areas.

Other minerals found in the ocean include zinc, lead, copper, silver, gold, phosphorite, salt, barite, and iron-manganese nodules; there are also crusts rich in cobalt, platinum, nickel, copper, and rare earth elements.

Clearly the oceans are among our most valuable natural resources, and awareness has risen about the necessity of protecting them. Industrial and municipal waste threatens many shorelines, and the depletion of certain marine animals by heavy fishing, the impact of pesticides and insecticides on marine life, and the disposal of hot water from power plants are all issues of concern.

SEAFLOOR

THE SUBMARINE LANDSCAPE

Although the seafloor of the ocean is hidden
from view, modern exploration has revealed
a diverse and interesting submarine landscape.
If we look at Earth from space, we see just
how much of the planet is covered by water,
and yet it has taken centuries for humans to
begin to explore submarine depths. Chapter 6
reviewed the early beliefs about the ocean
and detailed how recently explorations have
taken place. We weren't ready, in terms of
technology, to sound those depths until just
a few decades ago.

One of the reasons that ocean exploration
has taken so long to forge ahead is because
of how truly dark it is underwater. About
60 percent of all visible light is absorbed
within the first meter and about 80 percent
is gone at a depth of about 9 meters. In very
clear water, a tiny bit of light persists as far as
45 meters. But without light, there is also no
heat, and the farther one descends into ocean
depths, the colder and darker it becomes. In
addition, the weight of seawater, combined
with the weight of the air above, creates greater

water pressure as one descends. In fact, about
a thousand meters underwater, the water pressure is enough to crush a person as easily as
a raw egg. The water pressure at the bottom
of the Mariana Trench (located in the Pacific
Ocean, as you'll recall from Chapter 6) is
1.25 tons per square meter. That would be
equivalent to almost 16,000 pounds per
square inch, or the same as one person trying
to hold up 50 jumbo jets.

The first diving suit was developed in 1837,
with air pumped down to the person wearing
it from a device located above the water.
Modern self-contained underwater breathing
apparatuses (SCUBA) allow divers to get
oxygen when they breathe in, instead of all
the time; this yields a more efficient way to
explore the ocean. The first Aqua-Lung (a
trademark used for an underwater breathing
apparatus) was developed in the 1940s.

Early deep-sea divers also once suffered from
an often-fatal disorder called decompression
sickness, or the bends. If the divers came up
too fast, the decrease in pressure made the
nitrogen gas in their blood form bubbles, which
blocked the blood's flow. Modern technology
has resolved this problem as well, with the
invention of decompression chambers.

Advanced technology, such as the advent of
small submersibles (vessels capable of operating or remaining underwater), has allowed
explorers to delve deeper into the oceans in
recent years. Like space, our oceans are among

the most fascinating frontiers of our time. Using submersibles, research scientists can employ instruments to measure, record, and collect samples of water, plants, and animals around the craft. A submersible can only go about 4 km deep, but it enables people to explore underwater volcanoes, hot-water vents, and a multitude of marine organisms.

EXPLORATION 7.1
MAKE YOUR OWN SUBMARINE

To better understand how a submarine works, poke about three holes in one side of an empty plastic bottle. Place several coins near the holes as weights. Fix a plastic tube over the neck of the bottle with modeling clay and lower the bottle into a basin of water. The coins will help the bottle sink to the bottom of the basin, as water enters the bottle through the holes.

Next, blow into the tube. As air forces water out of the holes, your sub will lighten and rise. It's a simple experiment, but it gives you a sense of how a real-life submarine can work.

The seafloor closest to the margins of continents was the easiest region to explore. Because sediment carried into the seas covers the edge of the continent, or shelf, there is a gentle rise as you move away from land and into the deeper waters of the ocean.

As you move into deeper water, the seafloor becomes the flattest geographic feature on the surface of our planet—the *abyssal plains*. Winding oceanic ridges may occasionally cross these smooth plains. And close to the margins of a tectonically active convergent plate boundary, you'll find the deepest waters of the oceans—oceanic trenches. Here, on the ocean floor, you may see isolated chains of volcanic mountains called seamounts (recall that seamounts were discussed in the section on volcanism in Chapter 4). Those that peek above the surface of the water form chains of islands. The seafloor, once humans were able to reach it and study it, became an exciting source of information about our planet.

Continental Margins

The *continental margin* is the area where a continental landmass meets the ocean floor and consists of the continental shelf, the continental slope, and the continental rise. There are two types of continental margins—passive and active. A *passive continental margin* is characterized by minimal tectonic activity. In other words, no plate rifting or subduction is taking place. A good example of a passive margin is the eastern coast of North America. The topographic relief of the seafloor has been reduced by erosion, and thick piles of sediment accumulate along the shoreline. This results in a slow and gradual slope out to the ocean depths. Nearest the shore, the seafloor is intimately tied to the margins of the continents.

On the west coast of North America, we find an example of an *active continental margin*. This is sometimes referred to as the "leading edge" of a continent, as it is the area where a plate of continental crust collides with an oceanic plate; in this case, North America is colliding with the Pacific plate.

Tectonic activity is present in these active margins, and the terrain is rough, with extensive mountain building and earthquake activity. Such conditions on land result in rivers that are somewhat short in length and thin deposits of sediments that enter the ocean.

Whether they are active or passive, continental margins can be subdivided into four sections:

• Continental shelf

• Continental slope

• Continental rise

• Submarine canyons

The *continental shelf* is an area where the continent itself is submerged beneath the ocean waters (Figure 7.1). It typically averages about 70 km in width. These shelves are found in abundance on the near-shore regions of all continents where the seas are relatively shallow. The average water depth on the continental shelf is about 60 meters.

Continental shelves are not flat; they slope away from the coast at a very low angle—usually not much more than 10 meters per kilometer. Their surfaces are generally smooth with gently rolling hills. Violent storms that stir up near-shore sediments often leave a sediment ridge in their wake that runs parallel to the shore. These ridges can be up to 10 meters in thickness.

A curious feature at the edge of the shelf is known as the *continental break*. This feature marks the location of an ancient shore when sea level was at its very lowest point. At this time, when Pleistocene glaciation was at its peak—at the end of the Cenozoic era, between 1.8 million to 11,000 years ago—most of the continental shelf was exposed above the surface of the seas, forming what we might call a coastal plain. When the glaciers melted, the sea level eventually increased, reaching its present level about 3000 years ago.

The farther away from the coastline we move, the more drastically the depths of the ocean and the steepness of the seafloor increase. Eventually, we reach the *continental slope*, which was created over a great period of time by the accumulation of sediment washed into the oceans from the continent. This slope is a sharp drop where the water depth increases dramatically over a short distance. For instance, it is not uncommon to find depth increasing by several thousand meters over a distance of just a few kilometers.

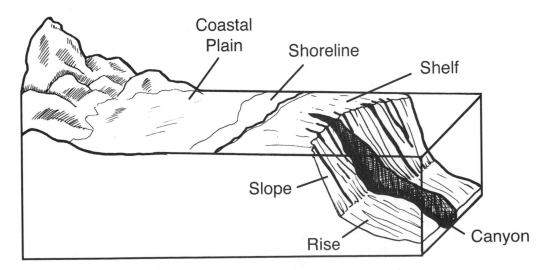

Figure 7.1—Continental Shelf, Slope, Rise, and Submarine Canyons

The boundary between the continental crust and oceanic crust is also marked at the base of the continental slope. These slopes are typically steeper when they come in contact with active plate margins. The steepness of these slopes can range from one degree to ten degrees, but they usually average about four degrees.

Continental slopes are almost always covered by thick accumulations of sediment. If the sediment becomes too thick on a fairly steep slope, it can slump and produce spoon-shaped scars on the face of the slope. Faulting on a continental slope can also create basins that trap sediments over an extended period of time. Petroleum is one of the important resources that can be found in these basins. You'll recall from Chapter 6 that the bacterial breakdown and subsequent heating by tectonic activity of organic material buried in ocean bottom sediments produces petroleum and natural gas.

At the very base of a passive margin, a feature called a *continental rise* can be found. This is an area where sediments have found their way far from the continent and have settled to make a very gentle wedge or rise. The slopes are not steep; they never exceed one degree. The rise serves as a blanket that covers the transition from the continent to the ocean basin. Low relief hills often punctuate the rise, perhaps formed by sediments that have slumped off of the continental slope.

It has been suggested that a certain type of current carried virtually all the sediment that makes the continental rise. These are known as *turbidity currents*, a downslope movement of dense, sediment-laden water created when sand and mud on the continental shelf and slope are dislodged and thrown into suspen-

sion. As the sediment fans out onto the ocean floor, it loses velocity and settles out of the current. Sediment can ultimately reach a thickness of several kilometers.

In addition to turbidity currents, swift oceanic currents can scour away loose sediments, forming a *submarine canyon*—which is, in effect, a channel—on the seafloor. The waters of terrestrial rivers (imagine the waters of the St. Lawrence Seaway flowing from the Great Lakes) that enter the sea and interact with the continental margins have carved many canyons. These currents not only carve canyons, they also carry sediments far toward the deep ocean floor.

Submarine canyons can be caused by a seaward extension of a valley that was cut on the continental shelf during a time when sea level was lower, or by turbidity currents that carved a canyon into the outer continental shelf, slope, and rise. These canyons can be deep and are always found running at an angle perpendicular to the coastline. They are V-shaped and often have smaller tributaries that connect to them. Some of these canyons even rival the Grand Canyon, which was carved by the Colorado River. Imagine underwater canyons as impressive as the Grand Canyon and you get a sense of how dramatically fluvial forces carve Earth's surface—even under water.

Basin Floor

More than half of our planet consists of sediment-covered basaltic crust beneath the oceans. These areas, the flattest sites on Earth, are called the abyssal plains. They are very level areas of the deep ocean usually lying at the foot of the continental rise. The plains are so flat that they hardly vary more than one meter in height per 1000 meters of distance. They are found extending from the edge of the continental margins into the wide expanses of the oceans. The very level abyssal plains are composed of vast accumulations of sediment—in some cases more than 5 km thick—that cover the basaltic oceanic crust.

Mounds, or *abyssal hills*, are periodically found distributed over the abyssal plains. They average about 200 meters tall and are by volume the most ubiquitous topographic feature found on our planet. Close to 80 percent of the Pacific Ocean floor is covered by abyssal hills. It is suggested that these hills are the remnants of volcanoes or ridges that protrude above the blanket of overlying sediment. Such submarine hills can be isolated features, or they can occur in chains where they mark the position of a buried oceanic ridge.

Abyssal plains are more prevalent on the floor of the Atlantic Ocean rather than the Pacific Ocean. This may be a consequence of the trenches along the Pacific basin, which serve to capture sediments before they can move too far away from the coast.

Mid-Oceanic Ridges

Distributed across the ocean basins are a series of ridges called *mid-oceanic ridges*. These are continuous mountainous ridges on the floor of all the major ocean basins, varying in width from 480 to 4800 km. The rifts at the crests of these ridges represent divergent plate boundaries. The ridges, averaging between 1 and 3 km in height, have their origins tied to rifting zones where new oceanic plate material is being generated.

Submarine lava flows accumulate and can build a ridge in the middle of the ocean floor. All along the center of the ridge is a very narrow valley or rift in the oceanic crust. Since new oceanic basaltic crust is born and then spreads away from here, it is often referred to as a *spreading center*.

The Mid-Atlantic Ridge runs the entire length of the Atlantic Ocean basin, from north to south. (See Figure 7.2.) Transform faults lie on both sides of this ridge. These are faults that are

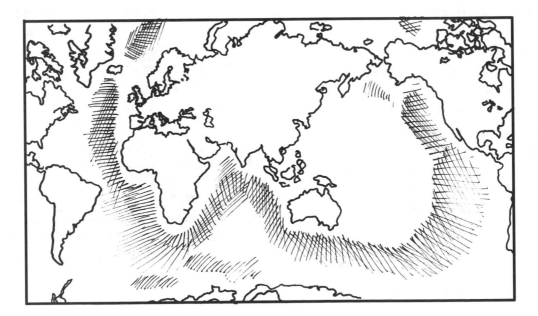

Figure 7.2—Mid-Oceanic Ridges

perpendicular to the spreading centers and result from the fracturing of the crust due to upwelling magma as it wedges its way to the surface.

As we move away from the center of the ridge, the ocean floor becomes older and gradually loses its rugged character as it is buried by sediment. Over time and with enough distance from the rifting zone, the mid-oceanic ridge merges almost imperceptibly with the abyssal plains and hills.

Oceanic Trenches

Where plates collide, oceanic trenches are often found. The deepest waters of the ocean occur here. When one plate is subducted, or pushed beneath another, an arc-shaped depression on the ocean floor is typically formed. Trenches take on this shape because of the spherical shape of the Earth, in combination with interacting plates along a convergent plate boundary. Melting of rock and sediments along the subduction zone can also produce arc-shaped bands of volcanic islands called island arcs.

It is within the western Pacific Ocean that the deepest waters occur at Challenger Deep— the name given to the deepest section of the Mariana Trench. The Aleutian Islands, located along the northern portion of the Pacific Ocean and extending to Alaska, are part of an island arc that is associated with a deep oceanic trench. Perhaps the best-known example of a trench and island arc system is Japan. The islands of Japan are notorious for volcanic and tectonic activity (especially earthquakes). The Sea of Japan, found between the islands and the Asian continent, resides above the Japan Trench.

An interesting aspect of underwater volcanic cracks or vents is that they can emit hot springs into the icy cold ocean water. One vent, located about 2 km below the surface of the ocean near the Galapagos Islands, was found teeming with life. Scientists discovered that bacteria, and therefore sea animals, got their energy from sulfurous gases and minerals that come out of the vents. In a place where life could otherwise not be sustained, volcanic vents provided nourishment.

Seamounts

Scattered across the floors of ocean basins are isolated mountains and chains of mountains called seamounts. Always of volcanic origin, these mountains can rise more than a kilometer from the seafloor and often rise above sea level, forming islands. If the seamount is old, eroded, and subsurface, it is called a *guyot*.

Probably the best-known example of seamounts is the chain of islands that make up Hawaii. The Hawaiian Islands are linked to a somewhat older seamount chain known as the Emperor Seamount Chain. Curiously, these ridges across the ocean floor are not associated with any plate boundaries. In fact, they are found on the middle of the Pacific plate. The volcanic chains are produced as a result of the Pacific plate gliding across a stationary, deep-seated hot spot.

FUN FACT: Mount Kea, under the Pacific Ocean, rises 10 km above the seafloor. This makes it almost 2 km higher than Mount Everest, the tallest mountain on the planet.

Seafloor Sediments

As the rivers pour into the oceans, the buildup of sediment is pronounced. The greatest volume of sediment is obviously collected in these locations. There is still accumulation of sediment on the seafloor, however. It just tends to be a slower, less dramatic process than it sometimes can be at the mouth of a great river.

Land-based Sediment

As big rivers open into the ocean, you will find the largest deposits of land-based sediment—gravel, tinier pieces of rock and sand, and some volcanic ash. The bigger pieces end up collecting closer to land, and the tiny particles are washed farther out to sea.

Oozes

Particles of plants, shells, teeth, and bones are called *ooze*, and this substance covers about half of the deep-sea floor. The shells come from tiny marine snails, one-celled animals called *foraminifers*, and the hard remains of one-celled plants called *coccolithophores*. Because the deepest part of the ocean has a higher concentration of carbon dioxide (the gas that these animals exhale), and this gas combines with water to form a weak acid that dissolves seashells, ooze is not as likely to be found at the deeper levels.

EXPLORATION 7.2
HOW SEDIMENT SETTLES

To get a better picture of how sediment is distributed, fill a quart jar full of water and pour in a handful of coarse gravel, sand, and powdery clay. Stir the mixture well. Give everything a little time to settle and you'll see that the gravel settles first, then the sand reaches the bottom, and the powdery clay, at last, floats to the bottom of the jar.

Clearly, the sediment along the coastline—where the runoff from rivers, mountains, and other topographical features is prominent—is much more significant than deep on the seafloor. In the deeper part of the oceans, sediment may build up at a rate of only 0.5 to 1 cm every thousand years. However, the Ganges, the Yangtze, the Yellow, and the Brahmaputra Rivers—all in Asia—provide more than a quarter of the world's land-based sediment each year.

The reason that the sediment of the seafloor is such an important part of scientific study is that it represents about 175 million years of Earth's history. Studying the layers of sediment gives us valuable information about how Earth has changed over the eons from glacial movement, volcanic eruptions, and changes in sea level. Along with the research that has been conducted on land, samples of seafloor sediment help us to create a feasible history of how our world has developed from earliest times.

SUMMARY

Although much of our planet is covered with water, it has taken centuries for man to create the technology necessary for deep-sea explorations. The coldness and darkness of the ocean's depths and the obvious problem of water pressure have made it a technological challenge. Today, explorers are able to explore much of the seafloor, making continual discoveries.

The seafloor has two types of continental margins—passive and active. The passive margin is a place with little tectonic activity, such as the east coast of North America. The west coast of North America is a good example of an active continental margin, where the "leading edge" of a continent is colliding with an oceanic plate.

All continental margins have four components: continental shelf, continental slope, continental rise, and submarine canyons.

The continental shelf is where the land continent becomes submerged beneath ocean waters. When the land begins to slope downward into the ocean, it is called the continental shelf. At the point when the land continent is separated from the ancient shoreline is the continental break. When the Ice Age was at its peak, this would have been the actual shoreline.

Eventually, we reach the continental slope, where a sharp drop moves down to the ocean depths. This feature is created over a period of time as layers of sediment accumulate. On a passive margin, the sediment can slump down, creating a continental rise or gradual slope that covers the transition from the continent to the ocean basin.

Turbidity currents—movements of dense, sediment-laden water—create most of the sediment of the continental rise. Another important feature of our underwater world is the submarine canyon, perhaps carved by turbidity currents.

The basin floor is sediment-covered basaltic crust. This is the flattest part of Earth and is known as the abyssal plains. Mounds, or abyssal hills, are sprinkled across the abyssal plains. They can be remnants of volcanoes or ridges that protrude above the blanket of sediment. There are also mid-oceanic ridges, or continuous mountainous ridges, on the floor of all major ocean basins. The rifts at the top of these ridges indicate divergent plate boundaries. In places where plates collide, oceanic trenches occur. Here, one plate is subducted or pushed beneath another, and an arc-shaped depression is formed. Melting of rock and sediments along this subduction zone can also create bands of volcanic islands called island arcs.

Seamounts, which we discussed in the section on volcanism, are isolated mountains and chains of mountains, always of volcanic origin. An old, eroded seamount below the surface of the water is called a guyot.

Sediment in the ocean comes from two sources—land-based sediment and ooze. Land-based sediment may flow from rivers into the ocean, dispersing and gradually settling far into the ocean depths. Ooze—particles of plants, shell, teeth, and bones—covers about half of the seafloor. Sediment builds up at different rates in different locations, depending on the circumstances, but obviously, the ability to study the layers of sediment gives scientists some of the most important information about Earth's history.

SHORELINE

SHORELINE FEATURES

The shoreline is a dynamic place—always
changing, but still maintaining a set of
recognizable features. Most familiar to many
of us is the beach, a place where sediments
accumulate against the *water–land interface*,
the boundary between coast and sea. Like
the air–sea interface, which was mentioned
in Chapter 6, this is where both the land and
sea come together, with tides overlapping
the sloping beach or lapping up against rock
formations. For many, it is a place of great
pleasure—sun-warmed sand with the constant
swish of waves splaying across the shore.
For many others, the shoreline is a haven
for exploration, where sea meets land and
discoveries of marine life are abundant.

The shoreline is rich in wildlife habitats, and
it provides a dramatic illustration of the forces
of the ocean working upon the land. In this
chapter, we'll explore many of these shoreline
features and how they continue to evolve and
change the surface of our planet.

Sand and the Beach

Beaches are accumulations of sediment that
occur along the *shoreline*, or the boundary
of the water–land interface. To many of us,
the beach is merely a sandy expanse intended
for recreational purposes; but it is so much
more than that. A beach is a dynamic
feature—the sand is always in motion, so the
beach is always changing. You can see this
clearly in one trip to the seashore where you
see the waves move to and fro, swishing sand
about. Although the rest of the beach appears
unaffected by wave action, the entire beach
can be affected by very high tides or by waves,
and it can be even more dramatically altered
by a severe storm.

The beach is often referred to as a "river of
sand." Sand (or any sediment) on the beach
generally moves in a zigzag manner known
as *beach drift*. This happens because waves
meet the beach at an angle, which pushes
sand grains at a relative angle to the shoreline.
However, when the water from the waves
slows and washes back toward the ocean, the
sand moves in a straight line perpendicular
to the shore. The sand or particles of sediment
are deposited in this zigzag fashion (See Figure
8.1.) and can be transported hundreds or even
thousand of meters in a given day.

Where waves break at an oblique angle to the
shore, a current moves parallel to the coast.
This is known as a *longshore current*. Since
these currents happen in the *surf zone*, an area

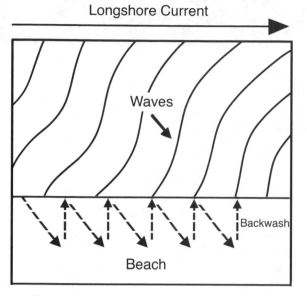

Figure 8.1—Beach Drift and Longshore Current

of turbulent water where waves rush onto the shore, fine sediment can be suspended in the water, and coarser sediment is pushed or rolled across the bottom. This process can produce elongated ridges of sand, known as *spits*, which extend from the land into the sea. These spits may form bars of sand that completely isolate a bay from the open ocean. Sometimes these sand ridges form tombolos, or sand bars that connect the mainland to an island.

The Sandy Beach

If a beach is composed of sand, the individual grains are usually derived from the weathering of continental rocks. The sand is most often composed of the mineral quartz. These beaches can often have quartz sand that is so pure that it can be mined later for melting and processing into glass.

On some beaches of the Hawaiian Islands, the sand is not quartz; rather, it is mostly composed of weathered, dark, basaltic lavas (fine-grained igneous rocks) and black, glassy, volcanic sand. These beaches have a unique black color. On other Hawaiian beaches and beaches in other tropical climates, the sand-sized particles consist of the broken shells of marine organisms and carbonate rocks like limestone. These beaches are very bright white or can have a pinkish color if reddish-shelled organisms contribute to the sediment mix.

A well-compacted sandy beach is easy to walk on, and may even be firm enough to allow car travel. This type of beach also tends to have a gentle slope toward the sea of no more than three degrees. This gentle slope allows sand to settle firmly, providing a more solid surface for one to traverse.

The Rocky Coast

When wave and current activity is intense, smaller sand grains cannot settle onto the beach environment. The beaches in these vigorous settings have sediments composed of coarse gravel and, sometimes, larger cobbles. If the wave action is strong enough to suspend and move all sand-sized particles, then the beach will be entirely a mixture of sand and gravel. Since gravel beaches are loosely consolidated, you can't walk or drive on them as easily as you can on a compacted, sandy beach.

As the sediment size of a beach increases, so does the slope. For instance, beaches composed of pebble-sized grains have slopes averaging about 15 degrees, while those made up of larger cobble-sized grains can have slopes approaching 25 degrees. A steeper slope increases the impact of wave action, allowing the sea to wash down larger cobble or pebble-sized grains. The beach is then not only steeper, but the sand underneath is not as tightly compacted, making walking or driving much more difficult.

The slope on any given beach can change in proportion to the current and wave strength across the shoreline. Strong currents and waves remove smaller sand grains, and thus the beach slope becomes steeper.

The Four Zones of Beaches

Based on the interaction of water and sediment, beaches can be subdivided into four zones: backshore, foreshore, inshore, and offshore. (See Figure 8.2.) The *backshore* is defined as the part of the beach farthest from the sea; it is typically dry but can be flooded by the highest of tides. This is where you might place your picnic blanket if you don't want to be surprised by an incoming tide. The *foreshore*, often called the low tide terrace, is the beach region upon which the daily tides oscillate; it is located between the average high and low tide levels. This is precisely the area that children flock to with their sand buckets because the sand is saturated with seawater and it is perfect for building castles and discovering shells. Farther seaward from the foreshore is an area where waves begin to pile up and break, called the *inshore*. This is where, on many ocean beaches, you'll see people standing in the way of breaking waves, enjoying the rush of cool water. Even farther seaward, beyond the break-

ing waves, is the *offshore* beach, the place where sediment can accumulate. This is far enough out that you might sail a small boat, in sight of the shore, but beyond the surf zone and breaking waves.

SHORELINE ENVIRONMENTS

The shoreline environment gives rise to many characteristic features found, to one degree or another, along most coastal areas. These may include salt marshes, deltas, barrier islands, reefs, and atolls.

One characteristic feature of a coastal area is a salt marsh. Salt marshes are defined as flat coastal wetland ecosystems that are inundated for some period of time, usually at high tide, by seawater. These areas are protected from wave action and are populated by plants that are able to tolerate high levels of salt. In order for a marsh to form, considerable sediment must accumulate. The sediment is usually a mixture of sand and silt.

The top portion of the salt marsh sediment is called a tidal flat. This is an area of the marsh that is alternately exposed at low tide and

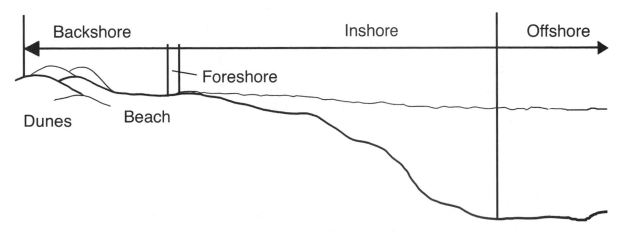

Figure 8.2—Beach Zones

submerged at high tide. Meandering channels snake their way across the salt marsh and serve as conduits for flooding at periods of high tide.

Salt marshes are generally not suitable for building or other human purposes, but they are rich in plant and animal life. Even walking through a salt marsh can be difficult for a human being, so these areas become important coastal wildlife refuges.

In places where a river carries heavy loads of sand and silt into the sea, a delta might extend into the ocean. Deltas—as you'll recall from our discussion of fluvial forces and the flow of rivers into the sea in Chapter 4—are fanlike accumulations of sediment deposited at the mouth of a river where it meets the coast. Not all rivers and streams produce deltas. Tidal and wave action can distribute sediment away from the stream onto nearby beaches or farther offshore onto the continental shelf. Deltas form only when the sediment load is so heavy that coastal processes cannot redistribute the sediments away from their point of entry into the sea.

Several factors influence the ocean's ability to transport river sediments—range of tides, tidal current strength, wave interaction along the coast, and the magnitude of longshore currents.

The sequence of events that produces deltas begins when the river's estuary becomes clogged with sediment. An *estuary* is a partially enclosed area that fills with oceanic waters at high tide and is commonly at the end of rivers where they meet the sea. The Chesapeake Bay on the eastern coast of Virginia is a prime example of an estuary, or flooded river valley. Freshwater pours into the Chesapeake from the Potomac, Rappahannock, Pocomoke, and James Rivers, while saltwater from the ocean floods in at high tide. The estuary therefore becomes a mix of both salt and fresh water.

Another example is the coast of Maine, particularly in the area of Acadia National Park, where the land was flooded by the post-glacial rise in sea level and became an irregular submerged coastline. The estuary steals away sediments that are on their way to the sea, and it must become totally filled with sediment before a delta can start to form. Because estuaries are places of transition from land to sea, and from freshwater to saltwater, they are often important refuges for wildlife. Here, they are protected from the full force of the ocean, while still enjoying unfettered access to it.

Although deltas pile up at the mouths of rivers, water still must reach the ocean. It does so by cutting small branching channels, called *distributaries*, across the growing delta. A delta's shape is a function of the rate of erosion versus the rate of sediment deposition. Rounded deltas indicate that the erosional coastal processes have been more dominant. A delta shaped like a bird's foot suggests that the river's sediment load was greater than the coast's ability to modify it.

Some 3 to 30 km offshore, *barrier islands* are often found parallel to the shoreline. Accumulations of sediment make these elongated barrier islands, which are composed of low ridges of sand that can be up to 30 km long and 5 km wide. They are very low in profile—usually not more than 10 meters in height above sea level. Barrier islands may have formed from pieces of land that were slowly separated from the shore by erosion. Alternatively, some barrier islands may have resulted from a rise in sea level after the extensive melting of glaciers, or at the end of the last glacial ice age.

In tropical areas, marine plants and creatures with calcareous bodies (containing or characteristic of calcium carbonate, calcium, or limestone) produce reefs along the shore. Coral reefs are massive structures made of limestone and invertebrates called coral polyps. The coral polyps, belonging to the same animal group as jellyfish and sea anemones, live together in colonies. When a coral polyp dies, its limestone "skeleton" remains, helping to build the barriers and ridges that comprise the coral reefs. This means that the reef is made up partly of these living animals and partly of their limestone remains.

Other plants and animals contribute to the structure, such as algae, seaweed, and mollusks. The reefs are built over time by the accumulation of the bodies of these carbonate-secreting creatures and calcareous algae. The algae serve to bind the reef together. The coral reefs cannot live without the symbiotic relationship they have with these special algae: The algae feed on the polyps, and the polyps use food made by the algae. The algae also help the polyps build their limestone skeletons. Despite the presence of the other organisms that thrive at the reef, the coral polyps and their remains give the reef its basic structure and beautiful color.

Reefs occur commonly in tropical and subtropical climates where the water must be above approximately 20°C year round. These structures grow only in shallow waters. Should the seafloor subside with time, the organisms that comprise the reefs grow toward the surface—keeping the structure within shallow water. Like other plants, the algae and seaweed need sunlight to live, so coral reefs can grow only in shallow, sunlit water.

Reefs grow very slowly over time, at perhaps a rate of one meter every thousand years. A coral reef is like a beautiful underwater garden, fragile and colorful. Once destroyed, it takes thousands of years for a coral reef to be rebuilt. Because they are such treasures, and because they grow so slowly, people have come to treat coral reefs with more respect and to guard their safety.

Atolls are continuous or broken rings of coral reef surrounding a central lagoon. (See Figure 8.3.) An example of this is Midway Lagoon, located about 4500 km west of San Francisco, near the northwestern end of the Hawaiian Island *archipelago*. An archipelago is a string of often-volcanic islands, reefs, and shoals that form along ocean ridges. *Shoals* are sandy elevations that form underwater, like sandbars, which can be hazardous to navigation because they are not usually visible from above the water level. The Hawaiian Island archipelago consists of 132 islands, reefs, and shoals stretching 2400 km.

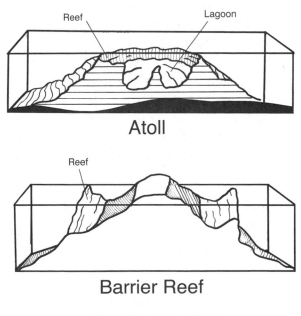

Atoll

Barrier Reef

Figure 8.3—A Coral Reef

The Midway Island group—located in the central Pacific Ocean, approximately 1850 km northwest of Honolulu and comprised of Sand and Eastern islands with the surrounding atoll—is an inactive U.S. military base with no indigenous population that began as a volcanic island, created over a hot spot nearly 30 million years ago. The islands eroded until they disappeared beneath the sea, but a fringing reef had begun to grow around the island's edge, creating an atoll. The movement of coral sand eventually created three islands. The original basalt that was Midway is now more than 150 m below the surface of the sea. The atoll is almost a complete circle, enclosing a lagoon, with the three islands nestling near the center point of the atoll.

SHORELINE EROSION

Waves that continuously crash against the shore produce a host of distinctive features. The most easily spotted of these features are *wave-cut cliffs*. As their name implies, these structures are formed by the undermining of the coastal land by the action of waves. As the waves crash into the faces of the cliffs, they wash away pieces of the wall and slowly scoop out the earth. With time, the process results in an overhang that becomes so overextended that it breaks off and falls into the sea. As the cliff erodes and scoops out part of the wall, it can also result in the formation of benchlike surfaces known as *wave-cut platforms*.

Land that extends into the ocean is subjected to intense wave erosion. Rock that is heavily fractured or relatively soft is removed the fastest. This has the effect of producing sea caves, and if two caves merge together, a *sea arch* results. Waves will eventually destroy such caves, and when they collapse, mounds of material called *sea stacks* are formed.

Since coastal areas are often heavily populated, humans have attempted to control the shape and erosion of the beach environment. Both slow, long-term change, and faster-acting changes induced by storms work to make the coast a very dynamic place. Piers or wharfs are sometimes used to influence the current or tide, or to protect a harbor or shoreline from storms and erosion.

In an attempt to keep a beach from losing too much sand, humans have begun to build barriers that trap sand. (See Figure 8.4.) These structures are called *groins*, and they are set up at an angle perpendicular to the shoreline. This configuration traps sand—keeping it from being carried away by longshore currents. Unfortunately, areas down current from the groin become depleted of sand and are thus subject to intense erosion. This situation results in the construction of multiple groins as property owners try to "harvest" their own supply of sand. Other human-made structures intended to mitigate shoreline erosion include jetties and seawalls. *Jetties*, pairs of structures that extend into the ocean at the entrance to a harbor or river, also protect against storm waves and sediment deposition. *Seawalls* are walls or embankments that help to prevent shoreline erosion. These structures share the same consequences as groins, in that they protect the shoreline on one side and contribute to the depletion of the shoreline on the other.

The problem, obviously, is that in addition to the natural erosion of the shoreline, human-made solutions to problems can create even more serious situations. Shoreline erosion is a problem that must be approached with effective long-term solutions that won't have a negative impact in the future.

The shoreline of New Jersey is an example of a place where too many of these structures have

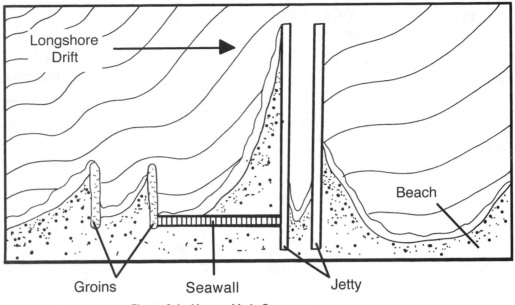

Figure 8.4—Human-Made Structures

been built, but these are not effective long-term solutions to beach erosion. A more appropriate solution is known as *beach nourishment*, the periodic addition of sand to the beach. The sand can come from a nearby lagoon or from inland dunes, and it would be trucked to the beach, or added at an upstream location and carried along by waves.

EXPLORATION 8.1
THE SHAPES OF SHORELINE AND HEIGHT OF TIDES

Obtain a square baking pan, a round baking pan, and a pie pan. Fill each of them to overflowing with water. Try picking up each pan and walking with it held in front of you. You will notice, no matter how carefully you walk, that the water is more likely to spill out of the square pan than the round pan or pie pan.

The entire ocean is affected by tides, but we really only notice this phenomenon along the shoreline. Consider the pans to be different shoreline shapes. Tides on low, gently sloping shores move in and out with little change, like in the pie pan. The more dramatic the edge of shoreline and sea is, the more dramatic the rise and fall of the tide will be.

SUBMERGENT AND EMERGENT COASTS

Although the beach, the salt marshes, deltas, and barrier islands can exist along any shoreline, one of the significant factors that impacts the nature of the beach is whether it is classified as a submergent coast or an emergent coast. A *submergent coast* is an area in which formerly dry land has been recently drowned, either by land subsidence or a rise in sea level; an *emergent coast* is an area in which land formerly under water has recently been placed above sea level, either by uplift of the land or by a drop in sea level. Changes in sea level over time have a drastic effect on the appearance of a coastline. With this in mind, shorelines can be classified by sea level changes as either submergent or emergent coasts.

EMERGENT VERSUS SUBMERGENT COASTLINES

- Emergent coast—sea level is falling
- Submergent coast—sea level is rising

EMERGENT COAST FEATURES

- Uplifted terraces
- Wave-cut platforms
- Wide beaches
- Larger salt marshes
- Exposed marine terrace

SUBMERGENT COAST FEATURES

- Drowned valleys
- Sea stacks
- Narrow beaches
- Small salt marshes

A coastline that has recently been inundated by rising sea level shows a markedly irregular profile. These submergent coastlines look this way because ocean waters first flood the low-lying areas such as river valleys, forming estuaries, while the ridges that separate the valleys poke above the rising sea. Estuaries such as these were formed as river valleys flooded, following a rise in sea level over geological time. They are characterized by little sedimentation and depths rarely exceeding 30 meters.

When a coastline is uplifted, new coastal lands are exposed as a result of the drop in sea level. The new coastline, once the sea level has dropped, has terraces or benchlike platforms that marked the position of the original coastline. If several episodes of uplift occur, a series of terraces or *paleo-coasts* is found moving away from the shoreline.

The coast of California, specifically Point Reyes National Seashore, is one of the better examples of this type of coastal behavior. Marine terraces are found there, and the most recent of these structures are exposed to intense erosion, thus forming a wave-cut platform.

SUMMARY

The interface between sea and land is a fascinating phenomenon, and circumstances along a shoreline can vary dramatically from point to point. Most of us are familiar with the shoreline at the beach, a place for recreation and leisure. But irregular rocky shorelines, like Acadia National Park on the coast of Maine, are well known for their rugged beauty.

Beaches are divided into four zones: the backshore, foreshore, inshore, and offshore. The shoreline also lends itself to many interesting features, including salt marshes, deltas, barrier islands, reefs, and atolls. Salt marshes tend to develop in areas where there is protection from wave action, but high tides tend to seep in on a regular basis, depositing sediment and cutting meandering channels off from floodwaters at high tide.

Deltas occur at the mouths of rivers, creating fan-shaped deposits of sediment. Barrier islands occur offshore as sediment piles up in elongated low-profile ridges just above sea level.

Shorelines are classified as either submergent or emergent. Submergent coasts have experienced a relative rise in sea level while emergent coastal areas have witnessed a relative drop in sea level. Most stretches of coastline have varied histories and can retain some features of both submergent and emergent coastlines.

What happens along the shoreline, that important interface of land and sea, obviously impacts life in both domains. Buildup of sediment may alter the flow of a river into the ocean, and a powerful storm can wash away sandy beaches that took generations to form. In an instant, humans can destroy a coral reef that took thousands of years to develop, but we can also be proactive about the restoration of beach areas that are prone to the extreme forces of wind and water. The shoreline remains a place where we can see the forces of both nature and humans on a day-to-day basis and understand clearly how a small change can have a major impact on the future of both land and sea.

CURRENTS

KEY TERMS

doldrums, gyre, acoustic tomography, boundary currents, upwelling, Coriolis effect, geostrophic current, Ekman spiral, thermohaline currents

THE MOTIONS OF THE OCEANS

The waters of the ocean are dynamic, always moving, and never still. Unequal heating and cooling of the sea, combined with winds across the surface of the water, create and drive currents. The winds themselves are also created as a consequence of the unequal heating of the surface of the planet.

Wind and the spinning of Earth cause surface currents. Temperature and salinity control the density of water, which in turn governs deep ocean currents. Ultimately, these currents transport warmer waters to the polar regions and cooler waters to the tropics, thus somewhat equalizing the distribution of heat on Earth.

Water doesn't necessarily move the way we think it does or the way it appears to. Waves move across the surface of the water, but the water doesn't actually move in a linear direction. As much as the waves appear to be moving toward the shore, the movement is not of the water particles but of the waves as a whole. Water moves up and down, almost like a ribbon or flag in the wind, flapping up and down but staying in one place.

In the previous chapter, we discussed how interconnected the land and sea are. Sediment washes into the ocean, and the ocean moves sand and sediment back onto beaches and into salt marshes. Neither the ocean beach nor the salt marsh could exist without the ocean. Similarly, the ocean is intimately tied to the power of the wind and currents; and these factors, in turn, have their effect on the continents.

Surface Circulation Patterns

The motion of the surface waters of all the major oceans is very similar, although the Southern and Arctic oceans have smaller basins, and, therefore, some differences in currents. Westerly flowing surface currents, called the North and South Equatorial currents, mark the equatorial region. A pair of steadily blowing *trade winds*—movements of air that come from the great deserts and flow toward the equator where they are deflected by the Coriolis effect—generate these currents. A thin, eastward-flowing current, known as the Equatorial Countercurrent, is situated between this pair of westerly flowing currents. This current is associated with the *doldrums*—a region of the ocean near the equator between the two belts of trade winds. The air converging at the doldrums rises high over Earth, recirculates poleward, and sinks back toward Earth. It doesn't go directly north or south because it is deflected by the Coriolis effect.

The doldrums are characterized by unpredictable weather events. The high amount of solar radiation causes intense heating of the land and ocean, resulting in various forms of severe weather, such as thunderstorms and squalls (sudden, brief, violent windstorms often accompanied by rain or snow). Hurricanes typically originate there. This equatorial region is also characterized by low pressure and is known as the intertropical convergence zone. The doldrums are also known for calms, periods when the winds disappear, trapping sailing vessels for days or weeks.

The equatorial currents are part of a larger, circular current pattern known as a gyre (Figure 9.1). The first arm of each gyre is an elongated, almost-closed circulation pattern that is confined to subtropical regions positioned approximately 30° north and south of the equator. An easterly flowing current found in both hemispheres forms the other significant arm of the gyre. In the Southern Hemisphere, this west-to-east flowing current is referred to as the West Wind Drift. It is the most prominent surface current found in that

hemisphere. Its counterpart in the Northern Hemisphere is called the North Atlantic Current, which is really just a continuation of the Gulf Stream current that flows along the eastern seaboard of North America.

The *Gulf Stream*—actually just a portion of a huge, slow-moving gyre—begins near the equator. We hear about it frequently since it often impacts weather in the United States. As the Florida Current, it passes through the Straits of Florida and along the southeastern United States. It is almost 80 km wide here, and then, north of Cape Hatteras, it is separated from the coast by a narrow southern extension of the cold Labrador Current. One of the densest concentrations of fog often occurs when the warm waters of the Gulf Stream meet the cold winds accompanying the Labrador Current.

The system of currents that exists in the Pacific Ocean is referred to as the North Pacific Current. The gyre of the Indian Ocean consists of the West Wind Drift to the south and the South Equatorial Current to the north.

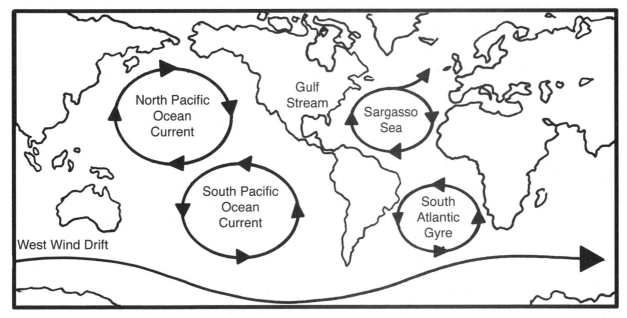

Figure 9.1—Gyres

EXPLORATION 9.1
HOW WINDS CAUSE
SURFACE CURRENTS

Fill a shallow baking pan with water. Use a hole-punch to cut 10 circles out of a piece of construction paper. Put the paper circles on the water, near the left side of the pan. Blow across the surface of the water, where the paper is floating.

You will notice that the paper circles move in a common direction around the outside of the pan. This is because your breath starts a surface current (a horizontal movement of water). The water travels away from where the wind starts the motion. In addition to the wind (or, in this case, your breath), the rotation of Earth, changes in the temperature of the water, and differences in the height of the ocean also impact currents.

Subtropical gyres flow clockwise in the Northern Hemisphere and counterclockwise in the Southern Hemisphere. Currents are often named for the area from whence they originate, making it a little easier for us to understand and remember Earth's major currents and circulation patterns.

The North Atlantic Ocean gyre spins clockwise. In the center of the circulating mass of water is a region known as the Sargasso Sea, with virtually no currents. This area of calm water is named after the Sargassum seaweed, which is found in abundance there.

The polar and subpolar regions have gyres that rotate clockwise in the north and counterclockwise in the south. Due to continental distribution, the high latitude gyres in the Northern Hemisphere are more prominent

HOW CURRENTS ARE MEASURED

There are many ways to measure the direction and intensity of current flow. Perhaps the easiest is to simply chart the path of a ship as it drifts across the ocean. Bottles with notes inside have been set adrift to help monitor currents. One such bottle, released in Perth, Australia, in 1962, was picked up five years later in Miami, Florida. A more sophisticated way to monitor currents is to use a free-floating buoy, but one that transmits data on its location. Other buoys are tethered to the seafloor, and they monitor currents at a specific site. Orbiting satellites can monitor current drift from above, as well. The three-dimensional flow of water can be studied by a process called acoustic tomography. Subsurface explosions generate sound waves that are transmitted through the sea. It turns out that these sound waves reach the receiver more quickly if the water is flowing toward the receiver. Deeper ocean currents have been tracked by monitoring the release of radioactive chemical compounds.

and better formed than those in the Southern Hemisphere, where no continents interfere with surface current flow. In particular, Antarctica is almost directly centered at the South Polar Region, allowing the West Wind Drift Current to flow uninterrupted around the globe. However, smaller clockwise gyres are found about the coast of Antarctica.

Boundary Currents

Currents that flow parallel to the equator eventually encounter continents and are then deflected either north or south into what are called *boundary currents*—because they flow along the boundary of the continents. These currents are significant in that they can transport heat from the tropics, produced by the warming of water by east-to-west currents, toward the polar regions. In the Northern Hemisphere, the western boundary currents are very strong, moving at a rate of hundreds of kilometers per day, while those in the east are much weaker and slower, moving at a rate of tens of kilometers per day.

The rotation of Earth on its axis has the effect of displacing boundary currents westward—resulting in swift, narrow, and deep ocean currents on the western edges of ocean basins. The Gulf Stream is a good example of this. Here, such currents cause water to pile up, forcing the pycnocline, a layer of ocean water with vertical density, to a deeper level. Usually the pycnocline level is between the surface and the deep ocean, as we discovered in Chapter 6. When the pycnocline is forced to go deeper, the western boundaries are then depleted of nutrients.

SIGNIFICANCE OF OCEAN CURRENTS

Seagoing vessels take advantage of the ocean surface currents. Voyage time can be significantly reduced if your ship travels with a current. Currents also bring equatorially warmed waters toward the poles. Where these warm waters move against the coast—for instance, in Great Britain—they moderate the local climate, making it warmer than it should be for the latitude. In the same way, cold polar water flows as a current toward the tropics, moderating this very hot zone during the summer months. In this way, these currents maintain a balance of heat distribution on our planet—excess heat from the tropics is transported to the polar region where there is a heat deficit, and excess cold from the Polar Regions is transported to the tropics where there is a heat surplus.

Upwelling and the Coriolis Effect

While the sea is depleted of nutrients on its western boundaries, the same currents create the opposite effect on the eastern boundaries. We just learned how the rotation of Earth on its axis displaces boundary currents, causing the pycnocline layer to a deeper level and depleting nutrients on the ocean's western boundaries. *Upwelling* has the opposite effect, as it is the process by which cold water from deeper layers replaces warmer surface water (Figure 9.2). Upwelling causes surface waters to shift away from the coast, resulting in broad currents with deeper waters moving toward the surface. This phenomenon occurs where wind moves toward the equator but parallel to the coast. It happens most frequently on the eastern boundaries of the oceans, particularly along California, Peru, and West Africa. This brings greater concentrations of such dissolved nutrients as nitrates and phosphates to the surface, providing nourishment for fish.

Because of Earth's rotation, currents are deflected to the right of their path of motion in the Northern Hemisphere and to the left in the Southern Hemisphere. Instead of the

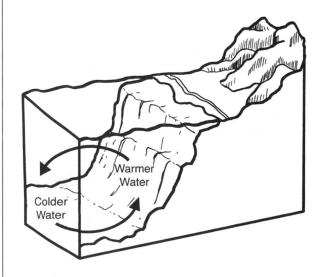

Figure 9.2—Upwelling

water flowing exactly as it is directed by the wind, the rotation of Earth causes it to shift direction, not always following the path of the wind. This is known as the *Coriolis effect* (Figure 9.3). The *Coriolis force* is an inertial force used by scientists and mathematicians to describe the motion of bodies in a rotating frame of reference. Although winds are important in generating currents, the Coriolis force causes currents to shift direction. When describing the effects of this force, such as the deflection of the winds and currents, the phenomenon is referred to as the Coriolis effect. These terms are sometimes used interchangeably, but they are best understood if you consider that the force moves a body from its path, and the effect is the new path that body is following.

Imagine surface currents moving parallel to the coast of South America, on the Peruvian side. Winds blow toward the equator parallel to the coast. Because of the Coriolis effect, the surface water movement is directed offshore; as this water moves away from the coast, deeper water upwells from depths of 50 to 300 meters, replenishing the nutrients of the surface water.

EXPLORATION 9.2
THE CORIOLIS FORCE

Imagine that you're riding on a rocket launched from the equator toward the North Pole. At the equator, prior to lift off, you are already moving at 1600 kilometers per hour. The motion is, of course, due to the eastward rotation of Earth on its axis. Upon launch toward the pole, the rocket moves across a surface that turns eastward at a uniformly slower speed with increasing latitude. Like a spinning wheel, the center of rotation, or the pole, has no lateral motion.

As the rocket moves northward, it retains its higher eastward velocity and so appears to move to the right if observed by an earth-bound onlooker. However, an observer from a removed spot—such as the Moon—would see that the rocket is really traveling in a straight line. It is the slower lateral motion of the planet as you move away from the equator that causes the apparent deflection of the Coriolis effect.

The Coriolis effect and resultant upwelling make eastern boundary currents suitable for the high productivity of marine organisms. These eastern boundary currents can also flow across the continental margin and transport cooler polar waters toward the equator.

Wind, temperature, salinity, and the rotation of Earth combine to ultimately shape the character of oceanic currents. The transfer of wind energy to surface waters is what primarily drives surface currents. The motion of water below the air–sea interface is governed by salinity, and salinity and temperature control water density. *Geostrophic currents* are the result of a balance between the wind, density, and the

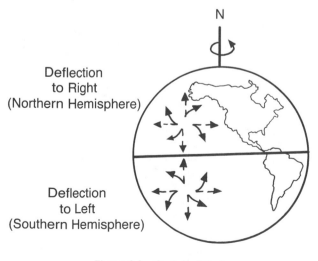

N

Deflection to Right (Northern Hemisphere)

Deflection to Left (Southern Hemisphere)

Figure 9.3—Coriolis Effect

EXPLORATION 9.3
UNDERSTANDING THE IMPACT OF EARTH'S ROTATION ON WIND AND WATER CURRENTS

Cut a 20-cm-diameter circle out of construction paper. Push the point of a pencil through the center of the circle. Place a drop of water on top of the paper, near the pencil. Now, hold the pencil between the palms of your hands, with the paper above your hands. Twirl the pencil in a counterclockwise direction. You'll see that the water drop swirls around in a clockwise direction. This is because the water is thrown forward and the paper moves out from underneath it. Similarly, wind and water currents in the Northern Hemisphere are turned toward the right because of the rotation. This is known as the Coriolis effect.

Coriolis force. Once the currents are in motion, they are deflected by the Coriolis force.

Subsurface waters move continuously in different directions and at different depths. The Coriolis force deflects each layer of water. Although the speed of the current lessens with depth, the overall result is that a spiral current is formed as it travels deeper into the sea. This deep, spiraling flow is called the *Ekman spiral*. The spiral may extend downward for as much as 200 meters, below the point at which wind no longer has any effect on the water.

Deep Circulation Patterns

The circulation of oceanic waters near the surface is not the total extent of current flow. Seawater moves in the deep ocean, and temperature and salinity control this motion. In this case, it is not the wind, but rather density differences acting under the influence of gravity that drive currents. (See Figure 9.4.)

Warmer, less salty water is less dense than cooler, saltier water. This cool, salty mass of water sinks and drives deep-ocean circulation. These currents are called *thermohaline currents* because of their cool temperature and heavy salinity. They are often below the surface of the ocean for a period of 100 to more than 1000 years.

It isn't difficult to understand how these currents operate. As the water comes into contact with the atmosphere, it is cooled, thus making it denser. Similarly, when water freezes into ice or evaporates, the net effect is an increase in its salinity, and therefore its density. The denser body of water, whether it is created by changes in temperature or salinity, sinks toward the ocean bottom.

In order to maintain a balance or equilibrium in the distribution of oceanic waters, the displaced deeper waters, which are less dense, move toward the area where the denser waters were formed. What this means is that cooler and less salty oceanic waters, formed near the polar regions, flow toward the equator, thus displacing warmer water.

The dense polar seas created in the Arctic and Antarctic regions are the source and cause of deep ocean circulation. The densest

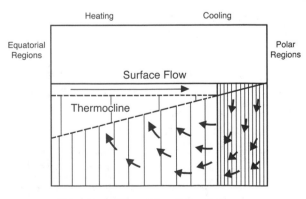

Figure 9.4—Deep Circulation Patterns

**EXPLORATION 9.4
UNDERSTANDING THE DENSITY
OF WATER**

Fill a one-cup measure about 3/4 full with water. Add 6 tablespoons of salt and stir. Pour in drops of blue food coloring to make the water a very deep navy color. Fill a glass bowl one-half full with water. Then, slowly pour the blue, salty water down the side of the bowl. You will see that the colored water sinks to the bottom of the bowl, forming waves under the clear water above it. When two bodies of water mix, the water with the most salt will move under the lighter, less salty water.

---

of all waters on the planet are created in the Antarctic where temperatures are cold enough during the winter so the surface water can freeze into ice. Saltier, and thus denser, water results because salts cannot be incorporated into ice. The crystal structure of the water doesn't allow salt, or NaCl, to be incorporated. Saltwater will freeze at a temperature lower than 0°C, and the salt concentration of the water increases as you get closer to the bottom.

Slowly, the denser water sinks to the sea bottom and then begins its sluggish journey across the ocean basins. This bottom layer is known as brine. Only centuries later may this water warm up enough to rise and appear at the surface again.

Density-driven deep ocean currents are somewhat like a conveyor belt. Warm waters in the upper layers of the sea move toward the poles. Here the water is chilled, eventually becoming more dense and sinking to the seafloor. The saline brine creeps toward the equator. As the waters warm, they upwell to the surface, only to begin the cycle again.

FUN FACT: The age of water is the amount of time that it has been in the deep ocean. As water becomes denser, it sinks into the deep ocean. Water age in the North Atlantic is between 100 and 750 years old. The waters of the deep Pacific Ocean are at least 1000 years old.

Carbon isotopes in seawater can be used to determine its age. We measure dissolved inorganic carbon in seawater, and thus how long it has been at depth, or not exposed to the atmosphere.

SUMMARY

The ocean waters are never still, but they are not necessarily moving in the way that we think they are. Currents are created by wind across the water, the spinning of the Earth, and the temperature and salinity of the water.

Surface circulation currents are known as gyres—larger, circular current patterns. Although there are different surface currents in various parts of the world, basically the Northern Hemisphere flows clockwise, and the Southern Hemisphere flows counterclockwise.

Currents flowing alongside the equator eventually encounter continents and then travel along the north or south boundaries, becoming what we call boundary currents. These boundary currents are deflected by the force of the Coriolis effect, resulting in swift, narrow, and deep ocean currents on the western edges of ocean basins and broader currents with upwelling on the eastern edges of oceans. The Coriolis effect also keeps currents from flowing with the wind. Earth's rotation helps to displace boundary currents, contributing to the displacement of layers of seawater. Upwelling is the vertical upward motion of

cold water—a process that brings dissolved nutrients to the surface.

The motion of water below the wind's reach is governed by salinity and temperature, which control water density. Ocean water moves deep below the surface. Cool, salty water sinks, and like a conveyor belt, may travel at deep ocean levels for a period of 100 to 1000 years before it reaches the surface again. The cooler and more saline oceanic waters, formed near the polar regions, flow toward the equator, thus displacing warmer water. The saltier, and thus denser, water that doesn't freeze at the polar regions, sinks to the sea bottom and travels slowly across the ocean basins.

Imagine the ocean as a complex system of layers. We discussed the surface zone, pycnocline zone, and thermocline (steep changes in temperature) and halocline (marked changes in salinity) zones. These layers do not mix freely, but travel, depending on the wind and the rotation of Earth. While brine from the poles sinks deep into the ocean depths and travels slowly to the equator, upwelling in other locations brings the nourishing pycnocline layer to the surface. The ocean is constantly on the move and much of this movement serves a purpose. The layers of water are alternated, warming the poles, cooling the equator, bringing nutrients to the surface for fish. The ocean is a powerful force that can also rage out of control, but much of what happens on a daily basis is important in maintaining the health of our planet.

WAVES AND TIDES

BEHAVIOR OF WAVES

In Chapter 9, we discussed different types of currents. The ocean doesn't appear to sit still, and, in fact, it probably experiences much more movement than we ever realized. We now know that what we see on the surface is only part of the story. Deep ocean currents keep water constantly in transit, like a conveyor belt. The up and down motion of currents is caused by changes in temperature and salinity, as well as the impact of wind and gravitational forces.

The next step in understanding the power of the ocean is to look at waves—disturbances in the sea that can be classified based on their origins. Wind, earthquakes, and the gravitational pull of the Sun and Moon cause these disturbances. Once created, they are best envisioned as oscillations of water in an up-and-down manner. This oscillatory motion (swinging back and forth with a steady, uninterrupted rhythm) decreases with depth. It is important to realize that open ocean waves do not move water laterally. Imagine a ship at sea. Waves are not pushing it along. The ship rises and sinks in elevation as the wave moves by.

Parts of a Wave

A host of terminology is used to describe how a wave behaves. The highest point of a wave is called its *crest*, and the lowest point is its *trough*. *Wave height* is defined as the distance from the trough to the crest. The distance between a wave crest and the next crest, or from any point on a wave to the same point on the next wave, is called a *wavelength*. How far a wave moves the water above or below sea level is the wave *amplitude*, which is equal to one-half the wave height. (See Figure 10.1).

Winds can be gusty and turbulent, and this may be reflected in the behavior of the waves. However, once the wind changes direction, the waves keep moving and then go through a gradual change to swells that are lower in height and longer in length. They may carry the storm's energy to distant shores. The waves that we watch may be a result of many differing winds and forces, but observing wave behavior is useful, and important, to those who are at sea as well as those who live along Earth's shorelines.

Waves are also classified by their *period*, which is defined as the amount of time it takes a wave to pass a specific point. The number of waves passing this point each second (or hour) is the *wave frequency*. The wave period can be as short as 0.1 second and as long as 24 hours.

The smallest waves are called *capillary waves*, and they have wavelengths of less than 1.75 cm and a period of less than 0.1 second. *Surface tension*, or the impact of wind against the surface of water, limits the size of the waves, and they are only found as small ripples on larger waves. Capillary waves, constrained by the surface tension, will never be more than ripples on the surface of the water.

Waves with periods up to five minutes are called *gravity waves*. Although these waves are induced by winds blowing across the open ocean, gravity is the force that is actually working to restore the sea to a calm surface. The longer the wind blows over a larger surface, the bigger the waves will eventually become. Waves with periods larger than five minutes include *tides*, periodic changes in the elevation of seawater, and seismic *sea waves*, rapidly moving ocean waves generated by earthquake activity.

Obviously, we don't have much to fear from capillary waves, the small ripples across the surface of the water. But it is important to observe tides, which can range from very low to very high (including flooding), and seismic sea waves, which can have a devastating impact on land. Awareness of major low or high tides and their impact on the shoreline, as well as the effect of seismic sea waves, can be important in the preservation of life, property, and natural shoreline features.

EXPLORATION 10.1 MAKING A WAVE

There are two easy ways to create your own wave. In the first, you and a friend can make a wave with a piece of rope. This is similar to the ribbon or flag on a pole. Each person takes one end of the rope and then together snap the rope to make a wave propagate across it. Experiment and see if you can vary the wave height and period.

Waves can also be made by dropping a stone in a pool of water. These waves, like an ocean wave, are an up-and-down cycle that moves out in all directions. Instead of moving away from a weather disturbance, like a storm, your wave moves away from the place where your tossed pebble hit the water.

TYPES OF WAVES
Wind Generated Waves

Most oceanic waves are created by the wind. Frictional drag from the air across surface waters creates tiny ripples that eventually develop into small waves. These initial waves appear choppy with V-shaped troughs and they propagate in the direction of the blowing winds.

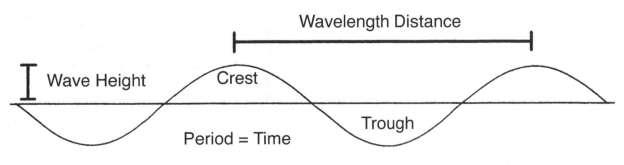

Figure 10.1—Parts of a Wave

Wave height increases proportionally with increasing wind speed. As the wave period grows, the velocity of the waves increases as well. How long the wind blows, and the *fetch*, or the distance over which the wind blows, control the overall size of a wave. Large waves are created only when the wind blows across a given area for a long period of time.

Waves formed by the wind are typically generated in storms. In the area of origin, the sea, ocean, or lake, waves can be chaotic and unpredictable. They then move away from their point of origin as a swell, or a group of waves that resemble rolling hills in the open ocean and move away from the storm in all directions.

The waves then move out in sequence, longest waves followed by progressively shorter waves, away from the point of origin.

Since the waves with the longest wavelengths travel the fastest, they reach land sooner than waves with shorter wavelengths. As long as the wave is in deep water, water depth has no impact on it. As soon as it approaches shore, however, the water becomes shallower, and this influences wave behavior. The wave begins to feel bottom at a water depth equal to about one-half its wavelength. Some energy is used in moving small particles of sediment back and forth, and the wave slows. The faster waves behind it catch up, decrease in wavelength, and the wave grows higher. Finally, the wave is unable to support its height and it collapses into a familiar splashing mist of foam, and the wave advances up the shore. Such tall waves have crests moving more rapidly than their troughs, encouraging the wave to curl over at the top. If waves break in a slow and even fashion, they are called *spillars*. Waves that break over a short distance and crash abruptly onto the beach are called *plungers*.

Seismic Sea Waves

Sudden movements of the seafloor caused by an earthquake or landslide can produce large seismic sea waves called *tsunamis*. Typically, these seismically generated water waves occur in groups of three or four, separated by intervals of approximately 15 minutes. Tsunamis can be powerful, and they move at great speeds with very impressive wavelengths. A typical tsunami may have a wavelength of approximately 250 km and a speed of nearly 700 km per hour. (See Figure 10.2.)

Oddly enough, tsunamis are almost imperceptible in the open sea where they may only cause a rise in sea level of less than 1 meter. The situation is quite different as these seismic sea waves approach the shallow water near the shoreline, however. As a tsunami feels the floor of the nearby coastline, the wave begins to slow and pile up. On flat beaches, these waves can reach a height of 20 meters. The most impressive waves are created in V-shaped coastal inlets where the breaking water can reach heights of nearly 30 meters high. Often, before the arrival of a tsunami, the coastal waters may be drawn out to sea. At this moment, harbors or a beach may appear strangely dry before getting hit by the first seismic sea wave. It is almost like a giant vacuum has sucked the water out of the harbor, leaving boats stranded and fish flopping on the mud.

Four out of five tsunamis happen within the "Ring of Fire," a zone of frequent earthquakes and volcanic eruptions in the Pacific Ocean. More than 50,000 people have been killed by tsunamis in the past century.

The Pacific Tsunami Warning System, based in Hawaii, has been established to help save lives in the case of tsunamis. Its network of earthquake detectors and tide gauges detects quakes that may cause a tsunami, giving people some time to take precautions. In cases where no warnings were available, people, houses, and

FACTS ABOUT TSUNAMIS

Tsunamis are the most destructive waves in the ocean. Incorrectly called tidal waves, the tsunamis are really triggered by earthquakes, landslides, or volcanic eruptions.

The 1929 tsunami, off the Grand Banks of Canada, was preceded by an earthquake that measured 7.2 on the Richter scale. It caused $400,000 in damage—mostly to transatlantic telephone cables—and it killed 29 people. The impact was registered as far as Portugal. The heavy financial cost of this tsunami was due to submarine landslides and the damage to cables. This was the first documentation of turbidity currents, a downslope movement of dense, sediment-laden water created when sand and mud on the continental shelf and slope are dislodged and thrown into suspension.

A more recent tsunami hit Peru on February 21, 1996. Effects were observed for a stretch of about 590 km of shoreline. Because the shores of Peru are low and flat, the waves did not rise very high. Instead, they came 200 meters inland, covering an isthmus. This tide carried fishing boats 300 meters on shore and left them stranded there for days.

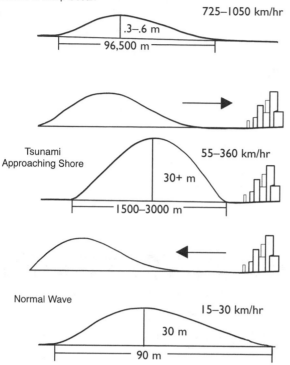

Figure 10.2—Tsunami Approaching Shore

boats were simply swept up in the giant force of the tsunami. Evacuating lowlands and shoreline areas when a tsunami is predicted may not save much property, but could significantly reduce the mortality factor.

CONSEQUENCES OF WAVES

Waves and the Shoreline

We focused on the beach in Chapter 7 and covered many significant aspects of the shoreline, including sandbars, spits, sea stacks, and caves. It is important, however, to consider the daily, constant impact of waves upon the shoreline. Certainly, a major event like a hurricane or tsunami can alter a shoreline in a few hours, but the steady pounding of waves and the flow of currents contribute their fair share to shaping the water–land interface.

The rate of shoreline erosion depends on the type of shoreline and the size and force of waves. During Hurricane Andrew in 1992, whole sections of Florida's beaches—and even buildings—were washed away. Weathering that might have normally taken years to change the face of the coastline took only a few hours. Normally, the shore may erode at about $1\frac{1}{2}$ meters per year. The process of erosion, the slow building up of other areas, and the creation of new shoreline features are barely perceptible.

Sections of the rocky California coastline change in a different way, however. Here, breaking waves chip off fragments of beach rock. These fragments are swept against other rocks, breaking off even more fragments. The water will also seep into the cracks of rock cliffs, making them larger, and eventually breaking large rocks apart. The chemical action of seawater will also dissolve minerals in rocks. At the same time, waves deposit sediment that builds up sandbars and spits, creating new formations along the shoreline. Waves and erosion are a constant—but often barely perceptible—process.

Wave Erosion and Refraction

Wave refraction was also touched upon in Chapter 8, in the discussion of beaches. We know that as a wave approaches the sloping bottom before the beach, it is bent and tends to orient itself parallel to the shore. The part of the wave nearest the shore touches bottom and slows down first, while the end that is in deep water continues forward at its regular speed. The result is a wave front that may approach nearly parallel to the shore, regardless of the original direction of the wave.

The impact of waves is concentrated against the sides and ends of headlands that project into the sea, while the force of waves is weakened in bays. Since the waves reach the shallow water in front of the headland before the adjacent bays, they strike it from all three angles. Over time, the result is a general straightening of an irregular coastline.

Tides Generated by the Moon and Sun

Tides can be thought of as very long period waves that are observed as the periodic rise (*flood currents*) and fall (*ebb currents*) of sea level. They are the product of the gravitational pull of the Moon and the Sun. In addition, the period of the tide is closely associated with the rotation of Earth on its axis. As our planet spins around once a day, coastal areas experience two high and two low tides each day.

The gravity of the Moon tugs relentlessly at the Earth—causing the oceans to rise or bulge in the direction of the Moon. Since Earth is spinning, centrifugal forces are at work, which also result in a bulge of water 180° opposite from the Moon. So, Earth has two bumps of water on opposite sides of the planet. This pair of elevated regions of seawater always remains in line with the Moon.

However, since Earth rotates faster than the Moon revolves around our planet, every point on the planet cycles through each of the two tidal bulges each day. Conversely, every point on Earth cycles through the two areas of lowered sea level as well.

The tide-producing force on Earth's hemisphere nearest the Moon is in the direction of the Moon's attraction, or rather, toward the Moon. On the opposite side of Earth—where the Moon's pull of gravity is at its weakest, the tide-producing force is in the direction of the centrifugal force, or away from the Moon. The bulges of water correlate with regions that experience high tides, whereas the areas of lower water mark low tides.

Spring Tides and Neap Tides

The Sun's gravitational pull also affects the intensity of the tides. When the Sun and Moon are in line with Earth, either at times of a full or new moon, the added gravitational tug creates very high and alternately very low tides. These are known as *spring tides* because there is such an excessive difference between tidal levels. Near the times of new and full moons, the Sun and Moon are aligned, and their forces are added together. Therefore, low tides and high tides will both be more extreme.

If the Sun and Moon are not aligned exactly with Earth—at the first and third quarter phases of the Moon, when the Sun and Moon are at right angles and each offsets the influence of the other—then there is not such a dramatic difference between high and low tide. These instances, where there are minimal differences between high and low tides, are called *neap tides* (Figure 10.3).

The timing and nature of tides is even more complicated than this. We have covered the basic causes and patterns of tides, but the height or time of actual tides at specific places can't really be predicted based solely on the position of the Sun and Moon. The shape of the coastline, the ocean basin, and existing weather patterns all contribute to the tides. The ever-present motion of the Moon around Earth, combined with the revolution of Earth around the Sun, makes tide prediction very challenging.

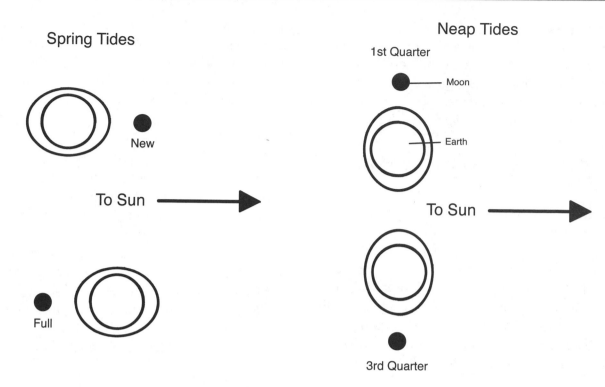

Figure 10.3—Spring and Neap Tides

If we combine all our knowledge about high and low tides, and take into consideration the existing topography and weather systems, then we can make predictions about tides. Such information is invaluable to fisherfolk and others who make their living near the sea, and it's always of interest to those who use the ocean for recreational purposes. In times of extreme high tides or stormy weather, tidal predictions can help people along the coastline prepare for possible flooding and its consequences.

Tidal Currents

The *tidal current* refers to the horizontal flow of water accompanying the rise and fall of the tide. We see this in the rising water of a *flood tide*, the period during which the sea flows as far as possible onto the land, and the lowering water level of an *ebb tide*, the period during which the tide recedes from the beach boundary. These currents are not particularly important in the open sea, but in bays, rivers, estuaries, and other narrow waterways, the impact can be substantial.

Tidal currents moving through narrow inlets may constantly move sediment out of small passageways that would otherwise close off a good harbor. Tidal currents in bays, rivers, and estuaries alternately flood the low-lying coastal zone, and then expose the drowned portion of the land. This land is obviously not suitable for building or human occupation, but it provides an invaluable wildlife habitat. Tidal currents can also present a disadvantage, particularly in the case of a severe storm, where the natural flooding can be extended beyond usual boundaries, causing danger to life and property.

In a few select locations, the power of the tide can be harvested to create power. There needs to be a range between flood tide and ebb tide of more than 6 m and a narrow inlet to create strong tidal currents. This happens in only a few spots; but when it does happen, it can be a valuable energy source. To use such power, we need to build a dam across the mouth of a bay or estuary. As the tide rises, water flows through open gates. When the tide wanes, the impounded water gradually flows out, turning electrical generators.

HAZARDOUS CURRENTS

Gaps across an offshore sandbar can form "channels" that funnel water away from the shore. These channels, also known as rip currents or rip tides, can be dangerous to swimmers. They are not permanent features of the beach, as they shift with ever-changing wave conditions. Swimmers caught within one of these currents can be quickly pulled offshore.

Should you find yourself in this situation, it is best not to swim against the current but to swim parallel to shore. Rip currents are strong, but very narrow. It is possible to swim out of the current and then toward shore. If you're tired, finding a sandbar on which to rest may give you the strength to fight the current before you make your way back to shore. The water level at many sandbars is only waist-deep, and these areas are marked by lighter-colored water and foam on the surface.

Undertow, a current underneath the surface current moving in the opposite direction, can also be a hazard to swimmers. This seaward pull of receding waves after they break on a shore can be observed at the edge of the water–land interface. After a wave washes ashore, it pulls itself back in, taking the sand with it out to sea. When this happens farther offshore, you can literally feel the water underneath tugging you farther out to sea.

The problem is that such power is intermittent, and turbines are needed to keep energy at a constant level.

If all bays and estuaries with strong tidal currents were utilized, they may provide only about 2 percent of the world's water-generated power, but it can be an important local resource. Such electricity consumes no exhaustible fuels and produces no noxious waste. There is also much less disturbance to the landscape when tidal currents are used to produce power.

This idea isn't new; twelfth-century water wheels were used for grinding grain. Most of Boston's flour was produced by tidal mills in the seventeenth and eighteenth centuries. Other countries have used tidal currents to produce electricity in recent years, but the United States has not developed any significant ways to utilize this power source.

EXPLORATION 10.4
RIP CURRENTS

You can simulate a rip current by damming a small pool of water. Once the water has accumulated, cut a narrow depression across the dam. Notice how the water streams out as a very swift current. Now, imagine this sort of event on a large scale and how difficult and tiring it would be to swim against the current.

SUMMARY

Waves, undulations of water surfaces, can behave in a variety of ways. The highest point of a wave is the crest and the lowest point is the trough. The distance from one crest to another or from one point to the same point on the next wave is the wavelength.

Amplitude refers to how high above or below sea level a wave might rise. Waves are also defined by their period, the amount of time it takes a wave to pass a certain point. Wave frequency is the number of waves passing this point per second or per hour.

Capillary waves are the smallest waves, with wavelengths less than 1.75 cm and periods of less than 0.1 second. Gravity waves might have periods up to 5 minutes, and seismic sea waves are those with periods of longer than 5 minutes.

Most ocean waves are generated by wind, and they increase proportionally in height with increasing wind speed. The fetch, or the distance over which the wind is blowing, is another factor that controls the size of a wave.

Waves are generated in storms and then move away from their point of origin as a swell, or a series of rolling hills of water. When the wave hits the shore, if it breaks in a slow and even fashion it is called a spillar. Waves that break over a short distance and crash abruptly onto the beach are called plungers.

Seismic sea waves, caused by earthquakes or landslides, are called tsunamis. These waves rush toward the shoreline at the speed of a jet airliner, achieving heights of as much as 30 m. Obviously, such waves can have a significant impact on a widespread area once they hit land.

In addition to the impact of waves, currents are a constant and inevitable force working upon the shoreline. They slowly erode coast-lines and pile up sediment and deposits elsewhere, creating sandbars, spits, and other structures. Waves are refracted as they reach the shoreline, often causing them to hit headlands from all three sides, which minimizes the impact in bays. This process tends to straighten out irregular coastlines.

Tides are created by the gravitational pull of the Moon and the Sun, and they are closely related to the rotation of Earth on its axis. Flood tides, or high tides, occur when the sea level is highest, and ebb tides, or low tides, occur when the water recedes as far as possible from the beach.

The Sun's gravitational force also affects the tides, and it can cause very high and alternately very low tides, respectively called spring tides and neap tides. Although tides usually ebb and flow gradually, causing gradual changes to the land–sea interface, tidal currents can be quite swift in areas where there are narrow passages, inlets, or channels. Here, the tide can serve a useful purpose in keeping an inlet clear of sedimentation, or cause more damage by cutting away at land or human-made structures.

Although it can be difficult to perceive the impact of tides, waves, and currents on a daily basis, the force of the sea is constantly changing the land. Tectonic forces at work on land continue undersea as well. The ocean forms a significant portion of our planet, and with all the area where the land and sea interface, the constant action of waves, currents, and tides can mean no small impact on the world as we know it.

PART

3

METEOROLOGY

ATMOSPHERIC COMPOSITION AND LAYERING

THE SKY

Scarcely a day goes by when we don't glance skyward and marvel at the clouds, wonder about the weather, or relish the hues of color cast by the setting Sun. Over the past 400 years, the sky has become the subject of intense scientific study. Without a doubt, we know much more about the clouds and sky now than we did then. We can predict when it will be clear and sunny, when it will snow or rain, or when wind and storms are about to descend upon us. And yet, most humans continue to look at the sky with amazement on a daily basis. Understanding does not imply that we cease to marvel at this part of our world.

In the coming chapters, we'll explore advances in *meteorology* (the science that deals with the phenomena of the atmosphere, especially weather and weather conditions) and discuss the impact of the weather on our planet and in our lives. This chapter will focus specifically on atmospheric composition and layering, the 30 km from Earth's surface to the point where 95 percent of the atmosphere exists, before moving on to the last 5 percent of the atmosphere and beyond that into outer space. Our planet's atmosphere is unique in its composition and structure. It is the product of planetary formation, volcanism, and the work of organisms over great gulfs of geologic time.

In this chapter we'll focus primarily on the origin and layers of our atmosphere. Studying these layers, and how they function, will add to your understanding of meteorological events, like storms, clouds, and rains, that we will discuss in future chapters.

Origin of the Atmosphere

The *atmosphere* is defined as an envelope of gases that surround the surface of a planet. There is really no well-defined limit as to how far the atmosphere extends into space, although approximately 95 percent of Earth's atmosphere resides within about 30 km of the surface of the planet. The remaining 5 percent extends skyward and fades imperceptibly into the vacuum of outer space.

Our atmosphere is the product of changes that occurred over the 4.6 billion-year history of the planet. Asteroid impacts, volcanism, solar heating, and the influence of life have all contributed to the composition and structure of the atmosphere, as we know it today.

Early Earth was a hostile place in which to form an atmosphere. Constant impacts from comets and small asteroids continuously disrupted any atmosphere that tried to form about the planet. Early Earth was nearly molten from core to surface, and internal layering was created as heavier elements sank toward the interior of our embryonic world. With things in such constant flux, it was perhaps over a hundred million years before Earth took shape and the atmosphere was able to stabilize around it.

This process of density sorting, as heavier elements sank towards Earth's interior, is known as *differentiation*. This process ultimately formed the familiar structure of the Earth—the core, mantle, and crust. The atmosphere can be thought of as the outer-most, tenuous part of this layering, based on density. The planet's earliest atmosphere was totally alien compared to what we have today. It was composed chiefly of hydrogen and helium—two very light gases that are the most abundant elements found in the universe. However, because of their very light weight, our planet's gravity could not hold them. Hydrogen and helium "leaked" away into space over time.

Differentiation and the leaking away of hydrogen and helium did not leave us without an atmosphere, however. Intense volcanism spewed voluminous amounts of gases that would contribute to another young atmosphere. We discussed the process of outgassing in Chapter 6—the way gases, including water vapor, are released from the mantle and vented out from beneath Earth's surface through volcanoes. This new atmosphere contained no oxygen, but consisted primarily of carbon dioxide, water vapor, and nitrogen. As primordial Earth cooled, water vapor in the youthful atmosphere cooled, enabling it to exist in a liquid form. Intense rains, over millions of years, flooded the land and

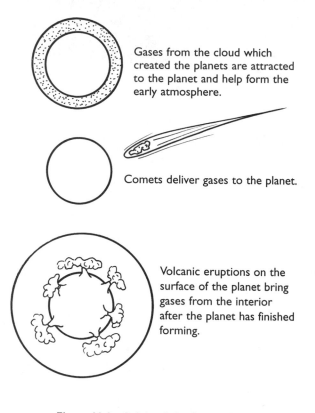

Gases from the cloud which created the planets are attracted to the planet and help form the early atmosphere.

Comets deliver gases to the planet.

Volcanic eruptions on the surface of the planet bring gases from the interior after the planet has finished forming.

Figure 11.1—Origin of the Atmosphere

ultimately filled the lowlands—making seas within the now familiar ocean basins.

There was no free oxygen in this early atmosphere. Free oxygen refers to oxygen in the O_2 state—oxygen that is not bound to rocks (in the form of silicates—quartz) or oxides (rusty iron oxides) on Earth's surface. Although the current atmosphere of our planet contains about 20 percent free oxygen, it took 4 billion years before plants were able to build oxygen up to that level. The other terrestrial planets, Mars and Venus, have no substantial free oxygen present in their atmospheres. The development of our atmosphere, with oxygen suitable for sustaining life, was a complex and time-consuming process. That process required the Sun to break up water molecules to produce a layer of ozone, it required that layer of ozone to allow life to exist, and it required photosynthesis to build up oxygen to the necessary level to support advanced forms of life. Ozone, a molecule of oxygen containing three oxygen atoms (O_3), is the most chemically active form of oxygen. It is found in the stratosphere at about 50 km, because here there is enough ultraviolet radiation from the Sun to cause the necessary collision between atomic and molecular oxygen.

Ultraviolet light from the Sun can photochemically break up water molecules. But, at most, the process can account only for about two percent of the oxygen presently observed in the atmosphere. Over time, this process naturally produced a layer of atmospheric ozone that shields the surface of Earth from harmful ultraviolet rays.

Fortunately, a layer of ozone is required for the healthy development of life; and it is this life on Earth that is the key to the present abundance of oxygen in our atmosphere. The origin and evolution of life on Earth dramatically changed the makeup of the early primitive atmosphere. One of the oldest known fossils belongs to cyanobacteria, an aquatic species of photosynthetic bacteria that contains chlorophyll, which is now one of the largest and most important groups of bacteria on Earth. Later, more sophisticated plant life, along with cyanobacteria, became the prime contributors to oxygen in Earth's atmosphere.

Plants use photosynthesis to make free oxygen and organic compounds from a reaction involving carbon dioxide, water, and sunlight. The present abundance of oxygen in the atmosphere is a by-product of the waste made by photosynthetic organisms.

CREATION OF THE EARLY ATMOSPHERE

Ozone is created when an atom of oxygen (O) and a molecule of oxygen (O_2) collide in the presence of a third, neutral molecule that acts as a catalyst by allowing the reaction to take place without itself being consumed in the process. Ozone is concentrated at about the 50-km height of the stratosphere because this is where the crucial balance exists. The ozone absorbs the ultraviolet radiation from the Sun in sufficient amounts to produce atomic oxygen, and there is enough atmospheric density to bring about the required collisions between atomic and molecular oxygen.

Atmospheric ozone protects life on Earth from the harmful ultraviolet rays of the Sun. Nitrogen is the most abundant gas in the atmosphere, and when it is combined with other elements to form solid nitrate compounds, it becomes important in the metabolism of plants and animals. Certain kinds of bacteria fix free nitrogen as nitrates, making it available for plants and for animals that live on plants. Green plants then give off oxygen as a by-product of their food-making process (photosynthesis). The level of oxygen in the atmosphere then remains at a fairly constant level.

The emission of gaseous wastes by humans (particularly carbon dioxide and fluorocarbons) has shifted this delicate balance in the atmosphere, which can deplete the ozone layer and increase the harmful effects of the Sun's ultraviolet rays. While it took 4 billion years for the atmosphere to reach approximately 20 percent oxygen—optimum for sustaining life—humans have managed to shift this delicate balance in only a few hundred years.

The first free particles of oxygen combined with rocks at the surface of Earth in a process called *oxidation*. Almost all elements react with oxygen to form compounds called oxides.

The corrosion or rusting of iron is a particularly common example. It was only after the surface became highly weathered or rusted by the oxygen that it could start to build up within the atmosphere. It would take almost three billions years before oxygen would represent ten percent of the atmosphere, and it was not until approximately 400 million years ago that the current level was finally considered sustainable.

Composition of the Atmosphere

Nitrogen and oxygen make up virtually all, or about 99 percent, of the atmosphere of our planet. Most of the rest of the remaining one percent of atmospheric gases is composed of *inert argon*, a trace element originally detected by a spectroscope. Argon is a colorless, odorless, tasteless gas, of which very little is found in air. (It's used today in making lightbulbs and fluorescent tubes.) Small amounts of other gases are also included in that one percent.

HOW A SPECTROSCOPE WORKS

Spectroscopy is the scientific study of the wavelength-dependent properties of light. It basically requires a prism to be used in conjunction with a lens. A spectroscope is a device which allows light from a burning substance to enter at one end of a tube, pass through a lens, and then be dispersed into spectral colors by a prism. Each element of a star, for instance, may produce a unique set of spectral lines of different intensities. Spectroscopy allows us to determine the composition of planets and stars too far away, or too hot, to visit.

OUR ATMOSPHERE

In order of decreasing abundance, the average composition of a dry sample of our atmosphere is as follows:

    78.08% nitrogen

    20.95% oxygen

    0.94% argon

    0.04% carbon dioxide

Although carbon dioxide makes up most of the atmospheres of Venus and Mars, it is found in very small quantities (0.04 percent) on Earth. It turns out that most of the carbon dioxide on Earth is locked up in a carbonate rock called limestone. However, even this small amount of carbon dioxide is significant, because it efficiently absorbs heat radiated by the surface of our planet. This has the effect of warming the air and is an important factor in controlling weather.

In addition to the above gases found in our atmosphere, there are other components (such as dust particles and water vapor) that can vary in abundance over time. Like carbon dioxide, these substances are found in minute quantities but can have a significant effect on weather and climate.

The atmosphere can lift small dusty particles from the surface and suspend them in the air. How far and for how long they are carried aloft depends on their size and density. These small particles lifted into the air collectively are called *aerosols*. They can include ash from volcanic eruptions, pollen, fine silt from the soil, soot and smoke from fires, and salts from the sea launched into the air by breaking waves.

Water is almost always present within the atmosphere in the form of a gas known as water vapor. Its abundance can vary from almost nothing up to about 4 percent. Water is an obviously important element of the atmosphere, because it produces clouds and related precipitation that is vital for the existence of life on Earth. It also plays a similar role to carbon dioxide in that it absorbs heat and thus warms the atmosphere.

Structure of the Atmosphere

Just as the ocean exists in layers, so does Earth's atmosphere. This layered structure exists from the planet's surface upward into the sky. The atmospheric pressure is greatest on the surface. Think about a column of air about 100 km tall. At the bottom of this column, the weight of the air exerts 14.7 pounds of pressure per square inch. As the distance above the surface increases, the atmospheric pressure decreases. (See Figure 11.2.)

At 16 km, you would have passed through about 90 percent of the atmosphere. As noted in the first part of this chapter, most of the atmosphere exists between Earth's surface

and 30 km. Scientists consider the altitude of 100 km to be the absolute limit of the atmosphere where only 0.00003 percent of all atmospheric gases remain. The troposphere is where all our weather occurs; airplanes fly in the stratosphere because it's stable. The mesosphere is where rock fragments from outer space burn up, and the thermosphere, where space shuttles orbit, is very thin.

EXPLORATION 11.1
THE STRENGTH OF AIR

Take one raw potato and two plastic drinking straws. Hold one straw about 10 cm above the potato, with the top end open, and jab it into the potato. Take the second straw, hold it at the same height, but put your thumb over the open end. Thrust it into the potato. You will see that the open-ended straw crumples on impact, and very little of it will go into the potato. The other straw stays straight and penetrates deeper.

The reason for this is that the trapped air inside the straw makes the straw strong enough to break through the skin of the potato. The force of the air against the inside of the straw keeps it from bending and the pressure increases as the potato enters the straw and compresses the air even more. Although air is invisible, this exploration helps us understand just how powerful air pressure can be.

In the bottom of our column of air, where the air exerts 14.7 pounds of pressure per square inch, it is also warmer than it is at the top of the column. Temperature, like pressure, also decreases with increasing altitude. This phenomenon is well known to visitors to a city that is situated at a higher elevation where the temperature is always cooler than the surrounding lowlands. Consider, for

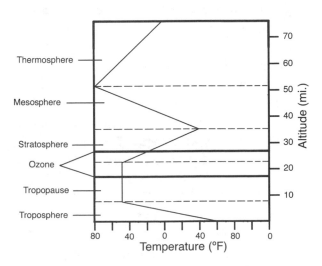

Figure 11.2—Atmospheric Structure

example, playing baseball in Denver as opposed to playing baseball in New York City. Denver, at a higher elevation (and less air pressure), is going to allow more balls over the fence. The athletes, however, are taking in less oxygen with each breath, so the game will probably be just as challenging. At Lake Tahoe, in California and Nevada, ski slopes reach elevations of 3060 meters, and the longest mountain descent is 9 km. Think about how much things could warm up in one slide downhill when you're traveling that far through the atmosphere! It is this temperature change with altitude that has been used to separate the atmosphere into four individual layers.

The Four Layers of Atmosphere

The lowest part of the atmosphere—the part we live in—is called the troposphere, and it has an average thickness of approximately 12 km. Obviously, this layer is important to us, since virtually all significant weather occurs there. This layer is marked by the vertical mixing of air. Within the troposphere, temperatures decrease at a constant rate of 3°C per 300 m of altitude. The upper edge of this lowest part of the atmosphere is called the tropopause; at this altitude the air pressure is only 10 percent that found at sea level (Figure 11.2).

Above the tropopause boundary is the *stratosphere*, the next atmospheric layer. This layer extends upward to 50 km and consists of two parts. The lower section of the stratosphere extends to an altitude of 20 km and is characterized by constant temperatures. The lack of temperature variation is due to relatively stable air that does not mix vertically—it flows horizontally. Above this height, the temperature gradually increases to the upper part of the stratosphere, the boundary called

the *stratopause*, found at an altitude of 50 km. The increase in temperature here is a direct result of the concentration of ozone. Since ozone absorbs ultraviolet light, it warms the atmosphere.

Human-made gases called *fluorocarbons* can deplete the ozone found in this important layer of our atmosphere, allowing harmful ultraviolet radiation to reach the surface. In other ways, human activity is predicted to increase Earth's average air temperature by 2°C over the next century. The atmosphere has always contained carbon dioxide. This gas, along with water vapor, accounts for the natural process known as the greenhouse effect, which warms Earth.

THE GREENHOUSE EFFECT

Certainly, you have heard of the greenhouse effect. But what is it, and how does it work? In a way, Earth's atmosphere acts very much like a blanket that covers the surface. It has the ability to warm the air. Approximately 50 percent of solar energy makes it to the surface of our planet. It warms the ground and is reradiated back into the atmosphere at wavelengths that are longer than the original light. Minor atmospheric gases, such as carbon dioxide, prevent this energy from escaping skyward by absorbing it and producing heat. You can see this at work in your car on a hot day. Shorter wavelength sunlight easily penetrates the windows of your car. The interior absorbs the radiation and emits heat energy at longer wavelengths. This radiation cannot easily escape through the windows and so the interior of the car heats up.

The addition of human-made gases created by aerosol sprays, air conditioning units, refrigerators, vehicle emissions, and energy consumption causes the natural balance of the atmosphere to tip. Humans have intensi-fied the natural greenhouse effect and are now further warming the atmosphere.

Above the stratopause, ozone is depleted in greater abundance, causing the temperature of the atmosphere to once again decrease with altitude. This layer of air is defined as the *mesosphere* and extends from 50 km above the surface to the mesopause, which is approximately 80 km above the surface. At the *mesopause*, the temperature is a frigid -90°C.

A rise in temperature above the mesopause marks the beginning of the last layer of the atmosphere, which is called the *thermosphere*. This layer is sometimes called the *ionosphere*, because it is where atoms experience the loss or gain of electrons and thus have an electrical charge. A bright display of ever-changing light caused by solar radiation interacting with the upper atmosphere in the region of the poles takes place in this thin upper layer. This light show is called the *aurora borealis* in the north, and the *aurora australis* in the south. High-speed electrons and protons from the Sun are channeled toward the polar regions by Earth's magnetic field; they enter the atmosphere and collide with air molecules to create light. These light shows also coincide with periods of sunspot activity and magnetic storms.

FUN FACT: Eskimos, who might often see strange lights in the sky, have an abundance of mythology associated with the aurora borealis. In some stories, the lights are associated with spirits guiding new arrivals to their world. The modern-day explanation is equally magical. Solar winds of tiny charged parti-cles envelope Earth in an ethereal bombardment. A magnetic shield, generated deep within Earth's core, turns the invisible barrage away, and then the solar wind finds gaps in the protective shield over

AURORA BOREALIS AND AURORA AUSTRALIS

The luminous displays of the aurora borealis, in the Northern Hemisphere, and aurora australis, of the Southern Hemisphere, can take many different forms. These light shows follow a solar flare, the explosive event associated with a sunspot. Earth's upper atmosphere, near the magnetic poles, is literally glowing for several nights. The lights can appear as vertical streamers, or expanding arcs, or as a quiet glow with a foglike quality. The auroral lights can appear in shades of red, yellow, green, blue, and violet, and are best seen in the most northern and southern latitudes.

The aurora borealis occurs through northern Norway, across the central Hudson Bay, through Point Barrow, Alaska, and through northern Siberia. It is visible in Canada and the United States, usually at the time of maximum solar activity.

the polar regions and collides with the molecules of the outermost reaches of the atmosphere to set off a series of reactions. Somehow the real explanation of the aurora borealis is as magical as the Eskimo mythology.

The absorption of short wavelength radiation by atoms of nitrogen and oxygen in this extremely high and thin layer of air causes the temperature to increase. Although temperatures can soar to more than 1000°C, the atmosphere is thinned and so this temperature is of a different sort than what we experience near the surface of the planet. The speed of air molecules defines its temperature; however, since the thermosphere is a place sparse in air, it has very little real heat associated with it. Not only did it take 4 billion years for oxygen to develop and create the balance of gases that we now know as our atmosphere, it also took a long time for scientists to distinguish the elements of the atmosphere and understand how nitrogen, oxygen, argon, and carbon dioxide worked together. Only at the end of the nineteenth century was there a clear understanding of what our atmosphere consisted of. More research helped to establish the layers of the atmosphere, and then there was all of outer space to explore. Our understanding of the world—how it was created, the processes through which life was sustained and through which an atmosphere developed that was suitable to support plants, animals, and humans—is no more than a speck in the history of the world. Although we have seen remarkable advances in the study of the atmosphere—and outer space beyond that—in the twentieth and twenty-first centuries, we are not far away from understanding how Earth was first formed and how life came to be.

Climactic Differences and Adaptation

Perhaps even more interesting is the way that plants and animals have adapted to the harsh extremes of our planet's environments. For instance, a human could easily freeze in the Arctic, or die of heatstroke in the Sahara Desert, but certain animals inhabit these areas and thrive. The animals of the North Pole, for instance, a place where no plants can grow, are strictly carnivorous. Some adapt by escaping the worst of the winter by taking shelter in insulated dens made out of snow; polar bears grow thick coats of fur, and seals and whales develop thick layers of fat. Some polar birds will mate and then fly south for warmer weather.

In the desert, snakes can bury themselves rapidly to escape the hot sun, and also to wait for and surprise their prey. The chameleon, another desert animal, can change its color to that of its environment to escape notice. Kangaroo rats, able to live wholly without water, for instance, can defend themselves by kicking sand into a snake's eyes. The Mexican desert of Chihuahua supports antelope jackrabbits, tarantulas, scorpions, and a wide range of lizards—animals you are not likely to find in another, more temperate environment.

In the tropical forests you will find many cold-blooded species of reptiles, amphibians, and fish, which don't need to keep their body temperatures constant. Consider other extreme environments—the swamps of Florida, the northern forests of Canada or Russia, and environments along Earth's seashores—all have animals ideally suited to live in these places. They manage to protect themselves from predators, find food and water sources, create appropriate habitats for their young, and generally prosper.

This is not, of course, by complete chance, but is a result of somewhat predictable environments and the ability of animals to adapt to these environments. You may have learned about Charles Darwin's study of finches on the Galapagos Islands. The birds that prospered on each island were slightly different from those of other islands, and different from those on the South American continent. Over time, through the process of natural selection, animals either adapt to survive, or slowly die off. The same process occurs with plants. Interference from humans has hurried the process of extinction along in many, many places. But given predictable seasons or ranges of temperatures and rainfall, wildlife (better than humans) seems to cope quite nicely with the polar regions, the deserts, the tropical rain forests, and the whole range of environments in between.

We explain the lack of kangaroos elsewhere besides Australia, the presence of tapirs in both Asia and South America, and other curious distributions of animals to the early shifting and breaking apart of landmasses, before the continents were fully formed in their current configurations.

SUMMARY

The Earth's atmosphere began with the process of differentiation and the leaking away of hydrogen and helium. Intense volcanism followed, spewing voluminous amounts of gases into the environment. As the Earth cooled, and heavy rains fell, the stage was set for the development of an atmosphere that would sustain life.

Over a period of 4 billion years, plants, first cyanobacteria, then other life forms, began the process of photosynthesis and made free oxygen and organic compounds from a reaction involving carbon dioxide, water, and sunlight. Over time, the oxygen level increased from about 2 percent to 20 percent, capable of sustaining life as we know it.

Nitrogen and oxygen make up virtually the entire atmosphere, but its other components can vary with time. They may be present in minute quantities, but they can be significant in terms of weather. Water is also almost always present in the atmosphere in the form of water vapor.

Just as the ocean exists in layers, so does Earth's atmosphere. The layered structure extends from the Earth's surface up about 100 km. Temperature and pressure vary in the different layers.

The part of the atmosphere closest to Earth's surface is called the troposphere and it extends for about 12 km. At the highest level of the troposphere is the tropopause. Above that boundary is the stratosphere, which ends in the stratopause at about 50 km. Above the stratopause, ozone becomes depleted and the mesosphere extends from there to a height of 80 km at the mesopause. The last layer of the atmosphere, the thermosphere, or ionosphere, extends to about 100 km, where only 0.00003 percent of all atmospheric gases remain.

Earth's atmosphere is about 20 percent oxygen. However, the introduction of other gases into the atmosphere, by humans, has tipped the balance slightly, damaging the protective ozone layer and increasing the natural effects of the greenhouse effect.

The atmosphere took 4 billion years to develop, although it wasn't until the nineteenth century that humans understood the basic elements of the atmosphere and how they work. Today scientific studies include ways to stop the deleterious effects of human-made gases as well as investigation of outer space, beyond Earth's atmosphere.

CLOUDS

KEY TERMS

meteorologists, clouds, evaporation, condensation, sublimation, deposition, humidity, dew point, specific humidity, relative humidity, psychrometer, hair hygrometer, adiabatic, condensation nuclei, stratus, cirrus, cumulus, graupel, rime

CLOUDS AND WEATHER

The last chapter explored the layers of the atmosphere—something we don't actually see but that impacts our daily lives. It's more likely that people pay attention to what is visible—the fluffy white clouds on a blue summer's day or the dark storm clouds signaling bad weather. We've been conditioned, since early childhood, to anticipate certain kinds of weather as a result of certain clouds. There is a real science to this, however, and this chapter will discuss the different types of clouds, what they mean and how *meteorologists*, scientists who study weather phenomena, can actually predict weather patterns.

Water Vapor and Humidity

Clouds are actually small droplets of water and ice crystals that aggregate, or clump together, within the atmosphere. They can then produce precipitation in the form of liquid water and/or ice crystals.

Atmospheric behavior within the lowest portion of Earth's atmosphere, the troposphere, is critically dependent on the amount of moisture or water vapor in the air. This gaseous water can vary, typically between zero and 4 percent of the air by volume, but that is all it takes to create precipitation.

Water vapor easily mixes with the nitrogen and oxygen that make up most of our atmosphere. As gases, nitrogen and oxygen are very stable—it takes a temperature below -200°C for them to condense out of the air. The same is not true of water vapor, however. The temperatures near the surface of the planet are suitable for water to exist as a solid, liquid, or a vapor. Water freezes to ice in the polar regions. It is found as a liquid in rivers and oceans. And water evaporates as a gas to form clouds, which will ultimately condense, changing from a gas to a liquid, which then falls back to Earth as rain or snow.

Evaporation is the process through which water converts from a liquid to a gas, or water vapor. When it returns to a liquid, such as when it rains, the change is called *condensation*. If the water freezes, it forms solid ice; and when the ice melts, it converts back to liquid water. Ice can also skip the water phase and change from a solid to a vapor in a process known as *sublimation*. You might have seen this happen in the sublimation of dry ice (solid carbon dioxide), which turns into a vapor instead of a liquid. *Deposition* is the reverse of sublimation, when a vapor is changed to a solid. A good example of this is the formation of frost.

We're all familiar with hot, summer days when it feels like there's more water vapor in the air than actual air. The amount of water vapor present within the atmosphere is a measure of its *humidity*. Humidity is a function of air temperature, because warmer air can hold more water vapor than cooler air can. When the atmosphere cools, it reaches a point where the air is saturated with water vapor, and this causes it to condense into a liquid. That's why we experience a cooling effect right before a sudden rain on a sticky summer day.

You've probably observed how a cold drink left in a warm room forms water droplets on the outside of the glass. The interface of the cold container with the humid air causes water vapor to condense. The *dew point* is defined as the temperature to which a particle of air would have to be cooled in order to reach saturation. When the air's capacity, which is temperature dependent, is exceeded, excess vapor is forced to condense. Dew, fog, and clouds also result once the atmosphere reaches the dew point.

SPECIFIC AND RELATIVE HUMIDITY

Specific humidity is the ratio of the mass of water vapor to the mass of dry air in a chosen volume of moist air. This measure of the moisture content of air is not affected by changes in pressure or temperature.

Relative humidity, the measure with which we are most familiar, also describes the moisture content of air. It is the ratio of the amount of water vapor in the air at a specific temperature to the maximum amount that the air could hold at that temperature, expressed as a percentage.

Measuring Humidity

Relative humidity is most commonly measured using a *psychrometer*, a tool consisting of two identical thermometers mounted side by side, which can measure both dew point and relative humidity. One of the thermometers, called the dry-bulb, measures the air temperature while the other, a wet-bulb, has a damp wick wrapped around it that allows the thermometer to measure any decrease in temperature. This indicates the maximum amount of cooling that can result from evaporation.

The psychrometer is exposed to a flow of air by slinging it around on a handle or blowing a fan across it. Humidity is directly proportional to the amount of moisture that evaporates off the wet-bulb. If the two thermometers have identical readings, no evaporation has taken place and the air is saturated with water vapor. Therefore, the more significant the measured difference between the two thermometers, the drier the air is and the lower the humidity level is. Meteorologists can use this data to acquire the exact humidity level and dew point by consulting a table.

A more common but less accurate instrument used to measure humidity is called a *hair hygrometer*, an instrument that can be read without the use of tables. Hair has a tendency to react to changes in humidity. It lengthens when there is lots of water vapor in the air and contracts when the air is dry. The ability of hair to flex with humidity has been incorporated into a simple device that allows humidity to be determined directly. A change in the tension on the hair is measured on a calibrated dial indicator that reads between 0 percent and 100 percent. However, not only is the hair hygrometer less accurate than the

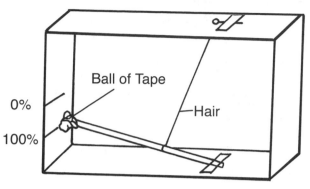

Figure 12.1—Hair Hygrometer

psychrometer, but it also responds very slowly to changes in humidity and often needs calibration.

Condensation and Cloud Formation

Cloud formation is closely related to the cooling of humid air masses. As a gas expands—such as the air found within the atmosphere—it cools in temperature. The opposite is also true; when air is compressed, it heats up. This change in temperature with expansion or contraction of gases is known as an *adiabatic* temperature change—a cooling or warming of air that is caused when air is allowed to expand or is compressed, not because heat is added or subtracted.

In Earth's atmosphere, this effect can be dramatic. Air that sinks down from high altitudes is warmed by an increase in atmospheric pressure. Inversely, air that climbs in altitude is under less pressure and begins to expand and then cool in temperature. The rate of adiabatic cooling has been measured at 10°C per kilometer of elevation above the surface. When the air is enriched in water vapor and cooled down to the dew point, condensation and cloud formation take place.

If the humidity is not in excess of 100 percent, cloud formation will not occur unless there are small particles of matter onto which the water vapor can condense. These *condensation nuclei*, bits of particular matter that serve as surfaces on which water vapor condenses, can include salt particles from the oceans, dust, and smoke. At ground level, such particles are not necessary—other objects like windows and blades of grass make good condensation surfaces.

Salt is perhaps the best of all condensation nuclei, because it has the ability to absorb and thus hold more water. Atmospheric salt particles are derived from the air–sea interface, where waves splash the salt into the sky. There are so many of these particles in the air that the humidity scarcely ever needs to reach 100 percent in order for clouds to form. Clouds can be thought of as a multitude of tiny water droplets suspended in the air. If the temperature is below freezing at the time of cloud formation, ice crystals will form instead. Typically, a cloud consists of some combination of water and ice droplets.

Types of Clouds

Clouds may appear to be chaotic masses moving randomly through the sky. A closer look, however, reveals that there is a high order of organization, making it possible to group cloud types based on their morphology (distinctive characteristics) and the altitude at which they are found. Meteorologists are particularly interested in clouds, because they are visible clues of what is happening in the atmosphere, and they can serve as reliable indicators of weather patterns.

Clouds have been classified into three major types (Figure 12.2). *Stratus* clouds, those found at the lowest elevation, completely cover the sky in layers or sheets. This blanketing of the sky makes it difficult to differentiate the individual clouds and it appears to be a mass of cloud cover. *Cirrus* clouds are the white patches of thin sheets at high altitude. They have a feathery look and can appear as wispy, strings of clouds. Finally, *cumulus* clouds are often puffy, white, and usually occur as individual or isolated groups of clouds. They look like a flat-bottomed cauliflower that reaches vertically into the sky.

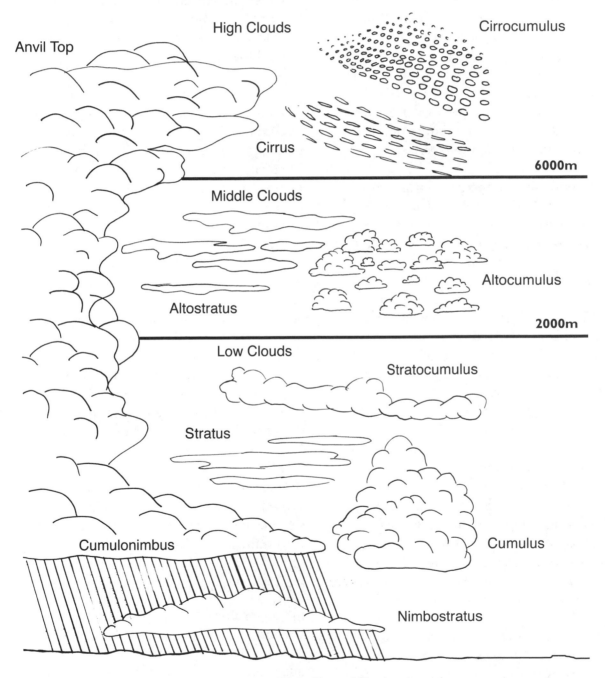

Figure 12.2—Types of Clouds

The classification of clouds can be even more finely tuned, depending on the altitude. Stratus clouds are found at lower altitudes than others and they are often associated with precipitation. A variation of this cloud type is the *nimbostratus*, which is Latin for "rainy cloud cover." The nimbostratus is thick enough to block the Sun entirely, and it is usually tied to continuously falling rain or snow that reaches the ground. Another variation is the stratocumulus cloud, which indicates fair weather and is characterized by long rolling chains or patches of clouds. These low clouds form at altitudes of less than approximately 2000 meters.

Clouds found at intermediate altitudes, or between 2000 and 6000 meters, are prefixed with the word "alto." *Altostratus* clouds are layers of stratified gray to white clouds that cover most of the sky, and often indicate drizzle or light snow. However, they are still thin enough so that a hazy disk of the Sun can shine through them. Clumps of fluffy white clouds at this medium altitude are called *altocumulus* clouds. Because of their appearance, they are sometimes referred to as "sheep-back clouds."

Another cloud type, the *cumulonimbus*, transcends all levels of altitude. These clouds move in a vertical fashion and are found anywhere from 500 to 18,000 meters off the ground. They are associated with bad weather—including storms, heavy rains, and tornadoes. As an impending storm takes shape, this cloud type towers far into the heavens like a mountain, even developing a hooked-over top that looks like an anvil head.

At the other extreme in elevation, above 6000 meters, are high clouds that are variants of the cirrus cloud. These clouds consist of only ice crystals because of the cold temperatures and low humidity found high in the atmosphere. They are not rainmakers, either. The relatively uncommon puffy white masses are called *cirrocumulus* clouds, while those that are more common are formed in sheets or layers and are called *cirrostratus* clouds. It is the cirrostratus clouds that give the sky a milky glow and produce halos or rings around the Sun and Moon.

The final cloud type is one with a base that extends virtually all the way to the ground. In common language, a cloud that extends to the ground is called *fog*. It differs from its cousins at higher altitude only in the manner in which it forms. As we learned earlier, clouds are produced as a consequence of humid air rising and then cooling with altitude. Fog also forms by the cooling of warm, humid air, but without the need for high elevations in the atmosphere.

Some fogs form when air, laden with water vapor, travels across a cool surface—such as snow-covered ground or even a cold oceanic current. Other fogs form on clear and cool nights when the surface cools quickly by radiation, causing the envelope of air near the surface to drop below the dew point. Fogs can also form when humid air sweeps up a mountaintop resulting in cooling and condensation. Finally some fogs occur as a consequence of evaporation, which has the effect of increasing the amount of water vapor within the atmosphere near the surface.

Precipitation

In meteorology, *precipitation* is defined as any form of water—such as rain, snow, sleet, or hail—that falls to Earth's surface, or the quantity of such water falling in a specific area

CLASSIFICATION OF CLOUDS

Cloud Family and Height	Cloud Types	Characteristics
High Clouds		
Above 6000 meters	Cirrus	Delicate white patches or thin sheets
	Cirrocumulus	Puffy white masses
	Cirrostratus	Formed in sheets or layers and giving the sky a milky glow, forming a ring around the Sun or Moon
Middle Clouds		
2000–6000 meters	Altocumulus	Fluffy white clouds, known as "sheep-back clouds"
	Altostratus	Gray to white clouds, covering the sky
Low Clouds		
Below 2000 meters	Stratocumulus	Low, rolling chains or patches
	Stratus	Clouds completely covering the sky
	Nimbostratus	Rainy cloud cover
Clouds of Vertical Development		
500 meters and above	Cumulus	Puffy white clouds, either isolated or in a group
	Cumulonimbus	Vertical cloud formations associated with bad weather

within a specific period. In order for droplets of water to fall from the clouds and reach the ground, they must first become large enough to make it to the ground without totally evaporating. The average size of a cloud's water droplets is about seven times smaller than the width of a single human hair, so the chances of reaching Earth at that size are minimal. A droplet of this size would take about two days to fall through 1 km of air.

Fortunately, there are ways for water droplets to join together, or coalesce, in a way that makes this trip to Earth possible. At high altitudes, water droplets can freeze into small ice crystals. These crystals will grow or coalesce into larger snowflakes. As they fall to lower elevations, the snowflakes warm and begin to melt. The resulting water droplets, which began their journey as ice crystals, are then large enough to make it to the ground.

Clouds at lower altitude, where the temperatures are too warm for ice crystals to form, have another way of forming precipitation. One theory is that as water droplets begin to fall from the clouds, they sweep up other, smaller droplets, in a process involving countless collisions until they are big enough to survive evaporation en route to the Earth's surface.

EXPLORATION 12.1
HOW WATER DROPLETS COALESCE

Take a plastic see-through lid, like a deli container or coffee can lid. Fill an eyedropper with water. Hold the plastic lid in your hand, bottom side up. Squeeze as many separate drops of water as you can onto the lid. Quickly turn it over and use the point of a pencil to move the tiny drops of water together.

This illustrates the attraction that water droplets have for each other. Water droplets, on the plastic lid or in the clouds, will join together to form heavier, larger drops.

SURFACE TENSION OF WATER

Surface tension is a filmlike behavior at the surface of a fluid, such as water. This behavior makes it easier for an object to move when it's beneath the surface than when on top. It's the same process that allows little bugs to walk across the surface of water. The cohesive forces between water molecules produce surface tension, which is the result of the water's tendency to be attracted to similar molecules (i.e., they cohere more to themselves and not so much to the air above or below).

Liquid precipitation reaches the planet's surface as mist, drizzle, or rain. The difference between the three is based on the size of the water droplets. Mist consists of droplets less than 0.05 mm in diameter. Droplets that are larger than this but less than 0.5 mm across fall as drizzle. Anything larger, up to about 5 mm across, is called rain. The upper size limit is controlled by the surface tension holding the drop together. Bigger drops cannot survive flight through the atmosphere. Because of air drag effects, big drops will tear apart into smaller ones.

Snowflakes are another type of precipitation in the form of ice (Figure 12.3). There are several types of ice precipitation: snow, graupel, and hail. Snow falls as ice crystals with diameters between 1.0 mm and 2.0 cm. Larger frozen precipitation, with diameters up to 5.0 mm, fall as a soft and mushy ice called *graupel*. Anything larger makes it to the surface as irregular to rounded clumps of hard ice called *hail*. Another variation of icy precipitation is *rime*, a deposit of ice that freezes out of the air onto a surface that has a temperature below the freezing point of water. Sleet differs from graupel in that sleet is smaller. Basically, sleet is nothing more than frozen raindrops. Graupel, with a size between 2.0 and 5.0 mm, is larger. It's sort of a soft hail, made when rime forms on snowflakes. Rime is formed when water vapor (not rain), in the form of clouds of fog, freezes on contact with the ground or a surface object. Glaze is different from rime, in that it forms when rain freezes on contact with the ground or with other objects.

FUN FACT: The largest hailstone on record fell in Kansas in 1970. It weighed more than 700 grams and was almost 15 cm in diameter!

A meteorologist can accurately measure precipitation. A *rain gauge* is used to measure the amount of rainfall. A simple gauge can be constructed to measure the amount of rainfall to within 0.025 cm. Any accumulation less than this would be considered *trace precipitation*. The standard gauge consists of a small cylinder with a diameter of 2.0 cm, with a 20-cm funnel on top of it. This instrument design reduces evaporation and also allows rain depth to be magnified by 10; thus, high

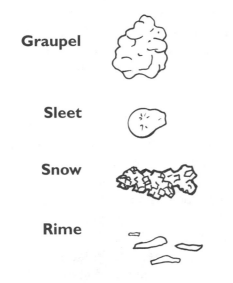

Graupel

Sleet

Snow

Rime

Figure 12.3—Frozen Precipitation Types

precision measurements can be achieved. Precipitation in the form of snow is measured in two different ways. Its depth is recorded using a meter stick, and its water quantity is measured from a given volume of snow.

You may wonder why it matters how much snow one place gets compared to another, or why someone would measure sizes of hailstones or amounts of precipitation, or why they would worry about the type of clouds overhead. As we said earlier in the chapter, the clouds provide clues as to what kind of weather is headed our way, and precipitation is essential to the continued health of our planet.

Water plays an integral role in all this, because in addition to absorbing or releasing heat energy, water vapor is the source of all clouds and precipitation. Some desert environments may go years without a drop of rain, while others, like Cherrapunji, India, may get 2644 cm of rainfall in a single year. Variations in weather and differing climates, temperatures, and environments help to

support a wide variety of plant and animal life. These significant differences promote diversity of life and impact the lives of humans in important ways.

SUMMARY

Clouds are actually small droplets of water and ice crystals that clump together within the atmosphere. The formation of clouds is critically dependent on the amount of water vapor found within the air.

Water can exist as a solid, liquid, or vapor on Earth's surface. Evaporation is the process of converting liquid to a gas. Condensation occurs when it returns to a liquid. Ice can also skip the water phase and go straight from solid to vapor in a process known as sublimation. Deposition, the reverse of sublimation; occurs when a vapor is changed to a solid, such as when frost forms on grass or windshields on cold, winter mornings.

Humidity is the amount of water vapor present in the environment and the dew point is the temperature to which a particle of air would have to be cooled in order to reach saturation.

Specific humidity is the weight of water vapor per weight of a chosen mass of air, including the water vapor. Relative humidity, the type we are most familiar with, describes the moisture content of air. We have two specific tools that can be used to measure relative humidity: the psychrometer and the hair hygrometer.

The formation of clouds is closely related to the cooling of humid air masses. As a gas expands, it cools in temperature. The opposite is true as well. When air is compressed, it heats up. This is known as adiabatic temperature change.

Humidity must be in excess of 100 percent before clouds form, unless there are small particles of matter onto which the water vapor can condense. The condensation nuclei, bits of particulate matter, can include salt particles from the oceans, dust, and smoke. At ground level there are lots of things that make good condensation surfaces. Because there is so much salt in the air from the oceans, the humidity hardly ever has to reach 100 percent to form clouds.

There are three main types of clouds: stratus, which are found at the lowest elevation; cirrus, which are found at high elevations; and cumulus, which may form in a vertical fashion. Within these three types of clouds are many specific formations that can be used by meteorologists to predict the weather. Fog also forms by the cooling of warm, humid air, but without the need for high elevations in the atmosphere.

Rain forms when water droplets, tiny specks of water, find a way to coalesce on their downward path. They might freeze and form into small ice crystals, or they might group together at lower altitudes as the result of countless collisions.

Liquid precipitation reaches the planet's surface as mist, drizzle, or rain, depending on the size of the water droplets. Snowflakes are another type of precipitation, and they fall to Earth in the form of snow, graupel, or hail. Snow is between 1.0 mm and 2.0 cm in size, while larger frozen precipitation falls as a soft and mushy ice called graupel. Rime is a deposit of ice that freezes out of the air onto a surface that has a temperature below the freezing point of water. Sleet is basically frozen raindrops, and glaze is different from rime in that it freezes on contact with the surface or other objects.

Precipitation can be carefully measured and supplements the knowledge meteorologists have about weather patterns. While levels of precipitation vary across the globe, these variations help to create different climates and a rich variety of plant and animal life, and they impact the way that humans exist on this planet.

WINDS

CIRCULATION OF AIR

Since the first ships sailed the seas, we have known that there were worldwide systems of Earth's air and circulation. Documentation existed in sailors' logs, and people spread the information informally. Today satellites and computers reinforce our understanding of air patterns, or circulation in the atmosphere.

Winds operate on both global and local levels, and the planetary circulation includes airflow close to the surface and in the upper air.

The unequal heating of the surface of our planet generates the winds that move clouds and storms across the sky. They are further controlled by the Coriolis effect, the deflective force of Earth's rotation, and lateral atmospheric pressure differences. Winds always blow from an area of high pressure to an area of low pressure. In this chapter, we'll explore how low-pressure zones draw in winds and spin them into storms. Winds associated with high-pressure areas flow outward and are typically accompanied by fair weather.

The winds of the Earth are somewhat predictable when considered on a global scale. Scientists have also designed instruments that accurately measure wind speed and direction, and they have studied patterns of pressure zones and wind systems around the globe. This knowledge is an invaluable key in predicting weather.

Air Pressure

The relative air pressure variations across the globe are responsible for the generation of winds. These winds that flow in a horizontal manner are an important factor that drives weather patterns. Air always flows from areas of high pressure to areas of low pressure. Pressure differences are a result of the unequal heating of the atmosphere by the Sun.

When weather forecasters talk about the *barometric pressure*, they are referring to the pressure of the air at ground level. This is caused by the weight of the air above pressing down, because gravity pulls the air toward Earth just like everything else. A *barometer* is an instrument used to measure air pressure. Barometers in the United States measure the pressure in inches of mercury, or rather how high the pressure would push mercury into a tube that has the top sealed off from air. Our usual pressure is 29.92 inches of mercury.

We already learned, in Chapter 10, that the pressure exerted by the air at sea level is 14.7 pounds per square inch. Meteorologists also use *millibars* (mb), the metric measure for pressure. At sea level, the standard air pressure is 1013.2 mb. Atmospheric pressure decreases steadily at first, as we move higher in altitude and then more rapidly with increasing altitude. At about 5 km of elevation, the pressure drops to 430 mb; at 10 km, pressure is 265 mb; at 20 km, the pressure is 55 mb; and at an altitude of 30 km, the air pressure registers at only 12 mb.

Commercial airlines cruise at about 10 km above the surface of Earth where air density is only about one-fourth as great as it is at sea level. The jet, therefore, has less force to push against.

Changes in atmospheric pressure are important in the prediction of weather. Falling air pressure means that clouds and precipitation are likely. Rising air pressure is an indication that clear weather is likely. Weather forecasters sometimes use a *mercury barometer* to measure atmospheric pressure in units called inches of mercury rather than millibars (Figure 13.1). It is a simple instrument consisting of a column of mercury within a pan. The height of the mercury in the column is a function of the pressure of the air pushing down on the open pan of mercury. What this means is that the height of the mercury in the column is equal to the weight of a column of air of the same diameter, extending from the surface all the way to the top of the atmosphere. At sea level, the standard atmospheric pressure is 29.9 inches of mercury—a value that is equivalent to 14.7 pounds per square inch, or 1013.2 mb. Changes in atmospheric pressure result in a shift in the column of mercury; that is, the level of mercury drops if the local air pressure should decrease, and it rises with an increase in local air pressure. The reading of 1013.2 mb is called one *atmosphere* of pressure,

EXPLORATION 13.1
MEASURING AIR PRESSURE

Cut the top inch or so off of a balloon, and stretch the bottom section of it over a small jar. Secure the balloon with a rubber band, and then glue the large end of a toothpick to the rubber lid and allow it to dry. Place this jar, with the balloon and toothpick, inside a larger jar. Cut the bottom off of a second balloon and stretch it over the mouth of a large jar (cut just enough to create an opening that will fit over the big jar). Secure it with a rubber band and then tie off the neck of the balloon. Watch the toothpick on the small jar as you pull up and push down on the balloon across the large jar.

Pressing on the balloon causes the air pressure inside the larger jar to increase. The compressed air pushes against the balloon stretched across the small jar. When this rubber lid is pushed down, the toothpick points upward. Pulling up on the balloon stem allows the air in the jar to spread out, which decreases the pressure. With less pressure on the small jar's lid, the air in the small jar expands, causing the lid to rise and the toothpick to point down.

a term used by physicists that is abbreviated atm.

This mercury barometer, however, is cumbersome to use, is easily broken, and must be compared to an aneroid barometer. While mercury barometers can give accurate readings, *aneroid barometers* or *barographs*, based on the idea of a vacuum, are more portable and easier to use. Barometers became popular pieces of furniture and have been designed in quite elegant ways as decorator pieces. If you want to use it to predict the weather, however, you need to get into the habit of looking at it every day and noting which way the pressure is going—up or down. It is not the same as looking at a thermometer and immediately knowing the temperature. Rising or falling atmospheric pressure only gives an indication of the weather to come, not necessarily what is happening at the moment.

The *barograph* is really the device of choice to measure air pressure. It consists of a metal chamber holding a vacuum that is sensitive to air pressure changes. The chamber is compressed with an increase in air pressure, while it expands with a decrease in pressure. The barograph works without a liquid and can be linked to a computer or a chart-recording device.

Again, the pressure differences across a horizontal distance cause winds. The greater the differences in pressure, the stronger the winds will be. Barometric pressure readings at weather stations across a region are used to design a map that has connecting lines of equal pressure called *isobars*. The weather map using isobars shows them as lines connecting places of equal air pressure.

A *pressure gradient* is a change in pressure over a given distance that can be inferred by the spacing of isobars. The closer the isobars, the greater the gradient and the higher the wind speeds will be. Widely spaced isobars suggest low wind speeds and pressure gradients.

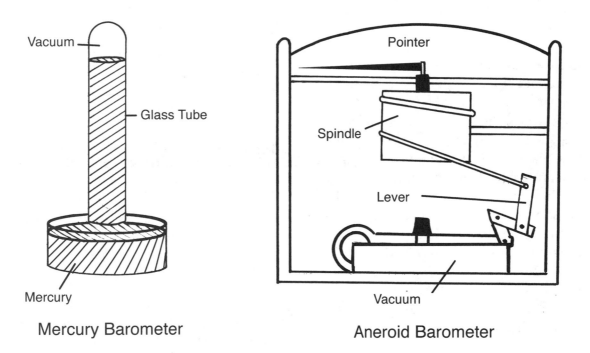

Figure 13.1—Types of Barometers

Cyclones and Anticyclones

Air masses never remain in one place. As soon as one forms, it begins to move from the area over which it gained properties of moisture and temperature, toward another part of Earth. As it moves, it intermingles with—and affects the stability of—air on Earth's surface. As air masses move and encounter other air masses, especially with different temperature and humidity, changes occur in Earth's weather.

Wind does not exactly flow in a straight direction from a high- to a low-pressure area. The Coriolis effect, once again, comes into play. It deflects winds in a direction perpendicular to the isobars or the direction of airflow. You'll recall from Chapter 9 that winds in the Northern Hemisphere are deflected to the right, while winds in the Southern Hemisphere are deflected to the left of their original course.

Wind speeds are also modified or slowed by frictional contact with the surface of the planet. This will weaken the Coriolis effect. In other words, the surface winds will flow at an angle of nearly 45°—not 90°—to the isobars. The lack of frictional surface drag, or resistance, on upper atmosphere winds allows them to flow in a direction parallel to the isobars, however. These are known as *geostrophic winds*—winds that move parallel to straight isobars, which result when the Coriolis effect and horizontal pressure forces are in balance. Because of the lack of friction, they are able to travel at speeds higher than those of surface winds.

Areas of high pressure within the atmosphere are commonly called *anticyclones*. In these high-pressure systems in the Northern Hemisphere, the surface wind spirals outward, away from the center in a clockwise motion; in the Southern Hemisphere, it spirals outward in a counterclockwise direction, due to the Coriolis effect. There is a decrease in pressure away from the center and toward the outer part of anticyclones. Isobars are circular with a high-pressure ridge at the center. Winds flowing from high- to low-pressure pockets typically move across the globe from higher to lower latitudes. Also, the air in these systems moves over the globe from higher to lower latitudes. In addition, the air in these systems descends from higher altitudes causing pressure increases that contribute to fair weather and clear skies.

In a low-pressure zone, or a *cyclone*, pressure increases from the central isobars toward the outer isobars. Cyclones, which we'll discuss in more detail in Chapter 14, are atmospheric systems characterized by the rapid inward circulation of air masses about a low-pressure center. The isobars are nearly circular with a low-pressure pocket at the center that is often referred to as a *trough*. In both hemispheres, the airflow converges inward as air rushes in from a high- to a low-pressure area.

CYCLONES

A cyclone can be anything from a tiny squall in a small area, or a major storm that blasts away at an area hundreds of kilometers in size. A cyclone can also start small, grow into a huge storm, or just plain fizzle out before it does much.

Cyclones are created when two different air masses meet—one warmer and moister than the other. The *front*, or atmospheric phenomenon created at the boundary between two different air masses, is marked by:
• Sudden shifts in the direction of the winds
• A rapid change in the weather
• Cloud cover and precipitation

THE FOUR SEASONS

The seasons occur due to the 23.5° axial tilt of Earth on its axis—in combination with its revolution around the Sun. The seasons are clearly evident in most places, except perhaps at the extreme of the equator or the polar regions. As the Earth revolves over the course of a year, there are variations in the relative lengths of days and nights and in the intensity of the Sun's heat. When the Sun's rays must traverse more of Earth's atmosphere before striking the planet's surface, then the heat is diminished. If the Sun's rays strike directly, and the day is long, then clearly the combination of the heat and hours of sunlight means conditions similar to what we call summer.

In Florida, for instance, the winter is scarcely noticeable, and people from the northern temperate zones tend to escape there during their regular season of ice and snow to enjoy the warm weather. If you go to the other extreme of the United States—say North Dakota or Maine—there is a more significant difference between summer and winter.

In those areas, it may be 35°C during the summer months and -15°C during the winter months. In these northern regions, summer may also appear to be shorter and winter may appear to be longer than in states at lower latitudes.

In the northern temperate zone, we consider spring to begin about March 21, summer on June 22 (the summer solstice, or the longest day of the year), fall on September 23, and winter on December 21 (the winter solstice, or the shortest day of the year). For anyone who has ever lived through the four seasons in the northern temperate zone, it's obvious that the weather doesn't always follow this predictable plan!

In low latitudes, or areas like India where wind and oceans determine much of the weather, we may dismiss the four season designations and talk about the "wet" season or the "dry" season.

Global Circulation

Let's now take a look at the motion of the atmosphere on a global scale. (See Figure 13.2). The same factors affecting airflow on a regional scale are at work, namely unequal heating by solar radiation and the Coriolis effect. In order to separate the impact of these two factors, it is probably easiest to try to imagine an Earth that does not rotate.

A nonspinning planet experiences only the influence of unequal heating by the Sun. Under these circumstances a simple convection system (the transfer of heat by a fluid system) is established. Extreme heating in the equatorial regions causes warm air to rise. When this rising air mass meets the tropopause (the top of the lowest layer of Earth's atmosphere), which acts to confine it, it begins to move toward the poles as an upper-level wind.

Cooling at the polar regions encourages the air to sink down and fall to the surface. At the surface, the air then flows toward the equator. The process begins all over again when the air is heated and rises skyward in the equatorial regions. From afar, an observer in space would see two mirror image *convection cells*, the transfer of heat by the movement of a mass or substance—one each in the Northern and Southern hemispheres, both transporting air from the equator toward the poles in an upper atmosphere low, and then cycling air near the surface from the poles to the equator.

These cells establish four pressure zones in each hemisphere. Two low-pressure areas are set up in each hemisphere, one in the equatorial part of the globe and another in the subpolar regions. Here, clouds and precipitation dominate since the air flows inward and then upward to higher altitudes. Two high-pressure centers are established in the subtropical and polar regions of both hemispheres where the air flows down and then outward onto the surface.

As an air mass forms, it takes on specific characteristics that vary with the region in which it originates. The air mass is named for the area in which it originates, usually because of certain temperatures and moisture content, but as it moves into other areas on the globe it often changes.

The rising air near the equator defines a pressure zone associated with ubiquitous precipitation known as the *equatorial low*. On the surface, tropical rainforests are found in the equatorial regions. At about 20° to 30° latitude in both hemispheres, the upper-level airflow begins to cool and fall toward the surface. A subtropical high-pressure center is formed here where the air is very dry, making surface conditions hot and arid. This is why most deserts distributed across the globe are found at this latitude.

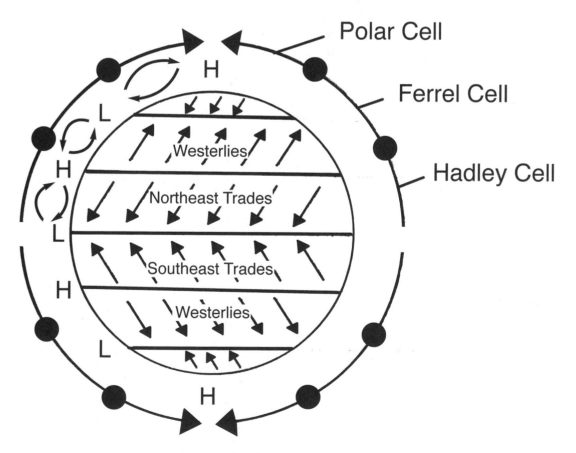

Figure 13.2—Atmospheric Circulation

The rise and fall of air masses around the globe, combined with the Coriolis effect, produces consistent wind patterns. Air that moves away from the subtropical highs is deflected in such a way that an easterly flow (the trade winds) dominates. Winds that move poleward from the subtropical highs are deflected in a manner that sets up the *prevailing westerlies*, a steady set of winds that flow from the west.

Situated at about 50° to 60° north and south of the equator are the subpolar lows—regions where the air rises, inducing a zone known for its abundant precipitation. Airflow is from the east here and establishes the reliable *polar easterlies*. These winds are produced at higher latitudes in the *polar high* regions where dry cold air sinks toward the surface.

MEASURING WIND SPEED AND DIRECTION

Two instruments, the cup anemometer and the weather vane, are used to measure wind speed and direction. A *cup anemometer* is a device with three cups on an axle that spins at a rate proportional to wind speed. Data from the instrument is sent to a dial indicator or fed to a computer. A weather vane consists of a needle with a fin that always points into the direction from which wind blows (Figure 13.3). For instance, an easterly wind blows from the east to the west. An exact direction is given in terms of degrees on a compass—with zero being equivalent to north, 90° equal to east, 180° equal to south, and 270° equal to west.

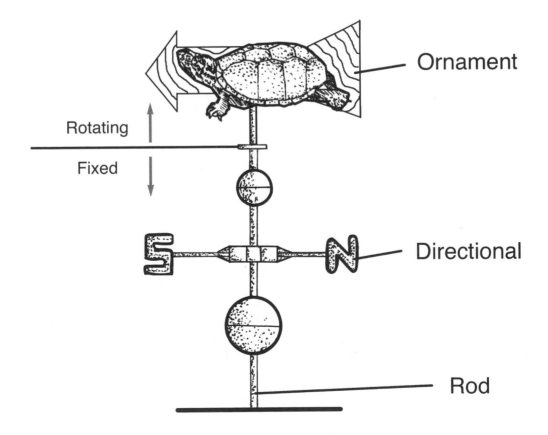

Figure 13.3—Weather Vane

Unfortunately, the flow of winds across the globe is more complicated in real life than it is on our model of a stationary globe. Rotation of Earth induces the Coriolis effect that makes the larger convection cells tear apart into a complex array of smaller cells of air flow. Three cells occur in each hemisphere. A *Hadley cell* consists of rising air at the equator that moves north and south until it begins to sink at about 30° latitude. This air then flows back toward the equator. Each *Ferrell cell* is made up of high-pressure zones at 30° latitude that circulate air poleward until a low-pressure zone lifts the air at about 60° latitude in both hemispheres. *Polar cells* occur between latitudes of 60° to 90°. They are characterized by a high-pressure down flow of air at the poles and a low-pressure up flow of air at 60° latitude.

Winds move the air masses into contact with other masses that have different characteristics, creating fronts and triggering various kinds of weather.

We have come a long way from the days when sailors knew, by word of mouth and other ship logs, what the weather and winds might be like in a particular region. Today, we have the history of winds, air masses, and weather, as well as the more specific science of meteorology that allows us to predict—based on years of research and daily and hourly measurements—what may happen in a particular area at a specific time. We've all watched the weather reports often enough to know that although meteorologists can tell us, more often than not, what is going to happen, the winds can shift, air masses can move, and variations in weather patterns are a fact of life.

SUMMARY

We have always known that there were predictable patterns to the Earth's air and circulation systems. For centuries, however, this information was transmitted by word of mouth and in ship logs. Today, with extensive scientific study and modern technology, meteorologists have identified specific patterns of global circulation, forces of air pressure, and how to predict weather patterns across the globe.

Air pressure variations are responsible for the generation of winds. These pressure differences are the result of unequal heating of Earth's surface. The pressure of the air is measured in millibars, and it decreases rapidly with elevation away from Earth's surface.

Meteorologists use this measurement of air pressure, or changes in atmospheric pressure, measured in isobars, to predict weather patterns.

Areas of high pressure within the atmosphere are called anticyclones and usually mean fair weather. Anticylcones move air in a clockwise direction in the Northern Hemisphere and counterclockwise in the Southern Hemisphere.

In a low-pressure system, or cyclone, pressure increases from the central isobars toward the outer isobars. The center is called a trough. Cyclones usually travel around the globe, from lower to higher latitudes, and are characterized by rising air masses and falling pressures that give rise to cloudy skies.

Global circulation is impacted both by unequal heating by solar radiation and the Coriolis effect. Warm air moves from the equator toward the poles in an upper atmosphere low, and then cycles air near the surface from the poles toward the equator. These patterns of global circulation establish four pressure zones in each hemisphere. There are two low-pressure areas in each hemisphere, one in the equatorial region and another in the subpolar regions. Two high-pressure centers are established in the subtropical and polar regions of both hemispheres, where the air flows down and then outward onto the surface.

The rise and fall of air masses around the globe, combined with the Coriolis effect, produces consistent wind patterns. Air that moves away from the subtropical highs is deflected so that trade winds dominate.

Winds that move poleward from the subtropical highs create the prevailing westerlies. The subpolar lows are at about 50° to 60° north and south of the equator and established the reliable polar easterlies. The winds at higher latitudes are produced in the polar high regions where dry cold air sinks toward the surface.

These global circulation patterns mean that meteorologists can accurately predict certain weather patterns, although it may sometimes rain when they say it will snow, or drizzle when they have predicted partly cloudy skies. Understanding air pressure and global circulation allows us a better picture of our planet's weather patterns and helps us know what to expect from week to week, no matter where we may live.

STORMS

KEY TERMS

air mass, warm front, cold front, stationary front, occluded front, lightning, forked lightning, tornado, Fujita scale, vortex, hurricane, Saffir-Simpson scale, storm surge

WEATHER EVENTS

People are fascinated by storms. They are always caused by the interacting of the boundaries of two contrasting air masses; but to those who witness them, the results are often unpredictable, dramatic, and memorable. Watching a funnel cloud swoop down to Earth and experiencing the intensity of a hurricane are not things you forget. High winds, hail, and lightning often accompany intense storms, making the experience even more dramatic. In this chapter, we'll explore the circumstances that converge to create powerful storms and how these weather systems impact our planet.

Air Masses and Fronts

An *air mass* is defined as a body of air that is composed of similar temperature and humidity. This can be a great body of air, up to 1500 km in width and several kilometers thick. A single air mass can impact an area on a scale of thousands to millions of square kilometers over a period of several days. The weather through the expanse of an air mass does not vary much.

When the bottom portion of the atmosphere slows over an area and has time to develop uniform temperatures and moisture properties, an air mass will form. We name the air masses based on the area in which they form. For example, an air mass produced over the sea is called a *maritime air mass*, while those that take shape over land are called *continental air masses*. Further classification is based on latitudinal origin. Air masses formed in warmer, low latitudes are called *tropical air masses*. Those produced in colder, high latitudes are called *polar air masses*. Combinations of these characteristics (sea–land and low latitude–high latitude) define the four types of air masses most often employed by meteorologists: continental tropical, maritime tropical, continental polar, and maritime polar.

CLASSIFICATION OF AIR MASSES

Continental tropical—formed over land at a low latitude

Maritime tropical—formed over sea at a low latitude

Continental polar—formed over land at a high latitude

Maritime polar—formed over water at a high latitude

Fronts

When two air masses of different origins encounter each other, the boundary between them forms a turbulent zone called a front. Frontal boundaries are very narrow—perhaps less than 200 km wide—compared to the overall size of the two interacting air masses. Since one air mass is typically cooler than the other, the warmer air has a tendency to flow up and over the cool air mass. The cooler and denser air behaves very much like a wedge that serves as a surface over which the warmer, less dense air can rise.

If warm air moves in and displaces an area of once-cooler air, the boundary is called a *warm front*. An increase in temperature and the appearance of cirrus clouds usually indicate the onset of a warm front. As the front moves forward, cirrostratus and then altostratus clouds form. Dense stratus and nimbostratus clouds—with their associated, moderate amounts of rain and/or snow—appear at the beginning of the front. Warm fronts progress relatively slowly across an area. They are characterized by a shallow front marked by a low-angled slope of warm air above cooler air.

A *cold front* is formed when cooler air replaces an area once occupied by warm air. The nature of the change in weather is usually much more violent than that associated with a warm front. This is due in part to the steepness of the front itself. In other words, warm air is pushed aside vertically, and in an abrupt fashion. As a cold front moves in, the temperature drops and tall cumulonimbus clouds take shape. Precipitation and winds can be intense, but only last for a short period of time since the cold air mass behind the front brings with it clearing skies.

Two additional fronts can also occur, and they are generally more complex in nature. When two air masses collide, so that the flow is nearly parallel to the front produced between cold and warm air masses, a *stationary front* is formed. In this case, the position of the front, relative to the surface, does not move.

Occasionally, a cold front can surpass or overrun a warm front—creating what is called an *occluded front*. In this case, the merger of two cold fronts effectively eliminates a warm front. Temperatures drop in this circumstance, although the opposite can also happen when a warm front overruns a cold front. In that case, temperatures may rise. The result is generally a lessening or weakening of the storm or weather system that precedes the occluded front.

Thunderstorms

Intense winds, hail, heavy rain, lightning, and thunder are characteristic of *thunderstorms*, which occur in conjunction with the onset of a cold front with the formation of cumulonimbus clouds. Such clouds can climb some 12 km in altitude, reaching the base of the stratosphere (the layer of the atmosphere immediately above the troposphere). Thunderstorms are triggered when warm and humid air is thrust upward into the sky. They usually occur later in the day, because their upward flight is aided by afternoon surface heating by the Sun. Most thunderstorms, for any particular area, last no more than 30 minutes to one hour. It is estimated that more than 2000 thunderstorms rage somewhere across the globe at any one moment in time. We've already discussed the phenomena of wind, hail, and rain, but lightning and thunder are significant aspects of any thunderstorm. Understanding thunder and lightning is important to your safety, and they are also interesting parts of the thunderstorm system.

Lightning is almost always a sign of an encroaching thunderstorm. The ancient Greeks associated lightning with Zeus, the king of the gods who would, as legend tells, hurl thunderbolts toward Earth. Today, we know that lightning comes from the development of cumulonimbus clouds, which form a separation in electrical charge. The frictional rubbing of individual ice particles and raindrops causes the bottom of a cloud to have a negative charge and the top portion to have a positive charge. These charges will build to millions, and even hundreds of millions, of volts before a lightning strike discharges the cloud. This process is not fully understood but is caused by the movement of precipitation within the cloud. There are several types of lightning. *Cloud-to-ground lightning* is the most dangerous. More than 100 people in the United States are killed every year by lightning strikes. A single electrical discharge carries an awesome 200 million volts of electricity. Since the surface of the Earth can be positively charged, the base of the cumulonimbus cloud, which has a negative charge, can send a stream of electrons from the cloud to the ground as a bolt of lightning. In other instances, lightning can move between oppositely charged areas of the same cloud. This *intracloud lightning* is the most common type of lightning. Lightning can also move between two oppositely charged clouds as *intercloud lightning*.

One of the most impressive kinds of lightning you can observe is *forked lightning*, when the bolt takes on the appearance of a branching network. On other occasions, you might not even notice the lightning at all because clouds and rain block your view. We refer to this as *sheet lightning* because, although we don't see the bolt itself, it illuminates the sky and clouds in a flash of light.

Thunder is a by-product of lightning. As lightning is actually the flow of electrons through the air, sound waves are generated when these electrons collide with air molecules. The noise is loud because lightning heats the air, causing rapid expansion and then contraction, resulting in the violent collisions of air molecules. These collisions produce sound waves that travel away from the lightning flash.

The distance of a lightning strike can be determined by listening to the thunder that follows. Sound within the lower atmosphere moves at a rate of about one mile in a 5-second period. Therefore, you can estimate how far off the lightning is by simply counting slowly after the flash until you hear the thunder. Dividing this number by 5 gives the miles between you and the storm. The rumbles we usually hear in a storm occur because a single bolt of lightning occurs over an extended area, so not all the sound waves reach us at the same time.

Tornadoes

A *tornado* is a small, very intense cyclonic storm characterized by high winds, usually produced along cold fronts in conjunction with a severe thunderstorm. They can have winds in excess of 400 km per hour. In the United States alone, more than 1000 tornadoes are spawned each year, resulting in an average of 80 human deaths with about 1500 injuries. In extreme cases, a mature tornado can carve a path almost 2 km wide that extends over a length of 80 km.

FORMATION OF A THUNDERSTORM

The three conditions required for thunderstorms to form are

- Moisture in the lower to mid levels of the atmosphere

- Unstable air—that is, air that will continue rising once it begins rising from near the ground

- A lifting force, or something that starts the process of lifting air, such as the heating of the ground. As the air warms, it becomes lighter, and lifts up. Advancing masses of cool air, which force warm air upward, also trigger thunderstorms. The air rising into a thunderstorm is called an updraft, and tornadoes form within a thunderstorm's updraft.

Fortunately, not all thunderstorms make tornadoes; in fact, less than one percent of all thunderstorms will spawn a tornado.

Although tornadoes can occur at any time of the year, in the United States, they peak between the months of March and May in the southern states (Figure 14.1). Peak tornado activity in the northern states occurs later, during the summer months. The average tornado moves at a speed between 30 to 80 km per hour and only lasts about 5 minutes while carving a path of destruction approximately 150 m wide.

Cumulonimbus clouds are the birth sites of tornadoes. High winds within such clouds develop into a *vortex*, or a rotating column of air that can reach from the cloud to the ground. These huge cloud systems include air pressures within the vortex that are much lower than the air outside it. All the air outside the vortex, or what we call a twister or funnel cloud, rushes into the vortex, sucking in all sorts of debris (and trailers, houses, trees, and anything else in its path). Things caught up in the vortex swirl upward in the cumulonimbus cloud. That's why, after a

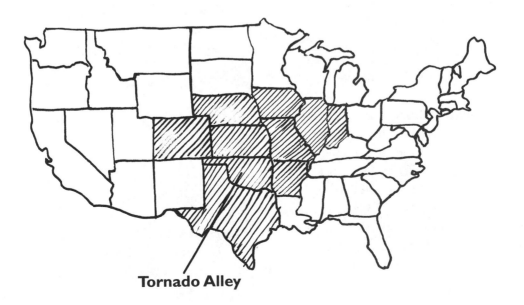

Tornado Alley

Figure 14.1—Map of Tornado Alley

tornado, people, animals, and other objects are often found some distance away, sometimes unharmed because they have been lifted by violent winds and then dropped or spun away from their point of origin.

As the air enters the low-pressure column, water condenses out, forming a cloudy funnel. This funnel usually develops from the cloud toward the ground. However, even if the funnel does not reach the ground, the surface winds may indicate the presence of a tornado, as the cloud has not yet developed. Debris picked up from the ground contributes to the darkening of the funnel cloud. If no material from the surface is incorporated into the twister, it can take on a white, cloudy coloration. In some instances, where the ground is made of red clay, the tornado can pick up the ruddy dust and then have an almost evil red hue.

Tornadoes are commonly associated with the nation's heartland—in a ten-state area, stretching from Texas to Nebraska. These are states that have seen F5 tornadoes (see chart, next page), although tornadoes of varying strengths have appeared in most of the United States. Tornadoes are as common in Florida as they are in Oklahoma, although Florida tornadoes are usually quite weak.

It is difficult to forecast tornadoes. Dr. Theodore Fujita (1920–1998), known as the "tornado sleuth," developed a machine that involves spinning a set of cups that force air to move upward very rapidly. This demonstrated that the vortex is accompanied by a cylindrical mass of air that drops downward outside the vortex at a high rate of speed. He also developed a scale for measuring the intensity of tornadoes.

EXPLORATION 14.1
TORNADO IN A BOTTLE

For this experiment, you'll need two empty, plastic, 2-liter soda bottles, duct tape, scissors, and a pencil. Fill one bottle half full of water and cover the mouth of this bottle with a strip of tape. Use the pencil to punch a hole in the center of the tape, making it slightly smaller than the circumference of the pencil. Smooth out the tape, then turn the second bottle so that the mouth of each bottle lines up with the other.

Dry any moisture from the necks of the bottles, then wrap strips of tape around the necks of the bottles to secure them tightly. Now, flip the bottles so that the bottle with the water is on top. Hold the necks of the bottles and quickly swirl them in clockwise circles parallel to the floor. Set them, still attached, on a table, with the empty bottle on the bottom. You might need to keep a steady hand on the bottles to keep them from falling over.

Watch as the water swirls in a funnel shape from the top bottle to the bottom bottle. The water moving through the small hole is similar to the spiraling tail of a wind tornado. The water movement is due to the action of several forces, as is the movement of a tornado.

Twist of color—Try adding 2 ounces of colored vegetable oil to the water (simply add a few drops of food coloring to the oil before pouring the oil into the water). Because oil is less dense than water, it will float on the surface of the water. When the oil and water swirl together, the less dense oil travels down the vortex first and creates a "colored" tornado effect. This can also be done with colored foam bath beads (which can be thought of as the debris that was swept up in the tornado).

The *Fujita* scale or "F" scale, developed by Dr. Fujita, is used to compare the force by which destructive tornadoes are classified. The F-rating is assigned only after damage has been assessed.

Tornadoes have been known to do some quirky things and have also caused major devastation. In 1931, a tornado carried an 83-ton railroad coach and its 117 passengers 24 meters through the air and dropped them in a ditch. In 1939, a student sitting in a tub full of water on the top floor of a dormitory in Georgia was picked up, along with books, clothing, and furniture, and deposited a block away, conveniently in thick shrubbery, which cushioned her fall. She walked away with cuts and bruises, but lost the braces off her teeth.

A strong tornado can also take many lives and cause incredible devastation. When 148 tornadoes struck an area stretching from Canada to Georgia on April 2 and 3, 1974, during what is known as the Super Outbreak, the death toll exceeded 300 and damages exceed $600 million—the worst such storm in half a century.

Tornadoes can also move capriciously across Earth, dipping up and down, so that we never know where they might hit next. The advent of *Doppler radar*, technology that allows detection of the initial formation and subsequent development of an intense rotating system, now gives us advanced warning of a tornado's impending strike. Although it is difficult to predict when a tornado will touch down, and exactly what path it might follow, people now have enough warning to seek cover before the funnel cloud is over their heads.

THE FUJITA SCALE

F0	64–115 km/h	Light damage	Fallen tree branches, small signs down, some uprooted trees
F1	116–179 km/h	Moderate damage	Roofs partially peeled off; houses, mobile homes off foundations or flipped over; moving cars pushed off road
F2	180–251 km/h	Considerable damage	Roofs torn off frame houses and mobile homes destroyed, can uproot or snap large trees
F3	252–329 km/h	Severe damage	Can overturn trains; pull the roofs and walls off well-constructed houses, toss cars into the air
F4	330–417 km/h	Devastating damage	Levels houses, tosses cars in the air, creates missiles out of flying debris
F5	418–508 km/h	Incredible damage	Can lift houses off their foundations, toss cars 100 meters, may damage steel-reinforced concrete structures

HOW DOES DOPPLER RADAR AID IN WEATHER PREDICTION?

Doppler radar is named for the Doppler effect, discovered by Christian Doppler in 1842. The Doppler effect is defined as a change in the observed frequency of a wave, as of sound or light, occurring when the source and observer are in motion relative to each other, with the frequency increasing when the source and observer approach each other and decreasing when they move apart. The motion of the source causes a real shift in frequency of the wave, while the motion of the observer produces only an apparent shift in frequency.

Later, scientists applied Doppler's principle to weather radar. When sound waves are broadcast from a radar antenna, they may come into contact with objects in their path, such as dust particles or ice crystals. If they come into contact with an object that is moving away from the radar, the sound waves will be reflected back at a decreased frequency (that is, fewer waves will be reflected back within a certain time period). If the object they come in contact with is moving toward the radar, the waves will be reflected back at an increased frequency. Using Doppler radar, meteorologists can get a picture of precipitation that allows them to track a storm's progress over time.

Hurricanes

A *hurricane* is a tropical cyclonic storm having winds in excess of 119 km/h. Hurricanes are the pinnacles of all tropical storms. They may start out as simple tropical disturbances, which are really nothing more than an unorganized group of thunderstorms. These storms, which always form over the ocean, are fed by warm, moist air above an ocean with temperatures over 25°C. (See Figure 14.2.)

Hurricanes have been described as heat engines that are powered by the latent heat released when water vapor condenses in vast quantities. This heat has the effect of warming the air, thus causing it to swirl up into the atmosphere.

When the winds begin to circulate with speeds between 37 to 63 km/h, a *tropical depression*, a slightly more intense storm, is formed. The tropical depression has winds that circulate in a slight rotary pattern at speeds approaching 65 km/h. If winds increase to the point where they blow anywhere between 64 to 117 km/h, the system is then called a tropical storm. Tropical storms are given names by the National Hurricane Center. A tropical storm becomes a hurricane, sometimes called a *typhoon*, once the wind reaches speeds of 119 km/h and up.

On average, hurricanes are about 600 km in diameter with winds that spiral in and then upwards assisted by steep pressure gradients. A circle of cumulonimbus clouds forms a ring at its center called the *eye wall*. The most severe winds and intense rainfall are found around this donut-shaped disturbance. At the base of a hurricane, winds are sucked inward. They swirl upward and then out, away from the center, at the top of the storm, which may be some 12,000 meters above sea level. In the Northern Hemisphere, hurricanes spin counterclockwise, with a distinct set of spiral arms extending away from the storm's center. At the very center of the hurricane is the *eye*, a relatively calm zone with an average diameter of about 12 km. Due to warm water requirements, hurricanes typically form during the late summer season, and only at latitudes within 20° of the equator. Hurricanes will not form at latitudes less than 5°, though, because the Coriolis effect, necessary to initiate a hurricane's spin, is too weak there. Once a hurricane moves across cool oceanic waters or land, it fades quickly in strength. This is because of the lack of warm, moist air in such environments, which is needed to power these giant vortices.

The *Saffir-Simpson scale*, with its five categories, was created to classify hurricanes based on their potential to inflict damage. This was developed in 1969 by Herbert Saffir, a consulting engineer, and Dr. Bob Simpson, Director of the National Hurricane Center.

One of the most damaging aspects of hurricanes is the storm surge, a rise in sea level associated with the storm. This can be anywhere from 1.5 to more than 6 m, and follows the low-pressure eye wall of a hurricane. When it makes landfall, this associated storm surge accounts for most deaths and property damage. In 1970, in the delta region of Bangladesh, which is mostly less than two meters above sea level, a storm surge combined with high tide and flooded the area. The official death toll was 200,000, but unofficial estimates ran as high as 500,000.

It is easy to understand how hurricanes can impact both the people and the property that lies in their paths. In 1992, Hurricane Andrew cut a swath through the northwestern Bahamas, the southern Florida peninsula, and south-central Louisiana. Damage in the United States was estimated to be near $25 billion, making Andrew the most expensive natural disaster in U.S. history. Andrew was classified as a category-4 hurricane. Fifteen people died as a direct result of the storm, and up to a quarter of a million people were left temporarily homeless. Because Florida had not experienced a storm of this intensity for more than 30 years, Andrew taught a whole generation of Floridians the importance of emergency preparedness.

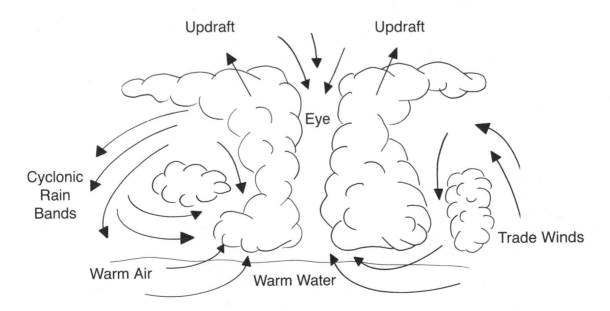

Figure 14.2—Hurricanes

SAFFIR-SIMPSON HURRICANE SCALE				
Type	Category	Damage	Winds (km/hr)	Storm Surge
Hurricane	1	Minimal	119–153	1.2–1.7 m
Hurricane	2	Moderate	154–177	1.8–2.6 m
Hurricane	3	Extensive	178–209	2.7–3.8 m
Hurricane	4	Extreme	210–249	3.9–5.5 m
Hurricane	5	Catastrophic	>249	>5.5 m

Another major storm, Hurricane Mitch, was one of the strongest and most damaging storms ever to hit Central America. Over a two-day period in 1998, this hurricane sustained winds of 290 km/h and dumped heavy rains over the region. Even as the storm moved inland, torrential rains caused catastrophic floods and landslides. People who lived along the major rivers were simply swept out to sea as floodwaters rose and riverbanks gave way. Hurricane Mitch was responsible for tremendous devastation, but it also transformed the surface of the land as it dumped a full year's worth of rain over a period of a few days. An estimated 5,660 people died; 12,270 were injured; and more than 8,000 were classified as missing—some never to be found. Roads, bridges, water systems, and energy and telecommunications systems were damaged or wiped out.

Hurricanes of the magnitude of Andrew and Mitch are rare. Emergency preparedness can help save lives when these storms do hit, but it is impossible to minimize the tremendous impact of such ferocious storms on the land. Massive flooding, landslides, storm surges, and winds can alter the landscape forever.

SUMMARY

Our lives are constantly being impacted by storms—thunderstorms, wind, rain, hail, tornadoes, and hurricanes—and predicting and understanding the various forces of these storms has helped humans to protect both their property and their lives. Sometimes, storms attain such magnitude that the landscape is permanently altered, something we can predict but never prevent.

Weather systems are triggered by different air masses, developing in different regions of the world that may collide elsewhere as fronts. When two air masses of different origins encounter each other, the boundary between them is a front. Depending on whether the air mass is warm or cold, different situations can develop. Warm fronts progress relatively slowly across an area.

Cold fronts, formed when cooler air replaces an area once occupied by warm air, cause more violent weather. A stationary front occurs when two air masses collide so that the flow is nearly parallel to the front produced between cold and warm air masses. This is a slow-moving weather system. A cold front can surpass a warm front, creating an occluded front, and effectively eliminating the warm front.

Thunderstorms arise from the onset of a cold front with the formation of cumulonimbus clouds. They are triggered when warm and humid air is thrust into the sky. Lightning is almost always the sign of a thunderstorm. There are several kinds of lightning, including cloud-to-ground lightning, intercloud lightning, intracloud lightning, and forked lightning. Thunder is a by-product of the lightning. Lightning is the flow of electrons through the air, and sound waves are generated when these electrons collide with air molecules.

Tornadoes are small, intense cyclonic storms with high winds, usually produced along cold fronts in conjunction with a thunderstorm. Tornadoes generally strike without much warning, causing loss of life, bodily injury, and property damage, but advanced weather forecasting techniques, like Doppler radar, have helped to reduce the casualties and injuries. Now people may have enough time to seek cover when these unpredictable twisters appear.

Tornadoes are measured on the Fujita scale, and can range from an F1, with branches and signs down, to an F5, with major devastation to property.

Hurricanes are tropical cyclonic storms, which often take longer to build up their strength, and thus allow people a longer time to prepare and seek safe locations. However, these can still be devastating storms, costing more and more in property damage as growing numbers of people build property along the shorelines. The Saffir-Simpson Scale measures hurricanes, based on the potential damage, wind speed, and storm surge.

While tornadoes may uproot trees, houses, and other structures, a hurricane can modify the landscape, creating major flooding and landslides. As we have grown more advanced in predicting weather patterns, we are often able to prevent loss of life and injuries to people from these major storm systems. The impact, sometimes permanent, on the face of Earth is beyond human control.

PART

4

PLANETARY SCIENCE

INTRODUCTION TO PLANETARY SCIENCE

KEY TERMS

planetary science, terrestrial planets, jovian
planets, Kuiper belt, ejecta blanket, impact basin,
complex craters, simple craters, flyby, orbiter,
lander, altimeter, topographic map, contour lines,
reflectance spectrometer

APPLYING EARTH SCIENCE TO OTHER PLANETS

All that we have learned in the previous chapters can be applied to planets found elsewhere in the solar system. Just as we have applied the principles of geology, oceanography, and meteorology to our planet, we can use the same principles in studying other planets. *Planetary science* takes the same principles of earth science and applies them to the study of the solar system.

Not only have geological processes been at work sculpting other planets, but in certain instances, the lessons of oceanography and meteorology can be applied as well. For instance, Mars may have once had lakes and oceans long ago, and a moon of Jupiter may now have a global subsurface ocean beneath its icy crust. Some planets have atmospheres—although not quite like that of Earth—ranging from the thick clouds of Venus to the dusty air of Mars, and from the striped clouds of Jupiter to the blue air of Neptune.

Terrestrial and Jovian Planets

Including Earth, there are nine planets that orbit our star called the Sun. These planets naturally divide themselves into two groups. Those closest to the Sun are called the inner planets, while those farthest away are called the outer planets. (See Figure 15.1.)

The inner planets are formally classified as *terrestrial planets*, because they have solid surfaces (*terra* is Latin for land). They are relatively small worlds, and they are situated rather close to the Sun. These planets are often called the earthlike or rocky planets because of their solid surfaces. The terrestrial planets are Mercury, Venus, Earth, and Mars.

By contrast, the outer planets are large worlds that are mostly composed of gas. They have many moons or natural satellites (small, terrestrial objects that revolve around planets). They are formally classified as *jovian planets* (named for Jupiter, the largest member of this class of planets), but they are also sometimes called the gas giants. These large and gaseous worlds include Jupiter, Saturn, Uranus, and Neptune.

Pluto is an oddity. It is not a jovian planet, nor does it exactly fit the criteria of a terrestrial planet. Upon discovery in 1930, it became known as the ninth planet. Since that time, astronomers have questioned its classification as an outer planet because of its small size and terrestrial characteristics. Pluto is a small, frozen world with a diameter less than that of Earth's moon. Recently, hundreds of tiny blocks of ice—all smaller than Pluto—have been found in the same orbit around the Sun as Pluto. This icy asteroid belt is called the *Kuiper belt*, and Pluto is its largest member. It differs in composition from the rocky belt of asteroids that orbits between Mars and Jupiter.

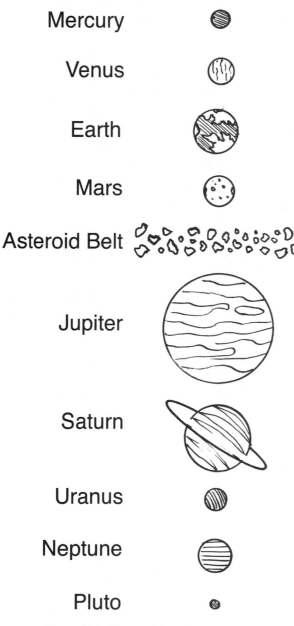

Mercury

Venus

Earth

Mars

Asteroid Belt

Jupiter

Saturn

Uranus

Neptune

Pluto

**Figure 15.1—Terrestrial and Jovian Planets
(Figures not drawn to scale.)**

Impact Cratering as a Geologic Process

As we study the terrestrial planets in the following chapter, attention will be given to features produced by the geologic processes. Volcanism and tectonism have played an important role in the evolution of planetary surfaces. Equally significant are the gradational processes that have worked to erode surfaces by the actions of water, wind, ice, and gravity. Our planet is changed significantly because of these factors, but so are others in our solar system. One of the most common surface-modifying agents known is *impact cratering*, the process by which holes on the surfaces of terrestrial worlds are caused by the fall of meteorites or even asteroids from space. In fact, it is a rare thing to find a terrestrial object in the solar system that does not exhibit a cratered landscape.

Earth's surface appears to be relatively free of these extraterrestrial holes, but this is misleading. Meteorites and asteroids heavily pounded our planet in its early history, just as they did all others. However, since that time, other geological forces have been actively at work, erasing most of the evidence of cratering on our planet's surface.

A casual glance at the Moon through a telescope reveals craters almost too numerous to count. Craters range from basin size to depressions less than 100 meters across, which are not readily visible with telescopes of common resolution. All impact craters are formed when meteoroids or chunks of space rock plummet from the sky. Upon impact, two shock waves are generated: one at the impact site and the other within the meteorite itself. One shock wave propagates through the meteorite and completely destroys it. The other shock wave moves through the planet's surface, compressing rock and sediment. When the surface decompresses or rebounds, material is ejected or thrown outward, forming a cavity called a *crater*. The material that is thrown out of the crater (*ejecta*) forms a deposit around the crater called an *ejecta blanket*.

Craters are classified into three divisions based on size. The largest are called *impact basins*, which are colossal holes with multiple-ringed mountains exceeding 100 km in diameter. Craters with central peaks and terraced walls, between 5 and 100 km in diameter are called *complex craters*. Craters less than about 5 km across have a bowl-shaped appearance and are called *simple craters*. (See Figure 15.2.) All three ranges are found on terrestrial moons and planets throughout the solar system.

Of course, it is difficult for us to actually explore each planet and moon in the solar system, but advanced technological equipment has enabled us to send both manned and unmanned explorations into space that bring back a wealth of specific information about other celestial bodies.

PLANETARY EXPLORATION STRATEGY

In an effort to learn more about the planets, robot and even human-piloted spacecraft have been sent on voyages to other worlds. *Space probes* are unmanned spacecraft that are sent past or into orbit around a specific planet or moon. They are equipped with scientific instruments that can send back all sorts of specific information about crater sizes, temperature, composition of the atmosphere and surface, etc. There is a logical sequence to the planetary exploration routine, from a simple flyby to the landing of human explorers. This strategy has been followed consistently, but only through to completion for our Moon (see the following table).

Simple Crater

Complex Crater

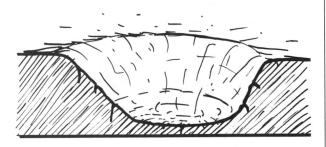

Impact Basin

Figure 15.2—Craters

Planet	Flyby	Orbiter	Lander	Piloted
Moon	X	X	X	X
Mercury	X			
Venus	X	X	X	
Mars	X	X	X	
Jupiter	X	X		
Saturn	X	X		
Uranus	X			
Neptune	X			
Pluto				

First in the sequence is an exploratory type of mission called a *flyby*. As the name implies, the spacecraft simply flies by the target and obtains a first look. Next is an *orbiter* mission, which circles the planet like a satellite in order to acquire information over a longer period of time. Orbiters pave the way for *lander* spacecraft. Lander-type vehicles make a soft landing at a predetermined site, occasionally being equipped with a mobile rover that can venture away from the initial landing base (Figure 15.3). The culmination in planetary exploration happens when humans actually set foot on another world. These are classified as *piloted* missions, because humans pilot the spacecraft.

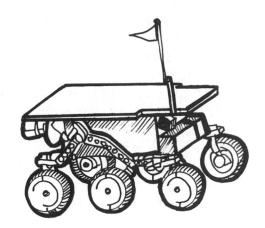

Figure 15.3—Mars Pathfinder Rover

Tools of Planetary Exploration

Space probes to the planets carry an array of scientific tools. The three most important are an imaging camera, an altimeter, and a spectrometer. These instruments are "flown" on virtually every type of probe mission to the planets.

As the old saying goes, "a picture is worth a thousand words," and in planetary science this holds very true. Cameras used onboard space probes are of the digital variety, and they are really not too different from those purchased at your local camera shop; however, they have a resolution far better than could reasonably be purchased by the ordinary photographer. Digital cameras work by dividing a scene into a myriad of picture elements, or *pixels*. The more pixels included in the image, the greater the detail that can be rendered. Each picture element has a brightness range between 0 (black) and 255 (white), and once they're put together like a great puzzle, an image is made.

Another important tool in modern planetary science is the altimeter. An *altimeter* is a device used to precisely measure elevation variation on a surface. An altimeter works by firing either a radar beam or laser at the surface while at the same instant recording the amount of time it takes for the signal to reflect back to a detector on the space probe. This information provides precise distances of the probe from the surface, which can be used to calculate topography. The information reported by the probe is used to create a topographic map. The *topographic map* is a rendering, or drawing of the planet's surface with *contour lines* that connect points of equal elevation above or below a predetermined level. The contour lines are drawn with uniform intervals of space separating them (for example, 10 meters). These lines then help us to see what the configuration, or relief, of the planet's surface might be. Alternatively, a computer program can manipulate the data into a three-dimensional digital elevation model of the terrain.

The third instrument that has been used to gather important information about the planets is a *spectrometer*, which is a device that can determine the chemical composition of rock and atmosphere. We've briefly discussed in previous chapters the use of spectrometers and how they use light to determine the elemental composition of an object. One such type of device, typically flown on planetary missions, is a *reflectance spectrometer*. It works by measuring the amount of sunlight reflected from a target at different wavelengths. A graphical display of the results is very much like a chemical fingerprint. In this manner the composition of a far celestial object can be determined.

SUMMARY

All that we have learned about Earth science—geology, oceanography, and meteorology—can be applied to the study of planetary science. Many of the same forces have been at work to modify the planets of our solar system.

Terrestrial and jovian planets are distinguished both by their distance from the Sun and the composition of their surfaces. Terrestrial planets are earthlike or rocky, while jovian planets are composed mostly of gas. Pluto, which is neither a jovian nor a terrestrial planet, is a bit of a puzzle. It is a small, frozen world, the farthest from the Sun in our solar system.

A significant factor that helps us to study the history of planets is the effect of impact cratering. Almost all the terrestrial worlds of the solar system show evidence of this geologic process. The fall of meteorites or even asteroids from space has created a range of topographic features, ranging from small craters to giant basins.

To study some of these features more closely, humans have developed a planetary exploration strategy. We usually begin with a flyby mission, cruising near the planet to gather information and pictures. Next we send an orbiter that circles the planet and captures more extensive information from all angles. Finally, a space probe might be landed on the surface of the planet. You can see from the chart in this chapter that this advanced stage of exploration has happened in only a few cases. Ultimately, piloted missions that set down on a planet's surface with human beings onboard are the goal. So far, our Moon has been the only place we have been able to complete such a mission.

Every space probe is equipped with certain kinds of equipment to help determine the mineralogy of a planet's surface, its atmospheric conditions, temperature, elevation, and many other features. Everything we discover about the other worlds in our solar system contributes to our understanding of Earth. Our planet experienced many of the same forces as other planets in the solar system. Continued study adds to our knowledge base of all the forces at work in our local part of the universe.

THE TERRESTRIAL PLANETS

KEY TERMS ────────────

ballistic trajectory, retrograde rotation, lunar maria, heavy bombardment, wrinkle ridges, sinuous rille, straight rille, scarp, sapping, Roche limit

THE INNER PLANETS

Over the past four decades, we have begun to seriously explore a new frontier—the solar system. How the other planets and moons were formed offers lots of clues as to how Earth took shape and what the future may hold for our solar system. Our neighborhood in space includes the nine planets bound to a star called the Sun. Of these worlds, the terrestrial planets are relatively small chunks of rock near the Sun. Farther out are the jovian planets—the giant, gaseous worlds—and Pluto, an odd, cold planet smaller than Earth's moon. Between the planets are smaller objects called asteroids and comets. These interplanetary stones date back to the beginning of the solar system. They are composed of the stuff that made the planets.

It is believed that the universe began to take shape about 15 billion years ago. Galaxies started to form about 13 billion years ago, and stars within the galaxies took shape shortly thereafter. Our solar system formed about 4.6 billion years ago, and life on Earth developed a mere billion years later, although hominids didn't make an appearance until about 4

million years ago. Refer back to the sidebar in Chapter 5 titled "Earth History Compressed Into A Year" (page 48) to get a sense of how long it took for life on Earth to evolve, and then put that into the context of 4.6 billion years from the beginning of the solar system.

The terrestrial planets, including Earth, orbit nearer to the Sun than the jovian planets. They also tend to have earthlike surfaces—rocky, hard topography similar to that of Earth. The geologic processes, oceanographic features, and meteorological phenomena of all these planets give us clues as to how Earth was formed, and ideas about how Earth fits into the solar system. Because we have studied Earth closely in the previous three sections of this book, it makes sense to first look at the other terrestrial planets and their similarities with Earth, along with the moons that orbit these planets, before we explore other aspects of the solar system.

One of the interesting points of comparison for all the planets is the length of the *revolution period*, or the time that it takes a planet to complete one full orbit around the Sun. We tend to think in terms of time on Earth (e.g., $365\frac{1}{4}$ days in an Earth year, and 24 hours in each Earth day), but every planet has slightly different periods of time. A year is technically defined as how long it takes a planet to complete one full orbit around the Sun, while a day is technically defined as how long it takes a planet to rotate once on its own axis.

Mercury

Mercury, named for the winged messenger of Roman mythology (Hermes was his Greek counterpart), is the nearest planet to the Sun. Mercury is much larger than our Moon and roughly half the size of Earth. It is a mere 60 million kilometers from the Sun and revolves around it faster than any other planet, at about 50 km per second.

Mercury takes only 88 Earth days to complete one orbit, where Earth takes 365 1/4 days. It rotates on its axis once every 58.6 days; on Earth, this rotation defines one day. What this means is that the Sun, if observed from Mercury, would rise and set three times in a two-year period. (See Figure 16.1.) Three days on Mercury last two Mercurian years (176 Earth days). This means that the planet spins three times on its axis for every two revolutions it makes around the Sun.

Because of the length of rotation, the side of Mercury facing the Sun has a long time to absorb its heating rays, while the other side has a long cooling period. Therefore, the temperatures can range from about 425°C to -150°C from one side to the other.

Mercury's Geology

The surface of Mercury is similar in some ways to that of our Moon. It is a gray terrain peppered with impact craters. The crater morphology, however, has some distinct differences from those of the Moon. Because there is a strong gravitational field, when an asteroid or meteorite struck its surface, the debris and rocks did not travel as far in the *ballistic trajectory* (the path of a projectile or other moving body through space in free flight) as they might have on the Moon, where

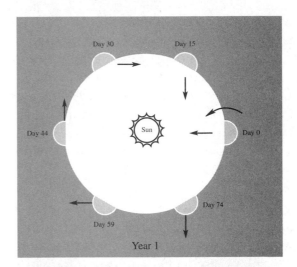

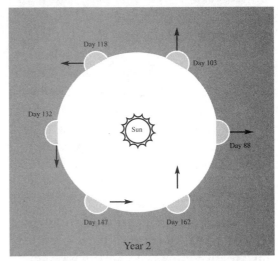

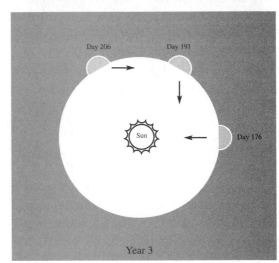

Figure 16.1—Length of Day and Year on Mercury (Arrow marks a fixed point on Mercury's surface.)

there is less gravity. In other words, the rocks simply don't fly as far on Mercury as they would on the Moon, because there is more gravity on Mercury. On the Moon, when a crater was created there was little gravity to hold back rocks sent flying by the impact. What is observed on Mercury in the ejecta pattern is how it hugs the crater rim. Most of the terrestrial planets and moons of our solar system show signs of impact craters. Unlike Earth, where there have been other significant forces at work on the surface of the land, these early asteroids and meteorite impact sites on other planets provide significant information about how the solar system and its planets and moons were formed.

Like the Moon, Mercury has several impact basins. The largest one ever photographed is named Caloris, and it is probably the most dominant feature on the planet. There also appears to be more craters with a prominent, bright-ray pattern.

The smooth plains regions of Mercury seem to be considerably brighter than those observed on the Moon. Some of these plains are thought to be volcanic in origin. It has been suggested that they are the result of lava flows that spilled onto the surface billions of years ago, much like the *lunar maria*, large dark areas on the Moon created by lava flows. (*Maria* is the plural of the word *mare*, which is Latin for sea.) This material fills the large, circular impact basins. The intercrater plains of Mercury are brighter and are likely composed of impact crater and basin ejecta—not lava flows. The only dark, maria-type material on Mercury seems to fill the interior of the basin Caloris, and this material is believed to be lava.

Mercury also has numerous ridges, believed to have been formed by compression when the crust collapsed due to shrinkage during core formation. Those ridges are thought to be thrust faults or low-angle normal faults— where part of the crust pushed up and over nearby crust, forming these ridges as the crust contracted during core formation. Mercury has a large core, and when it solidified, its volume decreased, resulting in crustal compression. Think of Mercury as an apple pie and remember how the crust cracks as the interior cools and contracts when it is finished cooking.

Because Mercury doesn't have a natural satellite (Mercury and Venus are the only planets without moons) a precise figure for its mass is not known. The gravitational tug of the planet could be felt by space probes, however, and this allowed a cursory determination of mass to be made. Mercury is a dense world with a large central core of iron. Since it is considerably smaller than Earth, its surface gravity is only 38 percent that of ours. Usually a planetary magnetic field only exists when the planet has some liquid metal, like iron and nickel, below its surface or at its core. Since Mercury's core is expected to be solid metal, rather than liquid, the reason for its weak magnetic field is still unanswered. When the *Mariner 10* space probe flew by Mercury, its trajectory was modified in such a manner that it was possible to calculate its mass (via Isaac Newton's law of gravity). Based on the size of the small planet, it had a significant gravitational tug that was interpreted to be the result of a large core. The magnetic field is weak, but might be explained as a remnant frozen into the iron core.

Mercury's Environment

Mercury is too small, too far away from us, and too close to the Sun for it to really be explored well. Space probes have managed a single flyby mission, and although the unusual orbital and rotational relationship meant that most pictures came from only one side of the planet, we have been able to understand some things about Mercury. It was once thought that Mercury always kept the same side towards the Sun, but it was later discovered that this is not the case.

By sending radio signals to Mercury and measuring how and when they return, scientists have been able to determine some of the planet's characteristics. It was through radar that we learned that frozen water ice might exist within craters near the poles of Mercury. It is possible that these areas are hidden from the Sun's direct light and therefore have been able to remain frozen.

Mercurian Meteorology

Mercury has almost no atmosphere, but it does have traces of hydrogen and helium gases that blow away from the Sun. Some of the atmosphere consists of sodium, which comes from atoms blasted off the surface of the planet by solar winds. Because the surface is so hot, they quickly evaporate into space. Unlike Earth and Venus, which have more stable atmospheres, Mercury's atmosphere is constantly replenished. In other words, it has virtually no atmosphere; it is a volcanically dead world and is so small that it really cannot retain an atmosphere. The traces of hydrogen, helium, and sodium quickly evaporate as they enter the planet's atmospheric zone. Since the planet has no air and no clouds, forecasting the weather on Mercury would be simple: unbearably hot all day (about 425°C) and freezing cold at night (about –150°C).

Venus

Venus, which at one time was thought of as a twin of the Earth, is located some 105 million kilometers from the Sun. Although Venus is roughly the same size as our planet, about 12,000 km across, the similarities stop there. The second planet is not the swamp oasis dreamed up by imaginative science fiction authors of years past; rather, it is the most hostile of the terrestrial worlds, literally a hellish place, with temperatures in excess of 480°C.

Venus is unusual in other ways, too. For example, the planet's day (rotational period of 243 Earth days) is greater than its year (revolution period of 225 Earth days). In addition, the planet spins in what scientists call *retrograde rotation*; that is, it is rotating backwards. Being farther from the Sun, Venus moves at a slower pace than Mercury, about 35 km per second.

FUN FACT: Venus is the easiest planet for stargazers to spot in the sky. Its surface is covered by dense clouds, which reflect sunlight. Because it is closer to the Sun than Earth is, it never gets very far from the Sun if viewed from Earth. Every 7 months, Venus goes through a period where it is the brightest object in the western sky in the evening, 20 times brighter than the star Sirius. Three and a half months later, it rises earlier than the Sun, appearing to be a brilliant morning star. Venus would appear the same to viewers from any part of our world.

Venusian Geology

Early observations of Venus revealed the planet to have continental masses embedded in a lowland, which accounted for most of the crustal geography. Impact craters are found on the planet's surface. These craters, like those on Mercury, have very small ejecta blankets. Volcanoes, lava flows, possible sand dunes, debris-flows, and faults have all been photographed.

Several Russian Venera space probes landed on Venus and were able to send back some pictures before the intense heat caused them to stop functioning. These images showed a barren, rocky surface with medium to large rocks scattered over lava fields, and about as much sunlight as on Earth during an overcast day. They also portrayed a surface color of dark orange, which is believed to be caused by the reddening of light coming from the Sun through the thick atmosphere.

The same geological processes that produced many of the surface features found on Venus have done the same on other planets, but it is here that the similarities seem to stop. Venus is unlike any other planet.

Venusian Meteorology

Because Venus is so close to the Sun, it is believed that the intense heat has boiled away any water or oceans that may once have existed there. A runaway greenhouse effect is apparently at work, where penetrating solar radiation is reradiated by the planet's surface at a longer wavelength and cannot make it back through the gaseous atmosphere into space. Therefore, Venus is like an oven, with uniform, blistering temperatures all over. In addition to being incredibly hot, the atmosphere is also incredibly dense—so dense that pressures are not all that dissimilar to those found at the bottom of the Earth's deepest ocean (remember the Mariana Trench from Chapter 7 and the idea of a single person holding up 50 jumbo jets?). Even more, the Venusian clouds are filled with sulfuric acid droplets. Although this environment is

exceedingly interesting from a geologic point of view, explorers to Venus would certainly be crushed, poisoned, or burned on contact.

Space probes have found that the upper atmosphere of Venus has high-speed winds and a permanent cloud layer beginning about 30 km above the surface and extending to an altitude of 80 km or so. No water is present in these clouds; only the dangerous, highly corrosive sulfuric acid droplets mentioned above. These clouds cover the whole planet, so if you landed on Venus, you wouldn't see anything above the surface of the planet—just more clouds.

Earth's Moon

We have already covered most aspects of Earth science—the geology, oceanography, and meteorology. It is important to note, however, that while Mercury and Venus do not have natural satellites or moons, the Earth—next in line from the Sun—does have a very impressive moon, our only natural satellite.

Our Moon is neatly divided into two provinces: the bright cratered highlands and the darker, relatively smooth maria. The maria are younger terrains composed of dark basaltic lava flows. They are the lowlands of the surface, created by colossal impact basins. The cratered highlands dominate the Southern Hemisphere, and these rugged terrains date back to the early history of the Moon. They were formed during an early epoch of the solar system known as the *heavy bombardment*, a period of intense strikes by meteorites and asteroids. Moons and planets swept up much of the remaining debris that did not go into the formation of planets within the solar system.

Undoubtedly, the most prolific features on our Moon's surface are the impact craters. These cavities, produced by meteorite collisions, range from humble bowl-shaped forms to basins hundreds of miles across.

FUN FACT: Here's an example of how craters were formed. First, a projectile hit the surface. As a result of that impact, a shock wave traveled downward, compressing the underlying rock. With the rebounding of the compressed material, a crater was formed. As a result, we have a small bowl-shaped hole with an associated ejecta blanket of rubble. Many of these larger impact basins (filled with lava) on the Moon are known by names such as the Sea of Tranquility or the Sea of Fecundity. It is not uncommon to find craters within craters, and the features are analogous to the look created when a rock is dropped directly into mud.

Winding lunar features are found on the maria that are generally attributed to volcanic and/or tectonic processes called *wrinkle ridges*, appearing as creases on the surface of the Moon. These ridges might have originated when the mare surface was compressed. Like a loosely fitted rug, or the crust of an apple pie as it cools, the crust buckled under the stress. Alternately, or perhaps in conjunction with, wrinkle ridges may have formed when thicker lava oozed out of linear fissure vents.

On the floors of some sections of maria are channels that, at first glance, resemble dry river beds. These channels once had fluid flowing through them, but not water. The fluid was molten lava. At one time, the liquid rock flowed beneath the surface through lava tubes. The maria, or lowlands, were formed within the impact basins after an impact, but were then further modified by the flow of lava. These conduits carried the basaltic lava that filled the maria found in impact basins. Once

the lava drained entirely out of the lava tube, the roof could no longer support itself, and so it collapsed, forming a dry channel now called a *sinuous rille*.

EXPLORATION 16.1 OBSERVE THE MOON THROUGH A TELESCOPE

The wonderful surface of our closest satellite can easily be seen through a telescope. The Moon's surface is an awesome sight, and even when viewed through a *small telescope with low magnifying power*, the dark maria and bright highlands are readily distinguishable. (See Figure 16.2.) Note the density of the craters on the highlands.

The best time to observe the Moon is when its phase is either a crescent or quarter. At this time, shadows cast by mountains and crater walls highlight the surface features. When the Moon is full is the best time to look for bright rays extending from fresh lunar craters, such as Tycho and Copernicus. The larger lunar craters (called basins) have Latin names, like Mare Imbrium for Sea of Rains, or Mare Serenitatis, for the Sea of Serenity. You can find maps of lunar maria, with the names of each one, to guide you as you search the Moon's surface on your own.

Stretching across both the maria and the highland are features known as *straight rilles*. These linear depressions are believed to have been produced by faulting. Extensional forces pulled the crust apart here, causing a central block of material to drop down into what we refer to as a graben.

Why the Moon exists at all is a mystery. We know that it once appeared as a much larger orb in the sky than it is today. Billions of years ago, the Moon orbited much closer to Earth.

Over the eons, it has slowly increased its distance. Today, it orbits Earth at a distance of about 385,000 km. A billion years ago, it was significantly larger in the sky. This is somewhat different from when you see the Moon on the horizon and it appears larger, which is an optical illusion.

Several ideas were offered to explain why Earth should have a natural satellite almost a quarter of the size of the planet itself. One suggestion was that the Moon was a captured object. In this theory, its birth took place elsewhere in the solar system. As it strayed too close to Earth, our planet's gravitational field snagged the Moon. In another hypothesis, the Moon was forged as a double planet with Earth. It is suggested that the Moon was here from the very start. Both objects condensed from the solar nebula, forming a sort of twin planet.

It is ironic that for years after the lunar landings astronomers still couldn't explain why the Moon exists. Rocks brought back from lunar missions were amazingly similar to those existing here on Earth. We now believe that our Moon was formed in a cataclysmic event shortly after Earth's birth. Our planet was probably struck by a Mars-sized *planetesimal* (any small body thought to have orbited the Sun during the formation of the planets). This object grazed the edge of the Earth, plowing through the crust and deep into the mantle. The new Earth and Moon were born from this collision. A combination of elements from both Earth and the impactor formed the Moon, although Earth ultimately absorbed much of the colliding planet.

Obviously, such a large collision would create a great amount of heat; the rocks that came from the Moon showed evidence of having

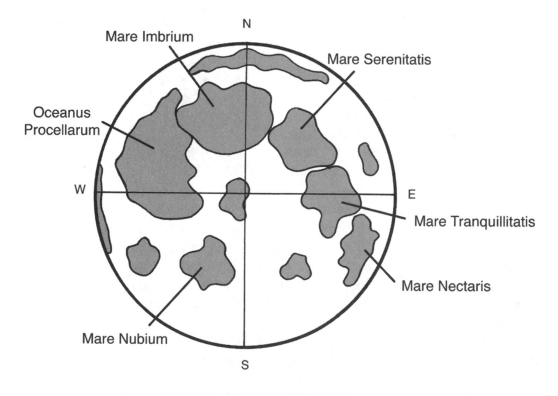

FIG. 16.2—OUR MOON'S SURFACE

melted and are devoid of any traces of water. Although we can't be certain that this is what happened, evidence supports this theory.

Mars

Mars, the red planet fourth from the Sun, is a world that ignites enthusiasm and curiosity about life elsewhere in the cosmos, even to this day. The Mars that Arizona astronomer Percival Lowell (1855–1916) purported has long since been disproved. He was passionately committed to proving the existence of intelligent life on this planet. Mars was once thought to be inhabited by a water-thirsty, dying civilization, more advanced than humans. Martian canal networks were seen littered about the planet, but it is now believed that they were an optical illusion as viewed through the telescope. These mythical features were disproved, even before the first flyby mission, but old beliefs die hard.

Geology of Mars

Mars is a cold, dry planet that is populated with a spectacular array of geological features—some of which are puzzling. The planet's day is somewhat longer than Earth's, and it orbits the Sun once every 687 Earth days at a distance of roughly 230 million kilometers. It is half the size of our world—only 6800 km in diameter.

In 2003, Mars was closer to Earth than it has been for 50,000 years. Everyone hurried to view the red planet through telescopes, and even the Hubble Space Telescope trained its cameras on Mars. People were able to see such details as polar ice caps and other markings on the planet's surface.

It has been observed that Mars has canyons, as well as volcanoes, craters, and polar ice caps. There are younger volcanic plains to the north, and ancient, cratered material to the south.

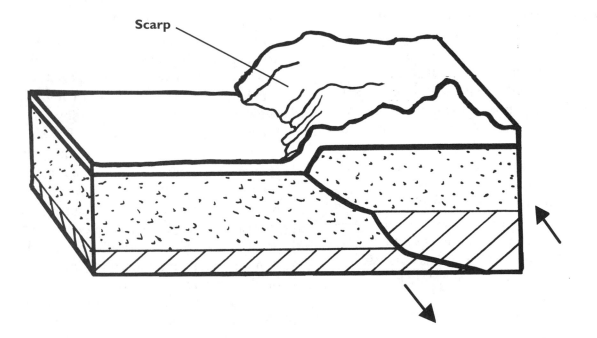

Scarp

FIG. 16.3—SCARP

These two terrain types are neatly separated by what has been called the highland/lowland dichotomy. This physical boundary is called a *scarp* (Figure 16.3); it is a line of cliffs that approximately separates the two hemispheres.

Two volcano-tectonic bulges lie in the northern lowland region, the Tharsis Bulge and the Elysium Bulge. Both have numerous massive volcanoes superimposed on them; however, those of the Tharsis region are larger and younger. Since Mars is believed to be a planet composed of a single stationary crustal plate, volcanoes are thought to have remained active for a great period of geologic time, thus allowing huge masses of molten material to be emplaced above the same hot spot. With no plate tectonics happening on Mars, a subsurface hot spot works on a single location over great periods of time. In this manner, large volcanoes like Olympus Mons can be built. On Earth, the lithospheric plates migrate away from the hot spot, so it is not possible for our planet to get volcanoes of that size.

There are at least 12 Martian volcanoes larger than any found on Earth; they are classified as shield volcanoes. As you'll recall from Chapter 4, this means they are composed primarily of layers of solidified fluid lava and resemble inverted bowls. The largest of the volcanoes is Olympus Mons, a mountain about the size of Texas and three times the height of Mount Everest. Surrounding these volcanic provinces and most of the major impact basins (Argyre, Hellas, and Isidis are the largest) is an area of highly fractured and faulted terrain.

FUN FACT: Names for features on planets and moons are chosen by the International Astronomical Union. Since Venus had been named for the Roman goddess of love (her Greek equivalent was Aphrodite), the Union chose to name all other features after famous women in history, from all cultures and traditions, including Edith Wharton and Emily Dickinson. On Mars, the name theme took a different approach. Large craters are named after deceased scientists who have contributed to the study of Mars; small craters are named after villages in the world with populations of less than 100,000; large valleys are named "Mars" in various languages; small valleys are the classical or modern names of rivers. In ancient Greek mythology, Phobos and Deimos were the horses that pulled Mars' (the war god's) chariot.

Water on Mars

Gradational forces, the movement of air and water over the surface of the planet, have been at work on Mars. Although the Martian air is thin, it is still quite capable of moving sand and dust, producing sand dunes and wind streaks about the craters. Evidence of fluvial activity occurs in the form of small valley network channels and massive outflow channels. It has been suggested that the valley networks, which are primarily confined to the southern cratered hemisphere, were formed by rainfall runoff. However, if this is so, it must have happened in the distant Martian past when atmospheric pressures were great enough to permit water to exist in liquid form. Others think the small channels might have been produced by a process known as *sapping*, the sublimation (conversion of a solid directly to a gas without going through the liquid state) of *permafrost* as an erosive factor. Permafrost is rock or soil that remains at or below 0°C for two or more years. In the geologic context of Mars, these small channels probably were formed over the course of tens to hundreds of thousands of years as the permafrost gradually sublimated.

Yet it is believed the larger outflow channels formed in a totally different manner. They are thought to have originated when subsurface volcanic eruptions melted underground ice. When this happened, massive volumes of water flowed downslope as the terrain collapsed, forming jumbled terrain and huge channels. Ice in the polar regions formed peculiar spiral valleys and layered materials. Finally, gravity worked as a gradational force, smoothing over rough surfaces. On Mars, tremendous landslides have been observed, especially along the slopes of Valles Marineris. This canyon represents numerous geologic processes at work, but especially tectonism and gradation. Much of the tectonism on Mars is related to crustal breakage related to the formation of impact basins. Huge basins produced radial and concentric fracture systems. The Tharsis and Elysium rises, or bulges, also produce crustal stress simply by their weight on the crust. Valles Marineris may have started as a break in the crust radial to Tharsis, and then was later expanded on by other geological processes such as wind, water, ice, and gravity.

Martian Meteorology

In spite of all the differences between Mars and Earth, humans are still fascinated with the possibility of visiting this planet. It resembles the American Southwest with its dune fields and rolling hills. But even if the topography looks familiar, the climactic conditions present tremendous challenges.

Mars has a thin atmosphere composed mainly of carbon dioxide, and it is fairly cold—rarely getting above freezing, even near the equator at midday. One space probe took images of dust devils moving across the surface, and, on occasion, the entire surface of the planet is covered by gigantic dust storms that represent a global weather phenomenon that is still not completely understood today.

To actually visit Mars, we would have to provide astronauts with a significant power supply—for lights, heat, and to process air. Because of the complex technology and cost of such an experiment, we have to content ourselves for now, with the close-up views made available to us by telescopes and space probe missions.

The Moons of Mars

Mars has two small moons. Phobos, measuring some 22 km across, orbits the red planet at an altitude of about 6000 km. Deimos has about half the diameter of Phobos and is situated 20,000 km away from Mars.

Prior to the space age, not much was known about these satellites. Because of this, some interesting speculation arose. One scientist, the Russian astronomer Iosef Shklovskii, speculated in 1959 that these moonlets were actually hollow, artificial objects. This reasoning was based on the decaying orbit of Phobos. Its orbit appeared to be accelerating as it dropped slightly closer to Mars. In fact, this moon will probably creep into the powerful *Roche limit*, or zone of destructive gravitational tidal forces, in approximately 40 million years.

This situation facing Phobos was attributed to the Martian atmosphere. Phobos is dragging against atmospheric gases, which has the effect of slowing the moon down, causing it to fall toward Mars. However, the only way this model could work is if the moon has a very low density—one that is 1000 times less dense than water. If Phobos were a natural satellite, its density should be closer to four times that of water, and being a heavy object, it should not suffer drag effects from the thin atmosphere. So, Shklovskii speculated that Phobos, and probably Deimos, were hollow spheres. It was even suggested that they were space stations constructed by an advanced civilization that once thrived on Mars.

Even more, it was suggested that the reason astronomers failed to discover the pair of moons initially, was that they weren't there. The Martians hadn't launched them into orbit yet. Obviously, the idea of Mars being populated by intelligent life has been a hard rumor to put to rest!

Astronomers now believe that Phobos's decaying orbit is related to gravitational tidal interaction with the Martian core, not to be confused with tides that are related to water. Tides are not merely an effect of water, but also a force of gravity. In fact, gravitational tides can literally stretch and squash a planet or moon. We now know that the moons of Mars are small, asteroid-like bodies. They may, in fact, be captured minor planets.

SUMMARY

In spite of all the significant differences between Mercury, Venus, Mars, and Earth, it is fascinating to compare the different geological processes and their atmospheres and weather systems, and to consider how similar they are to the processes that shaped our world.

How all this happened still remains much of a mystery, although the study of our Earth and how it formed and the exploration of space have given the scientific community valuable information in recent years. We can see, by observing other planets, that our Earth is not the center of this universe (as was once believed); nor is it as unique as we once thought. Other terrestrial planets orbit the Sun, and they have volcanoes, sand dunes, and some atmosphere or gravity. Earth is unique in that its environment supports human life, but how the rest of the solar system developed, and how it continues to change and evolve, is of critical interest to scientific study today.

Explorations in the past 40 years have made us more familiar with all nine planets, the Sun, numerous moons, and the asteroids and comets that move between them. This chapter looked, in detail, at the terrestrial planets—those that have rocky surfaces like the Earth.

Mercury is our closest solar neighbor, situated a mere 60 million kilometers from the Sun. Its terrain is similar to Earth's Moon, but it is much larger, about 6400 km across. It is a dense world with a large central core composed of iron.

Venus used to be considered a twin of the Earth because it is about the same size, but beyond that there are few similarities. It is the most hostile of the terrestrial worlds, with temperatures exceeding 480°C, a runaway greenhouse effect at work, an incredibly dense atmosphere, and clouds filled with sulfuric acid droplets.

Mars, fourth in position from the Sun, is called the red planet, and has long been the subject of science fiction fantasy. Today we know that it is a cold, dry planet, populated only with a spectacular array of puzzling geological features.

Gradational forces, the movement of wind and water, have been at work on the surface of Mars. The presence of volcanic-tectonic bulges is also obvious, as are volcanoes and craters. Although the other planets in our solar system appear to lack an environment that would support the kind of life that we are used to, it is clear that the geological processes, occurring over billions of years, have not been dissimilar to those experienced by Earth.

THE JOVIAN PLANETS

KEY TERMS

jovian, Great Red Spot, belts, zones, orbital resonance, Cassini division, shepherd moons, albedo

THE GIANT PLANETS

Jupiter and Saturn are the largest worlds in our solar system. They are significantly different from the terrestrial planets, which orbit near the Sun. Mercury, Venus, Earth, and Mars are sometimes called the inner planets, but they are most often referred to as Earth-like or terrestrial because they have solid surfaces. The outer planets—Jupiter, Saturn, Uranus, and Neptune—are low-density objects with gaseous atmospheres and mostly liquid interiors. As a group, they are called the Jupiter-like or jovian planets. The term *jovian* refers not just to Jupiter, but to all the planets that have characteristics resembling that of Jupiter. Each hosts a system of rings, a strong magnetic field, and a magnificent collection of moons.

Jupiter

Jupiter is the largest of all the solar system's planets. It is about 11 times the diameter of Earth and is 318 times more massive. The jovian planets also rotate faster than the terrestrial planets. Jupiter is some 144,000 km across, yet it spins once every 9 hours and

50 minutes. This state of rapid rotation has a profound effect on the shape of Jupiter. It is flattened at the poles, and it noticeably bulges at its equator. Because Jupiter is nearly 800 million kilometers from the Sun, it takes almost a dozen years to complete one orbit. Since the planet's day is so brief and the year is so long, there are over 10,500 Jupiter days in each Jupiter year.

EXPLORATION 17.1
FIND JUPITER AND SATURN IN THE NIGHT SKY

Of the planets visible to the naked eye, Jupiter ranks second only to Venus in brightness. When Jupiter is at its faintest, it still shines more brilliantly than the brightest star, Sirius. Like Jupiter, Saturn glows in the night sky as if it was a bright yellow star, and it can easily be found without the assistance of a telescope. Since Saturn is approximately twice Jupiter's distance from the Sun, it is appreciably fainter and moves more slowly against the fixed stars as it orbits the Sun.

You can learn where to find these worlds by contacting your local planetarium. If such a facility is not present within your town, there are two magazines that are concerned with the night sky and the motion of the planets. *Astronomy* and *Sky and Telescope* are both readily stocked at most good bookstores. Keep in mind that Uranus and Neptune are far too faint to see with the naked eye. A telescope is required to see these worlds.

Although ancient skywatchers identified Jupiter, and named the massive planet after the Roman king of all noble gods (his Greek counterpart is Zeus), they didn't really know much about the planet until after the advent of the telescope.

In the winter of 1610, Galileo, an Italian astronomer armed with a small telescope, saw Jupiter as no one had ever seen it before. He reported sightings of strange stripes on a disk around the planet's middle, and he is credited with discovering its four moons, which are now collectively called Galilean moons. Later, with the aid of telescopes, astronomers were eventually able to determine Jupiter's size, rotational period, and mass; and they were also able to identify major atmospheric characteristics such as composition and circulation patterns.

Jupiter's Atmosphere

The planet's trademark sign, the *Great Red Spot*, is one of its most enigmatic features. This is believed to be a hurricane that has been blowing for at least 350 years. This storm is larger than Earth. And, instead of being a region of low pressure, like hurricanes on Earth, the Great Red Spot is a region of high pressure that pokes up above the cloud tops. A great white oval located below the Red Spot is another whirlwind.

The planet is also distinguished by sweeping bands of color in the upper atmosphere, parallel to the planet's equator. A large equatorial band runs around Jupiter's middle, with alternating dark and light bands above and below the equatorial belt. The dark-colored bands are known as *belts* and the light-colored ones are called *zones*.

The large ovals, such as the one located near the Great Red Spot, are large atmospheric disturbances that move through the belts or zones.

Unlike the terrestrial planets, the surface of Jupiter is gaseous; therefore, observations focus more on the zones and belts, the Great Red Spot, and the beautiful colors of this planet. Jupiter also has the strongest gravity of all the known planets, as befits the largest planet in the solar system. Because of its strong gravitational field, Jupiter retains many of the gases originally present in the solar nebula. Hydrogen and helium are the primary atmospheric constituents, while ammonia, methane, and other substances are found to a lesser extent. Generally, roughly 80 percent of the atmosphere is hydrogen, and most of the rest is helium.

The higher clouds are made of ammonia ice, and deeper clouds are formed of water vapor, water ice, and other gases. The mean cloud temperature is about -121°C at the top, and about 100°C a hundred kilometers down.

As you approach the interior of Jupiter, the pressure becomes so great it is hardly right to call it an atmosphere. Deep inside Jupiter is a region of very dense hydrogen that exists in a liquid state, but because of the high pressure it has the characteristics of some metals. This is called *metallic hydrogen* and it can freely move electrons around. This, as in the liquid-metal outer core of Earth, is what gives Jupiter such a strong magnetic field.

The beauty of Jupiter's clouds lies in the mixture of colors present. For instance, a palette of blue, white, orange, red, and brown gives the planet its dazzling appearance. These colors not only reflect atmospheric chemistry, but also the depth and temperature at which the clouds are found. Cloud decks located deeper within the atmosphere are warmer than those on the planet's fringes. Red clouds, due to their extremely cold temperatures—approximately -140°C, are thought to reside farthest out. In contrast, the rare blue clouds, which have the warmest temperatures, lie deeper within the planet and are only visible through holes in overlying clouds. Above the bluish clouds are found brown and then white cloud patterns.

THE COLORS OF JUPITER'S CLOUDS

The exact chemistry of cloud coloration is still somewhat of a mystery. Sulfur may be the primary coloring agent. Its color is dependent on its association with other elements. The variety of colors seen in the clouds of Jupiter could be due to sulfur's varied molecular structure. Alternately, organic or carbon-bearing compounds have been suggested as a possible coloring material. As life on Earth is centered about organic molecules, some researchers have speculated on the possibility of floating "baglike" creatures among the jovian clouds. Phosphorous has also been proposed to account for the red hue of the Great Red Spot.

Cloud Circulation

The fascinating manner in which the colorful clouds of Jupiter and other jovian planets circulate is a result of several factors. For instance, the gaseous/fluid nature of these planets allows for the construction of symmetrical cloud bands. On Earth this is not possible. Solid landmasses disrupt the natural flow of air,

---

EXPLORATION 17.2
MAKING THE CLOUD BELTS OF JUPITER

In a tall, clear container (perhaps a juice pitcher), you can model the appearance of the atmosphere of a jovian planet. Mixing colored fluids of different densities can simulate the parallel belts and zones. Fill your pitcher two-thirds full with water. Use red or orange food coloring to match the color of the planet Jupiter. Next, pour in a few ounces of motor oil. Since the oil is less dense than water, it will settle in a layer above the water. Now, with a stirring stick in hand, mix the fluids in a circular motion. Watch as the cloud bands appear before your eyes!

---

producing a more complex pattern in atmospheric circulation. On the jovian planets, however, there are no continents or mountains to get in the way. Also, there is virtually no temperature variation from the poles to the equator. So, the meteorology of these planets is not driven by the transfer of heat from the equator to the poles, as happens on Earth. Jupiter radiates more internal heat than what is received from the Sun. In addition, the big planets spin very rapidly and this, combined with all the above, produces the observed parallel stripes and circulation characteristics so unique to this remarkable world.

In any case, the dominant features, alternating dark belts and light zones, can be described in terms of rising and sinking gas and are the work of the Coriolis force produced by planetary rotation (Figure 17.1). The stripes are the result of parallel high- and low-pressure bands that are separated by regions of high-speed winds. Bright zones are areas of high pressure (rising warmer air) while the dark

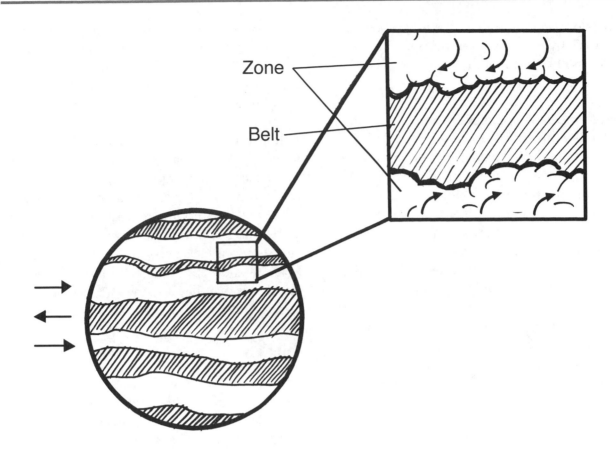

Zone

Belt

Figure 17.1—Jovian Belts and Zones

belts are places where the gases are falling (sinking cooler air), producing a region of low pressure.

The expanding gases of the zones and belts are affected by Jupiter's swift rotation. The Coriolis force deflects gases to the right in the Northern Hemisphere and to the left in the Southern Hemisphere, just as it does here on Earth. Once deflected, the moving air shears across the edges of adjacent belts, giving rise to lateral high-speed winds. Saturn's equatorial winds reach 320 km per hour, but those of Jupiter have been clocked at more than 650 km per hour. This explains how these spectacular winds produce areas of such intense turbulence and give rise to vivid swirls and spots.

Spots and most atmospheric movement are set in motion by events that occur deep below the tops of the clouds. Although there are subtle differences, the interiors of Saturn and Jupiter are quite similar.

Geology of Jupiter's Moons

Galileo's discovery of Jupiter's four largest moons was quite significant. It supported the emerging heliocentric or Copernican model of the solar system. In other words, these new worlds proved, beyond a shadow of a doubt, that not every celestial body revolved around Earth.

The four Galilean moons were eventually named from Roman mythology. Three of the moons (Io, Europa, and Callisto) bear the names of some of Jupiter's lovers, while the other (Ganymede) is taken from the mortal who was chosen to be the cupbearer to the ancient god.

Space probes have explored this jovian system in detail. Some of the most memorable images were those taken of Io. No less than nine erupting volcanoes were discovered. Additionally, some 200 volcanic craters, or calderas, were found. This satellite's surface is blanketed with yellow sulfur compounds, and it is so young that it lacks the impact craters so common to other terrestrial bodies.

Because of their proximity to the giant planet, the moons Io and Europa are locked in an orbital resonance that produces strong tides. *Orbital resonance* is a phenomena that occurs when two orbiting bodies have periods of revolution that are in a simple integer ratio so that they exert a regular gravitational influence on each other. This may serve to destabilize one of the orbits. The tides that are caused by this phenomenon result in internal heating—heating that gave rise to Io's volcanism and melted Europa's interior, perhaps forming a subsurface ocean.

With a surface area equivalent to that of Africa, Asia, and Europe combined, Ganymede is the largest natural satellite in the solar system. Like Europa, it's a ball of cold ice, but it may lack the internal ocean layer. Ganymede also has a series of grooves that crisscross the surface. They are, perhaps, analogous to graben valleys on Earth, and are probably the result of tectonic activity during the early history of this moon.

However, the outermost of the Galilean satellites, Callisto, shows very little more than a surface literally covered by impact craters.

After its formation, the only geologic activity this moon experienced was the fall of meteoric material. Callisto's surface undoubtedly dates back to a period of heavy meteorite bombardment more than four billion years ago.

Although most of our information about Jupiter's moons is based on the Galilean moons (since they are the largest of Jupiter's moons), we do know that Jupiter has at least 60 other satellites. More moons are discovered on a regular basis as technology improves. While the four largest moons have been studied more intensely, all we know about the plethora of smaller satellites is that they are small and rocky, and some are likely covered with ice.

Saturn

Galileo observed Saturn through his telescope, but he was thoroughly confused when it didn't appear to be round, but more like three separate bodies connected. Saturn showed two odd appendages—one on either side of the planet's disk. He explained the planet as three side-by-side worlds. Later, with better equipment, it became clear that Saturn was one world surrounded by rings. The telescope that Galileo used in the early 1600s didn't afford him the clarity to make accurate observations.

Understanding what was going on with Saturn was somewhat complicated—not only by the images that early telescopes gave us, but because Saturn is tilted, our view of it changes over time as it orbits the Sun. As we see it from Earth, the disk of rings shifts orientation as the orbit progresses, moving from an edge-on view (at which we see nothing more than a line) to the maximum angle, back to the edge-on view, and then the maximum angle again, but from the opposite hemisphere.

These rings, which so perplexed Galileo, have been the subjects of extensive study.

We know now that the rings themselves are made up of ice chunks and small ice-covered rocks. They don't touch the planet's surface. The innermost ring visible from Earth is more than 10,500 km above the surface. From edge to edge, the rings that we can see are about 300,000 km in total width, but are not continuous.

The major rings are labeled alphabetically, depending on when they were discovered. The larger rings are composed of smaller rings, called ringlets, and there are also gaps between the rings. The largest of these is called the *Cassini division* for Italian astronomer and mathematician Giovanni Cassini (1625–1712). These gaps are caused by gravitational interactions with Saturn's

larger moons, which push and guide the ice chunks and rocks into particular orbits. The smaller moons also have influence on the rings and are called *shepherd moons*. The rings are much larger in extent than what we are led to believe by observing them from Earth. Space probes, on the other hand, have discovered faint rings far above the planet.

Saturn is the second largest planet in the solar system. Its density is slightly less than that of water. In spite of its large size, if you could find an ocean big enough, Saturn would float like a beach ball.

Saturn, like Jupiter, has an active atmosphere; but because it is farther from the Sun, its cooler temperatures allow the formation of a high-level haze, which blocks our view of

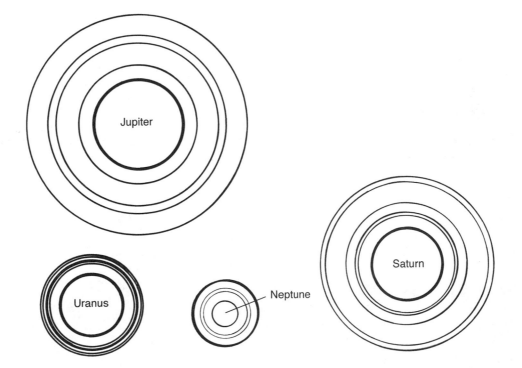

**Figure 17.2—Rings of the Jovian Planets
(Objects not drawn to scale.)**

the deeper cloud layers. The winds on Saturn are slower than Jupiter's, peaking at about 320 km per hour.

The inner portion of the planet is thought to be much like Jupiter's, with a metallic hydrogen mantle within the planet. Because the planet is less massive, however, the core is probably smaller. It also has a magnetic field, which is why scientists believe it has a metallic hydrogen interior. There could also be some inner regions or a core of rock, but because the pressure is so intense, any probe would be crushed. Because any type of landing mission is out of the question, we must content ourselves with pictures from afar.

Saturn's Atmosphere

Saturn's atmosphere is composed mainly of hydrogen and helium, with methane, ammonia, and other gases playing a lesser part.

PLANETARY SEASONS

Planetary seasons are caused by both axial tilt and revolution of a planet around the Sun. Seasons on some planets, like Mercury, are scarcely noticeable. However, the seasons are always opposite in the two hemispheres, because one pole is tilted toward the Sun, while the other is tilted away from the Sun. Scientists have actually been able to establish approximate dates for the vernal and autumnal equinoxes and the summer and winter solstices on other planets (Figure 17.3).

Really, the only significant difference between Saturn and Jupiter is that Saturn is slightly cooler, being farther from the Sun.

One unusual phenomenon on Saturn is a weather event that happens periodically. During Saturn's summer, in its northern hemisphere, a large bubble of warm gas rises

PLANET	vernal equinox / spring begins	summer solstice / summer begins	autumnal equinox / autumn begins	winter solstice / winter begins
Mercury	n/a	n/a	n/a	n/a
Venus	2/24/00	4/01/00	5/28/00	7/22/00
Earth	March 21	June 21	Sept. 23	December 22
Mars	5/31/00	12/16/00	6/12/01	11/02/01
Jupiter	August 1997	May 2000	March 2003	March 2006
Saturn	1980	1987	1995	2002
Uranus	1922	1943	1964	1985
Neptune	1880	1921	1962	2003

Figure 17.3—Seasons on Other Planets (Northern Hemispheres)

to the surface of the planet and is then dispersed by high-speed atmospheric winds. Since it is warmer, this bubble can rise above the hazy regions in the atmosphere and reflect sunlight. It then becomes visible on the planet's surface as a white storm. Although we know this happens, scientists still don't have an answer as to *why*.

Geology of Saturn's Moons

Saturn has a system of satellites that is dominated by one large body—a moon called Titan that orbits the planet every 16 days. Other satellites have been named Iapetus, Rhea, Dione, and Tethys, after the Titans in ancient mythology. Later discoveries included Enceladus, Mimas, and Hyperion.

Mimas orbits on the outer edges of Saturn's ring system. It is saturated with craters. Enceladus has a grooved terrain, blanketed in places by smooth deposits. The eruption of water and slurries of water ice may have formed these deposits.

Tethys' most noticeable feature is a big crater called Odysseus, which is more than 40 percent of the diameter of the moon. Dione's surface is streaked with a network of mysterious bright wispy marks. Rhea also exhibits these marks and shows evidence of having been struck by colossal meteorites long ago.

Titan has a dense atmosphere and a thick, ruddy cloud layer. It may even have an ocean of liquid ethane and methane with islands of frozen land. It has been proposed that its chemically rich atmosphere and ocean may even have spawned primitive forms of life.

Uranus and Neptune

Like Jupiter and Saturn, Uranus and Neptune have an atmosphere composed of hydrogen and helium gas. It is impossible to land a probe on such a surface, so we must rely on information sent back from one probe expedition, *Voyager 2*, which has gotten close enough to send back reliable information. *Voyager* observed Uranus in early 1986 and then explored Neptune in 1989.

Both Uranus and Neptune have tenuous ring systems, but because the small icy rocks they are made of are very dark, they are hard to see. Reflectivity is extremely important in planetary study; Saturn's rings are very easily seen because of how well they reflect light. The term given to describe an object's ability to reflect light is *albedo*. The rings around Uranus and Neptune have what is called low albedo, meaning they are not very reflective. Albedo ranges from 100 percent (a perfect mirror) to zero (a flat piece of black velvet). The rings of Uranus and Neptune have relatively low albedos.

Atmosphere and Interior

Uranus is more than 2865 million kilometers from the Sun, while Neptune is more than 4490 million kilometers away. The interiors of Uranus and Neptune are, in some ways, different from the larger jovian planets because of their smaller size. Their interiors are not as unusual as those of Jupiter and Saturn, or as alien to our understanding. They do have a small, terrestrial, rocky core at their center. Beneath an outer layer of gaseous hydrogen and helium is a region of liquid hydrogen. Between this layer and the rocky core is a thick mantle made of a liquid to icy substance. This mantle material likely consists of a combination of highly compressed water, methane, and ammonia.

The ammonia commonly found on Jupiter and Saturn has frozen out of Uranus's atmosphere, taking with it the beautiful colors that are usually visible as belts and zones. The atmosphere of Uranus is almost completely featureless, except for the blue-green tint of the atmosphere which is caused by the presence of methane gas. Small clouds do appear in the upper atmosphere, although we are unsure how they arise.

Uranus also has an unusual rotational axis. It is tipped so much that one whole half of the planet is in darkness while the other is in constant light. This is a unique situation for Uranus. Since its spin axis is tipped at about 90°, one hemisphere (north and then south) experiences long periods of darkness while the other has a long period of daylight—even though the planet rotates fairly rapidly on its axis. This is not true of the other planets, because as they rotate with a nearly straight, almost up-and-down spin axis, day and night happen on a daily basis. Uranus, because of its unusual tilt, would appear to have much longer nights and days. If Uranus was closer

THE PLANETS AND THEIR MAJOR MOONS

THE SUN

- MERCURY

- VENUS

- EARTH
The Moon

- MARS
Phobos
Deimos

- JUPITER
Metis, Adrastrea, Amalthea, and Thebe
Io
Europa
Ganymede
Callisto
Leda, Himalia, Lysithea, Elara, Ananke, Carme, Pasiphae, and Sinope
Recently discovered moons

- SATURN
Pan and Atlas
Prometheus and Pandora
Epimetheus
Janus
Mimas
Enceladus
Tethys, Telesto, and Calypso

Dione and Helene
Rhea
Titan
Hyperion
Iapetus
Phoebe
Recently discovered satellites

- URANUS
Cordelia, Ophelia, Bianca, Cressida, Desdemona, Juliet, Portia, Rosalind, Belinda, and Puck
Miranda
Ariel
Umbriel
Titania
Oberon
Caliban, Sycorax, Prospero, Setebos, Stephano, and Trinculo

- NEPTUNE
Naiad, Thalassa, Despina, and Galatea
Larissa
Proteus
Triton
Nereid

- PLUTO
Charon

to the Sun, this might make a difference, but the temperature is hardly affected at such a great distance.

Neptune, since it is even farther away, is even colder. The average temperature in the upper atmosphere is about -212°C. Its atmosphere consists of some methane, mixed with the same gases found on Uranus, primarily helium and hydrogen. Because it takes Neptune 165 Earth years to orbit the Sun one time, no human will ever live to see a complete Neptunian year.

Neptune is a light green to blue color, like Uranus, but images from the *Voyager* space probe show some more dramatic atmospheric activity. This is probably because the obscuring haze has frozen and sunk lower in the atmospheres. Both dark and light regions exist, but there is no prominent banding. Neptune also had a Great Dark Spot when *Voyager* flew by in 1989, which was a storm feature within the atmosphere, or a region of high pressure.

The Moons of Neptune and Uranus

There are many frozen, interesting moons orbiting Neptune and Uranus. Uranus has five satellites of intermediate size and at least another 15 smaller moonlets. The moons display craters, faults, and evidence of the eruption of ice lavas across their surfaces. Miranda, one of the moons of Uranus, has proven to be the most fascinating. An odd *chevron feature*, a bright V-shaped feature, stands out against a heavily cratered terrain. There is some evidence that Miranda was fractured a number of times in its formation. Gouged in the crust is an eminence canyon, which has cliffs many kilometers high.

Oberon, another moon of Uranus, with its spotty pockmarked surface, has bright areas that are probably ejected deposits produced by meteorite impacts. The moon Titania has supercraters called impact basins. Umbriel is the darkest of Uraninan moons, and it shows little evidence of any kind of geologic activity other than cratering. Finally, there's beautiful Ariel, with its cratered and fractured landscape.

Neptune's largest moon, Triton, is of prime interest to astronomers. This moon is actually larger than the planet Pluto. Triton revolves around Neptune in a retrograde or backward fashion. This satellite also has a thin atmosphere composed of nitrogen and methane. Thin clouds and some haze cover parts of this moon. In the very coldest of areas, atmospheric gases have condensed onto the surface, producing a spotted appearance. Other regions are blanketed by strange frozen deposits erupted through crustal fissures. Some of these flows look like bright lakes that have iced over. But the most remarkable discovery of the *Voyager* spacecraft, which explored these moons, was Triton's volcanoes. These features were detected as streaks that emanated from dark spots. The streaks are interpreted as ash deposits carried away from the eruption site by winds in the thin atmosphere.

PLUTO

We've saved Pluto for last because it is really hard to classify. It doesn't quite fit in with the terrestrial planets, nor is it a jovian planet. It lies at the farthest reaches of the solar system, an odd, frozen planet that we'll probably never fully explore. It seems to be more like a jovian moon than an actual planet. It is the smallest of all the planets, and is thought of as the last planet. It takes Pluto 248 Earth years to complete one full revolution around the Sun. While Earth's orbit is a nearly circular path around the Sun, the orbital path of Pluto is more long and narrow. Because of this extremely elliptical orbit, Pluto travels nearer to the Sun than Neptune for 20 of the 248 Earth years it takes to complete a revolution. From 1979 to 1999, Pluto could actually be referred to as the eighth planet from the Sun.

Pluto's Moon, Charon

Charon is Pluto's only moon, and compared to the planet, it is quite large. Pluto and Charon can be thought of as twin planets. In Roman mythology, Pluto is the ruler of the underworld, while Charon is the ferryman who guided his ship of the dead across the river Styx. Given the great distance of Pluto and Charon from the other planets and the Sun, and the extreme cold of both the planet and its moon, the mythology of the underworld, or land of the dead, seems appropriate. Nothing could survive in this environment. From the surface of Charon, our Sun would appear as only a bright star, causing temperatures to climb scarcely above -212°C.

Pluto and Charon are the last of the planetary outposts, and they haven't been explored up close. They are so far away and bear so little resemblance to our world, that it is hard to imagine what they might offer. Space probes of this century will probably eventually tell us more.

SUMMARY

The jovian planets are so unlike Earth and offer environments so hostile to space exploration that much more study has focused on our Moon and the other terrestrial planets. However, many prominent features of the jovian planets and their moons show evidence of some of the same forces that have been at work on Earth for millions of years.

Jupiter is the largest planet, with a rapid rotation, interesting rings, and the fascinating Great Red Spot. This feature is believed to be a hurricane that has been raging for about 350 years, but unlike hurricanes on Earth, it is a region of high pressure that reaches above the cloud tops.

Like other jovian planets, Jupiter has a gaseous surface, which makes landing on the planet impossible (not to mention the extreme temperatures). However, space probes allow us to study the fascinating rings and the beautiful clouds of Jupiter. These give us much information about the origin of the planet, its composition, and its atmospheric movement.

Jupiter also has many moons—more than 60 and more to be discovered. The four Galilean moons, among the largest, have been explored more closely, and show many common features like volcanoes, calderas, impact craters, and faults.

Saturn was a difficult object to study because as Galileo viewed it through his primitive telescope it appeared to be three worlds in one. Today we know that these interesting earlike appendages are actually rings, but the unusual orbit allows us to see them straight on, as a single line, and then to the maximum angle of ring opening.

The famous rings of Saturn are made up of ice chunks, a feature shared by other jovian planets. The larger rings are made up of smaller rings, called ringlets, and there are also gaps between the rings.

Saturn's density is slightly less than that of water, so if it was possible to find an ocean big enough to hold it, it would float like a beach ball. It also has an active atmosphere, although the winds are slower than Jupiter's, peaking at about 320 km per hour.

Saturn's moons are dominated by one large body called Titan. Titan has a dense atmosphere; a thick, ruddy cloud layer; and it may even have an ocean of liquid ethane and methane with islands of frozen land.

The other jovian planets, Uranus and Neptune, have an outer atmosphere of hydrogen and helium gas, just like their neighbors Jupiter and Saturn. They also have tenuous ring systems, which are almost impossible to see because of their lack of reflectivity.

The interiors of Uranus and Neptune are different from Jupiter and Saturn because of their small size. Like their larger cousins, they may have small, terrestrial-sized, rocky cores at their centers, but there is a thick mantle of a liquid to icy substance, probably made of compressed water, methane, and ammonia, within an outer layer of gaseous hydrogen and helium.

Both planets are very cold, being so far from the Sun, and both feature a collection of frozen, exotic moons. On the moons we can see many of the same features of other moons—craters, faults, and the evidence of eruption of ice lavas across their surfaces.

Pluto, the last planet in our solar system, is more like a terrestrial planet, but lies beyond the jovian planets. It is the smallest, coldest, least explored planet in our solar system. It also has a moon, Charon, which is quite large, but because both are so far away, we haven't truly explored them yet and know less about them than all the other planets that orbit our Sun.

In spite of the differences of the jovian planets, and the odds that we will never be able to land a space probe on their gaseous surfaces, we learn a lot about how the solar system was formed, how other planets developed, and what similarities Earth might share, by exploring as much as possible. The evidence of different atmospheres, gravitational pulls, rotations, and the geological surface features, including volcanic craters, grabens, impact craters, and gradational forces such as wind and water, help us to better understand what Earth may have experienced before humans even appeared.

ASTEROIDS, COMETS, AND METEORITES

GEOLOGY OF SPACE ROCKS

We've spent the past few chapters looking at how Earth fits into the solar system. Understanding the similarities and differences between Earth and the other planets brings us to a fuller knowledge of how Earth was actually formed and how the geologic and meteorologic processes continue today. We've also taken a look at the various moons of the solar system, leaving only asteroids, comets, and meteorites to explore in this final chapter.

Asteroids

Asteroid literally means "little star." Asteroids are irregular masses of rock and metal that range in size from small mountains to almost 480 km across. Asteroids and comets are potentially destructive impactors that have been around for eons. Most of the craters that you see on the moons and planets of the solar system date from the period of heavy bombardment, about four billion years ago. At this time, youthful planets were in the process of sweeping up debris. The planets formed through accretion; as the solar nebula collapsed, forming the Sun and planets, a flurry of dust and ice particles swarmed around the Sun. At first, these particles were too small for gravitational attraction to play any role. But within the cloud of dust and gas, minute particles began to stick together. Then larger clots appeared, in much the same way that dust holds to the teeth of a comb, through *electrostatic attraction*—the electrical charge built up due to friction between objects; friction removes some electrons from one object and deposits them on another object.

Soon, several larger objects emerged, which were called the planetesimals. They formed the nuclei about which the planets would grow. Their increasing gravities swept up excess material, and in this way, freshly created landscapes on terrestrial worlds became blemished with impact wounds.

Today, most of the remaining planetesimals, the asteroids, are found between the orbits of Mars and Jupiter. Pieces of these main belt asteroids are sometimes hurled inward toward the Sun. This can mainly be attributed to the gravitational pull inflicted on asteroids by Jupiter.

Most asteroids appear as faint, point-sized images, even with the best telescopes of today, and are easily lost among the myriad stars in the sky. By 1900, scientists had identified 300 asteroids. Today, more than 20,000 have been discovered.

Asteroid Types

The largest asteroid we know of is called Ceres, and it is about the size of the state of Arizona. Asteroids are categorized in terms of their composition. When the objects are primarily stony to stony-iron in construction, they are classified as *S-type* asteroids; when they are composed of metal-rich silicates and perhaps blocks of pure metal, they are classified as *M-type* asteroids; and when they are carbonaceous, they are classified as *C-type* asteroids.

ASTEROID TYPES

S-type = stony to stony-iron
M-type = metal-rich silicates
C-type = carbonaceous

Although most of the asteroids travel between the orbits of Mars and Jupiter, there are some interesting exceptions. A few of the asteroids have extremely elongated orbits that carry them between many of the planets. A few minor planets cut across the orbit of Mars and are dubbed Amor asteroids. It is expected that most—if not all—Amor asteroids will one day collide with the Red Planet.

A class of asteroids called Apollo asteroids or Earth orbit–crossing asteroids can pass quite close to Earth and, in fact, may one day strike Earth. The asteroid Hermes passes within 800,000 km of our planet—that's only twice the distance to the Moon. More than 500 of this type of asteroid measure a kilometer or more in diameter. Each year, astronomers discover several near-Earth objects (NEOs), which are asteroids with orbits that take them near Earth. These potentially pose a direct threat to life on Earth; the risk is quite low, but present

nonetheless. Because there are so many of these tiny objects out there, and the typical interval between discovery and closest approach to Earth is less than two weeks, it seems inevitable that we'll have a disaster at some point in the future. On the flip side, these chunks of rock are priceless in terms of research material, and if a very small asteroid could strike, say, an unpopulated area of Earth, scientists would find much to learn from it.

Comets

In addition to asteroids, substantial amounts of icy debris can be found at greater distances from the Sun. Astronomers believe a sphere of *comet nuclei* surrounds our solar system, nearly one-fifth of the way to the nearest star. These comet nuclei, similar to asteroids, are celestial bodies, observed only in that part of their orbits that are relatively close to the Sun. They have a head consisting of a solid nucleus surrounded by a nebulous coma and an elongated curved tail that appears when the coma is close enough to the Sun (Figure 18.1). Scientists believe that comets are made up mostly of ammonia, methane, carbon dioxide, and water. Occasionally, these deep-frozen snowballs fall toward the Sun.

As a comet nears the Sun, the ices in the nucleus begin to vaporize, forming a diffused and gaseous envelope around the nucleus called the *coma*. Together, the nucleus and coma form what is commonly referred to as the head of the comet.

Certainly the most spectacular part of any large comet is its tail. The tail usually begins to develop when the comet is between the planets Mars and Earth. Actually, the comet's tail is composed of two parts. The first part forms as a result of solar radiation pressure or a stream of particles called the *solar wind*. Minute dust particles are pushed out of the coma, creating the *dust tail*. The dust tail appears noticeably curved, tracing the comet's path around the Sun, and is usually yellow in color. The second component is made up of gas molecules and is called the *gas tail*. The gas tail is blue in color and always points directly away from the Sun.

The physical appearances and behaviors of comets are as varied as the appearances and behaviors of people; no two are alike. Depending on the amount and composition of material present in a comet and the close-

ness of its approach to the Sun, the tail may be almost nonexistent or may not develop at all.

The Impact of Comets

Although comets have low densities when compared to rocky asteroids, they can inflict considerable damage on a planet—even Earth. When a comet called Shoemaker-Levy 9 came too close to Jupiter's gravitational field, we got a glimpse of the potential for destruction. The comet probably became a satellite of Jupiter as early as 1858, but after years of orbiting Jupiter, it came too close and broke apart. At least 21 large fragments were

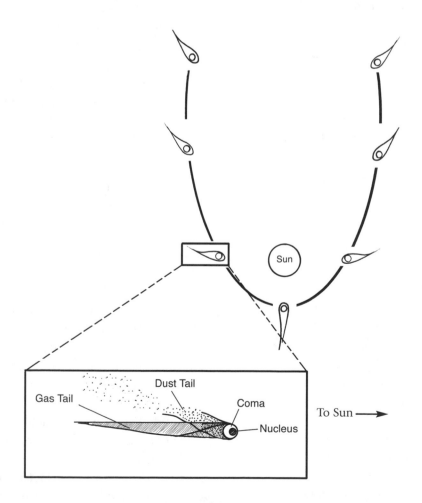

FIG.18.1—COMETS

formed in July of 1992, as the comet skimmed only 30,000 km above Jupiter's clouds. The following year, the comet was observed as it plummeted toward the giant planet. A train of comet fragments about 4.8 million kilometers long was seen extending through space. It wasn't until July of 1994 that the comet fragments actually rained down on Jupiter.

The fragments of Shoemaker-Levy 9 traveled very rapidly, flattening like a pancake as they hit Jupiter's surface. Remember that Jupiter has great atmospheric pressure—below the surface of the clouds, the pressure is great enough to liquefy hydrogen. As they slowed down, fireballs about the size of Georgia were created, which tunneled their way through the cloud tops. Within seconds of impact, each cometary fragment vanished in a spectacular explosion. Each detonation produced a blinding flash of light—releasing the equivalent of 6 million megatons of explosives. By comparison, the first nuclear bombs were equivalent to about 20,000 kilotons (or thousands of tons of explosives). The impact of a good-sized comet on Earth, for instance, could be far worse, in terms of impact, than what we saw with nuclear weapons.

Within minutes, a dark plume, part comet and part Jupiter material, rose upward through the atmosphere and emerged from the cloud tops. Jupiter shuddered and reportedly "rang like a bell." The Galileo space probe, then en route to Jupiter, was positioned so it could see the collision directly and the Hubble Space Telescope had the best opportunity to observe the dark blotches created by the impact.

METEOROIDS AND METEORS

Closely associated with asteroids are the meteoroids, small debris that can actually enter Earth's atmosphere. Some meteoroids are probably chips off of asteroids gone astray, but most are very small and much too faint to be seen even with the largest telescopes. Their presence becomes known only when they enter Earth's atmosphere.

If you have ever observed the sky on a clear, dark night, away from the lights and smog of the city, perhaps you've seen bright streaks of light moving quickly across the sky. These are called meteors, material that passes through our atmosphere. A fragment of a meteor that falls to Earth's surface is referred to as a meteorite.

To the ancients, meteors appeared as if stars had gotten loose from the sky and were falling to Earth, so they were called shooting or falling stars. Today, they are still popularly referred to as shooting stars, although we know that they have nothing to do with stars at all. Rather, meteors are the result of meteoroids that strike the Earth's atmosphere. The friction encountered during their rapid passage through the air makes the surrounding air hot and results in streaks of light appearing across the sky.

Meteorites

Meteorites are chunks of rock and metal that have fallen to Earth from space (Figure 18.2). Contained within this cosmic debris are the most ancient materials of our solar system. Here is where we find some of the best clues from space about our origin and the destiny of our planet.

Most asteroids occupy the planetary gap between Mars and Jupiter, as we learned earlier in this chapter. Asteroids occasionally collide with each other, sending meteoroids toward the inner planets. When they fall through our planet's atmosphere, meteoroids appear as shooting stars called meteors. Should the celestial stone survive its fiery flight to the surface of Earth, it is then called a meteorite. Freshly fallen meteorites display a smooth, dark surface called a *fusion crust*. This surface is created by melting as the stone falls through the atmosphere, but a meteorite's interior remains pristine, entirely unaffected by the fall.

Meteorites are named after the place where they fell. Thousands have been found worldwide, and a few have probably been found right in the area where you live. Although meteorites are fairly evenly spread across the surface of the world, an exceptionally large number have been found in Antarctica and the Sahara Desert in the past 20 years. These areas are so remarkably sparse in rocks, it makes finding dark-colored meteorites easy.

DEFINITIONS OF CELESTIAL BODIES

Asteroids—minor planets, most of which orbit mainly between Mars and Jupiter

Comets—compared to large, dirty snowballs, they are made of water, ammonia, methane, and carbon dioxide, which hold together small pieces of rocky materials

Coma—the nebulous head of a comet

Meteoroid—a small piece of debris in inter-planetary space

Meteor—a meteoroid that has entered Earth's atmosphere and appears as a "shooting star"

Meteorites—remains of meteoroids that actually strike Earth's surface

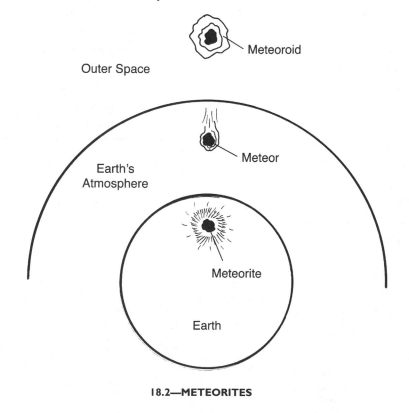

Outer Space

Meteoroid

Earth's Atmosphere

Meteor

Meteorite

Earth

18.2—METEORITES

Falling Stones

On April 26, 1803, a large fireball burst over the skies of Orne, France. More than 2000 stony meteorite fragments then rained down over the city. This incident established, without doubt, that stones could fall from space to Earth.

Since then, there have been many documented meteorite hits. In 1954, a celestial stone fell through the roof of a house in Sylacauga, Alabama, striking a woman who was sleeping on a sofa in the living room. Mrs. Hulitt Hodges received a painful "astroblem" (big bruise). Ironically, her home was located across the road from the Comet Drive-In Theater.

A meteorite hit a mailbox in Georgia in 1984, injured a child in Uganda, Africa, in 1992, and hit a car in Peekskill, New York, in 1992. Your chances of being hit by a meteorite are pretty slim, but the reality is that it has happened to people before, and we can expect it to happen again.

Origin of Meteorites

There are three main classes of meteorites—those that are rich in metals (nickel and iron), those that are made of stony material, and those that are made of both metallic and stony substances. These classes of meteorites may represent portions of a "differentiated" or layered minor planet or asteroid. Iron meteorites come from the cores of asteroids where iron accumulated when the minor planet was in a molten state. Since meteorites come from asteroids, or minor planets, they can consist of any part of the asteroid. Stony-iron meteorites are mixtures of stone and iron that settled at the core-mantle boundary. Some varieties of stony meteorites represent the upper part or crust of an asteroid.

COMPONENTS OF METEORITES

Like their terrestrial counterparts, meteorites and rocks are both composed of various proportions of minerals. The six most common meteorite minerals are:
- Nickel-iron—alloys kamacite and taenite common in all meteorites
- Pyroxene—silicate found in all stony meteorites and in some stony-iron meteorites
- Olivine—iron-magnesium silicate found in all stony and stony-iron meteorites
- Magnetite—iron oxide common in some stony meteorites and most fusion crusts
- Troilite—iron sulfide found in all meteorites in various amounts
- Serpentine—water-bearing silicate found in carbonaceous chondrites

A technique called *reflectance spectroscopy* has been used to link some meteorites to specific asteroids. A reflectance spectrometer can measure and quantify how much light of different colors or wavelengths is reflected from an asteroid. This reflectance data provides clues to the chemical nature of an asteroid and allows it to be linked, in some cases, to a class of meteorite.

About two dozen interesting meteorites have been recovered whose chemical composition is different from all other meteorites. Analysis of their age and physical characteristics suggests Mars is likely their source. These specimens were probably formed on Mars approximately 1.3 billion years ago. These meteorites belong to a group called SNC (pronounced *snick*). SNC is an acronym for the first three known falls of Martian meteorites: Shergotty, India; Nakhla, Egypt; and Chassigny, France.

Stony Meteorites

Stony meteorites are mostly rocky in composition and are about one and a half times heavier than ordinary igneous rocks. When they are cut and polished, bright flecks of metal are usually observed in a stony matrix. This matrix is composed mostly of the minerals olivine, plagioclase, and pyroxene.

There are two major types of stony meteorites: *chondrites* (which contain *chondrules*—small, rounded granules of some mineral, usually pyroxene and olivine) and *achondrites* (which do not contain chondrules).

Chondrites have the same basic chemistry as the Sun, except for the gases. They also contain some of the first materials to condense out of the cloud of dust and gas from which the Sun and planets formed.

Carbonaceous chondrites, an important variation in this group, show little evidence of heating or thermal alteration and probably form in the outer (and cooler) areas of the asteroid belt. Temperatures there are low enough to allow claylike minerals with water in their crystal structure to form.

Achondrites are stony meteorites that do not contain chondrules. These stones have been melted and are more like terrestrial igneous rocks than other meteorites. Achondrites are believed to be volcanic rocks from the asteroid belt.

Iron Meteorites

Meteorites are beautiful stones to behold. If an iron meteorite is cut open and the inside is polished smooth and treated with nitric acid, crystals of metal can be seen forming lines or patterns in a distinctive geometry.

These patterns are called *Widmanstatten figures* after a Viennese scientist who first described them in 1808. These patterns form as a result of slow cooling of the original body from which the meteorite came. Slow cooling, on the order of one to ten degrees per million years, allows the growth of large crystals, as you recall from Chapter 1.

Stony-Iron Meteorites

Stony-iron meteorites are mixtures of stone and metal. They are composed of about 50 percent nickel-iron and 50 percent silicate minerals. Certainly, a review of the materials within meteorites sounds much like the early geology sections of this book, and it should. The planets and asteroids have the same origins, and although atmospheres, temperatures, and other characteristics differ radically, the basic materials comprising the celestial bodies of the solar system are much the same.

SUMMARY

Earth science is the study of the rocks, oceans, and atmosphere that make up our planet. The significance of this field is that it synthesizes many seemingly disconnected fields of science. As we have learned, the Earth's surface, seas, and air all interact in such a way as to produce the world that we live in. No one process exists without the impact of the others.

Geology is the study of the physical nature of Earth. Minerals are the basic building blocks of igneous, metamorphic, and sedimentary rocks. The concept of plate tectonics, describing how lithospheric plates interact and move, has revolutionized the study of geology. Geological processes, ranging from fiery volcanism to the slow movement of glacial ice, have sculpted the surface of our world. Earth is a very ancient place, having a geological history reaching back to the formation of the solar system some 4.6 billion years ago.

An ocean of water covers more than three-quarters of Earth. Its origin is tied to the early history of our geologically active planet. The oceans are dynamic and teeming with life. The motions of these waters are primarily governed by an interaction with the winds of the atmosphere. Earth's atmosphere is a thin envelope of gas, extending from the surface to about 160 km above. Its role in shielding the surface from harmful solar and cosmic radiation is vital to the maintenance of the biological payload of the planet.

As we have learned, Earth science is more than just the study of our planet. Principles learned about geology, oceanography, and meteorology can be applied to other worlds found throughout the solar system. Only in recent times have astronomers developed techniques that have led to the discovery of planets orbiting about other stars. As we continue to learn more about these distant worlds, the lessons of earth science learned on our small planet will surely apply elsewhere in the cosmos.

In addition to the terrestrial and jovian planets, interplanetary space is filled with asteroids and comets. Meteorites, the chunks of rock that actually land on the surface of the Earth, are a wonderful resource for Earth scientists to learn about the connections between the solar system and the origin of our world.

GLOSSARY

aa lava
basaltic lava flow with a rough, jagged texture.

abyssal hills
mounds on the seafloor that average about 200 meters tall and are by volume the most ubiquitous topographic feature found on our planet

abyssal plains
the part of the seafloor that is the flattest geographic feature on the surface of our planet

achondrites
stony meteorites that do not contain chondrules

acoustic tomography
process used to study the three-dimensional flow of water

active continental margin
the "leading edge" of a continent, as it is the area where a plate of continental crust collides with an oceanic plate

adiabatic
change in temperature with expansion or contraction of gases

aeolian process
the transformation of Earth's surface by wind

aerosols
small particles lifted into the air

air mass
a body of air composed of similar temperatures and humidity

air–sea interface
the place where the seawater comes into first contact with the atmosphere

albedo
term given to describe an object's ability to reflect light

alluvial fans
fan-shaped deposits formed by a stream as it issues from a ravine onto a plain

altimeter
a device used to precisely measure elevation variation on a surface

altocumulus
clumps of fluffy white clouds at a medium altitude

altostratus
layers of stratified gray to white clouds that cover most of the sky, and often indicate drizzle or light snow

amplitude
how far a wave moves the water above or below sea level, which is equal to one-half the wave height

aneroid barometer
device to measure air pressure that uses no liquid

angular unconformity
when an overlying sedimentary rock layer is at some angle to the layer beneath

anions
negatively charged atoms

anticline
a fold that shows signs of having been bent upward so that two limbs of the fold aim downward away from the hinge of the fold

anticyclone
areas of high pressure within the atmosphere where surface wind spirals outward away from the center

aphanitic
igneous rock with crystals too small to be seen with the naked eye

aquaculture
fish farming

archipelago
a string of often-volcanic islands, reefs, and shoals that form along ocean ridges

asteroid
literally, "little star;" irregular masses of rock and metal that range in size from small mountains to almost 300 miles across

asthenosphere
a molten area within Earth at a depth of about 700 km

atmosphere
an envelope of gases that surrounds the surface of a planet

atmosphere (atm)
a reading of 1013.2 mb equals one atmosphere

atolls
continuous or broken rings of coral reef surrounding a central lagoon

aurora australis
a bright display of ever-changing light in the Southern Hemisphere caused by solar radiation interacting with the upper atmosphere

aurora borealis
a bright display of ever-changing light in the Northern Hemisphere caused by solar radiation interacting with the upper atmosphere

backshore
part of the beach farthest from the sea

ballistic trajectory
the path of a projectile or other moving body through space in free flight

barchan dune
common dune that is crescent-shaped with horns aimed downwind

barogarph
a metal chamber holding a vacuum that is sensitive to air pressure changes

barometer
instrument used to measure air pressure

barometric pressure
the pressure of the air at ground level

barrier islands
accumulations composed of low ridges of sand found parallel to the shoreline

basaltic lavas
a very fluid type of volcanic flow

batholiths
large magma bodies that solidified beneath the surface of Earth

bathythermography
the study of thermal effects on sound waves in seawater

beach drift
sand (or any sediment) on the beach generally moves in a zigzag manner

beach nourishment
the periodic addition of sand to the beach

bed forms
evidence of mud cracks, ripples, or rain drop imprints when layers of sedimentary rock are separated

bed load
sediment that is carried smoothly and evenly across the bottom of the streambed

beds
the thickest strata of sedimentary rocks

belts
the dark-colored bands that run around Jupiter's middle, above and below the equatorial belt

Benioff zones
narrow areas beneath a seafloor trench where earthquakes occur

biogenic sedimentary rock
rocks formed from the remains of organisms that built their shells and bones from ions within seawater

biogenic sedimentation
when living organisms take ions from seawater and use them to build shells and bones; when these organisms die, they form biogenic sedimentary rock

body waves
seismic waves that travel in all directions through the interior of Earth

bottomset beds
as a dune rolls over itself, the topset beds are created by sand from the bottomset beds

boundary currents
currents that flow parallel to the equator eventually encounter continents and are then deflected either north or south

Bowen's Reaction Series
a chart that models the mineralogy of igneous rocks

brines
pockets of salty liquids within sea ice

burial metamorphism
rock that is altered by the weight of overlying rock

C-type asteroid
asteroids that are carbonaceous

calcareous
containing or characteristic of calcium carbonate, calcium, or limestone

caldera
a crater that is enlarged by the collapse of the top of the volcano

capillary waves
the smallest waves that have wavelengths of less than 1.75 cm and a period of less than 0.1 second

carbon-14 dating
the technique of using radiocarbon to date recent rocks or events

carbonaceous chondrites
stony meteorites that contain chondrules plus water

carbonates
a group of minerals that have the carbonate ion (CO_3) bound with a cation

Carboniferous
a period of the Paleozoic era

Cassini division
the largest of the gaps between the rings of Saturn; named for Italian astronomer and mathematician Giovanni Cassini (1625–1712)

cataclastic metamorphism
small-scale deformation of rock, for instance, along a fault boundary

cations
positively charged atoms

Cenozoic era
the time from 66 million years ago to the present time

chemical oceanography
study of the gases and solids dissolved in the ocean

chemical sedimentation
a process that forms nonclastic sedimentary rocks

chevron feature
an odd, bright V-shaped feature that stands out against a heavily cratered terrain of Miranda, one of the moons of Uranus

chondrites
stony meteorites that contain chondrules

chondrules
small, rounded granules of some mineral, usually pyroxene or olivine

cinder cones
volcano made up of pyroclastic deposits with rubble-laden, steep slopes and a central pit

cirques glaciers
glaciers that occupy only a small section of a mountain

cirrocumulus
puffy white masses of clouds consisting of ice crystals found high in the atmosphere

cirrostratus
sheets or layers of clouds consisting of ice crystals found high in the atmosphere

cirrus
clouds of white patches of thin sheets at high altitude

clastic sedimentary rocks
rocks formed from the process of clastic sedimentation

clastic sedimentation
when particles suspended and transported by water or wind are deposited

cleavage
a mineral's internal arrangement of atoms, which cause a mineral to break in a specific way

clouds
small droplets of water and ice crystals that aggregate, or clump together, within the atmosphere

cloud-to-ground lightning
a stream of electrons that travels from the cloud to the ground as a bolt of lightning

coccolithophores
the hard remains of one-celled plants

cold front
boundary formed when cooler air replaces an area once occupied by warm air

color
an identifying characteristic of minerals

coma
a diffused and gaseous envelope around the nucleus of a comet formed as a comet nears the Sun and the ices in the nucleus begin to vaporize or sublimate

comet nuclei
the central core of a comet

complex craters
craters with central peaks and terraced walls, between 10 and 100 km in diameter

composite cones
volcanoes that consist of a combination of pyroclastic materials and lava

compressional waves
P waves, like sound waves, that travel by the compression and subsequent expansion of the material through which they pass

condensation
when water vapor returns to a liquid, such as when it rains

condensation nuclei
bits of particular matter that serve as surfaces on which water vapor condenses

conglomerates
clastic sedimentary rocks composed of pebbles or larger-sized grains

contact metamorphism
country rock that is inundated by an igneous magma

continental air mass
an air mass produced over the land

continental break
marks the location of an ancient shore when sea level was at its very lowest point

continental crust
lighter felsic minerals and rock that make up Earth's surface

continental drift
the theory that continents were actually moving across the face of Earth

continental margin
area where a continental landmass meets the ocean floor; it consists of the continental shelf, the continental slope, and the continental rise

continental rise
area where sediments have found their way far from the continent and have settled to make a very gentle wedge or rise

continental shelf
area where the continent itself is submerged beneath the ocean waters

continental slope
a sharp drop where the water depth increases dramatically over a short distance

contour lines
features of a topographical map that connect points of equal elevation

convection
transference of heat by circulation of heated parts of a liquid

convection cell
the transfer of heat by the movement of a mass or substance

convergent plate boundaries
created by the crashing or crunching together of different lithospheric plates

coral reefs
massive structures made of limestone and invertebrates called coral polyps

Coriolis effect
the rotation of Earth causes a moving object to shift direction

Coriolis force
an inertial force used by scientists and mathematicians to describe the motion of bodies in a rotating frame of reference

country rock
original, buried rock mass into which magma can intrude

covalent bond
when atoms with similar charges share electrons in order to be stable

crater
a cavity formed on the surface of a planet when meteorites or chunks of space rock strike it

crest
the highest point of a wave

Cretaceous
period of the Mesozoic era and time during which dinosaurs became extinct, also first flowering plants took hold

crevasses
large cracks that form in the top of a glacier

crosscutting relationships
a principle to explain why rocks of different ages are found together, such as when a fault or an igneous dike cuts across a layer of rocks, it must be younger than the sediments through which it cuts

crystal
a mineral that has grown in an orderly and symmetrical manner

crystal habit
the shape of minerals

crystallography
the formal study of minerals

cumulonimbus
towering clouds found at all levels of elevation that are associated with bad weather

cumulus
clouds that are often puffy, white, and usually occur as individual or isolated groups

cup anemometer
a device with three cups on an axle that spins at a rate proportional to wind speed

Curie temperature
magnetic grains of molten lava become aligned with a distinctive north–south polarity at 580°C

cyanobacteria
an aquatic species of photosynthetic bacteria that contains chlorophyll

cyclone
low-pressure zone within the atmosphere where surface wind spirals in toward the center

cyclosilicates
silica tetrahedra that are linked in a ringlike structure

decay constant
interval based on natural radioactive decay of certain elements; for example, when parent atoms of uranium are converted into daughter atoms of lead over a fixed interval of time

deep zone
the deepest ocean waters

deltas
fan-shaped deposits of sediment accumulating at the mouth of a river

dendritic
a channel that branches out, like a stream or a tree limb

deposition
the reverse of sublimation, when a vapor is changed to a solid

depositional history
evidence that rocks have been deposited at different times, or that there are layers within rocks

desert pavement
pebbles and cobbles left behind by wind

detritus
sediments that are the small pieces of rocks and minerals formed from erosion by water and wind

Devonian
a period of the Paleozoic era during which vertebrates called amphibians took to land

dew point
the temperature to which a particle of air would have to be cooled in order to reach saturation

differentiation
process of density sorting

dikes
plutons inclined toward the inclosing rock

disconformity
a surface that separated two layers of sedimentary rocks

distributaries
small branching channels that cut across a delta

distributary channels
passages of flowing water that carve their way to the sea

divergent plate boundary
new material is formed at spreading centers and the two lithospheric plates then make an oceanic ridge

divides
topographic highlands that isolate streams from one another

doldrums
a region of the ocean near the equator between the two belts of trade winds

Doppler effect
a change in the observed frequency of a wave, as of sound or light, occurring when the source or observer is in motion relative to one another

Doppler radar
technology that allows detection of the initial formation and subsequent development of an intense rotating storm system

drumlins
linear mounds of material sculpted by ice sheet glaciers

dust tail
part of a comet that is formed when dust particles are pushed out of the coma; it is noticeably curved, and usually yellow, the color of reflected sunlight

earthquakes
a vibration or movement of part of Earth due to motion along a fault plain

earthy luster
minerals that look like broken brick or dry soil

ebb currents
tides produce very long waves that are observed as the periodic fall in water at the beach

ebb tide
the period during which the tide recedes from the beach boundary

ejecta
the material that is thrown outward from the target surface during the formation of a crater

ejecta blanket
a circular deposit formed around a crater when ejecta is thrown outward from the surface of a planet during the formation of a crater

Ekman spiral
although the speed of the current lessens with depth, the overall result is that a spiral current is formed as it travels deeper into the sea

electrostatic attraction
the attraction between a proton and electron that causes particles of matter to adhere to one another

emergent coast
an area in which land formerly under water has recently been placed above sea level, either by uplift of the land or by a drop in sea level

eons
two very long segments of time in Earth's history: Precambrian and Phanerozoic

epicenter
the point on Earth's surface from which the earthquake waves seem to go out

equatorial low
a pressure zone associated with ubiquitous precipitation, defined by rising air near the equator

eras
divisions of eons

erratics
rocks of relatively large size moved from their origins by glaciers

estuary
a partially enclosed area that fills with oceanic waters at high tide and is commonly at the end of rivers where they meet the sea

evaporates
nonclastic sedimentary rock created by the evaporation of seawater within an enclosed basin

evaporation
the process through which water converts from a liquid to a gas, or water vapor

eye
the relatively calm center of a hurricane

eye wall
a circle of cumulonimbus clouds that forms a ring at the center of a hurricane

fault
any break, with evidence of displacement, that occurs within a brittle rock unit

faunal succession
principle stating that fossils are deposited in a logical order, with new species replacing older species

felsic
rocks that are light in color and are composed chiefly of minerals enriched in the elements silicon and aluminum

Ferrell cell
high-pressure zones at 30° latitude that circulate air poleward until a low-pressure zone lifts the air at about 60° latitude in both hemispheres

fetch
the distance over which the wind blows to create a wave

fire fountain
a curtain of flaming lava

fission track dating
method of dating rocks

fissures
vents in the earth through which lava erupts

fjord glaciers
deep valleys that are cut when valley glaciers reach the coastline

flood basalts
extensive lava flows

flood currents
tides can be thought of as very long period waves that are observed as the periodic rise in water at the beach

flood tides
the period during which the sea flows as far as possible onto the land

floodplain deposits
extensive flat sediment layers caused by flooding rivers

fluorocarbons
human-made, ozone-depleting gases

fluvial processes
the erosion and transport of sediment by water

flyby
an exploratory type of mission where the spacecraft simply flies past the target and obtains a first look

focus
the point from which seismic waves go out

fog
a cloud that extends to the ground

foliation
minerals aligned in one direction that cause rock to break along parallel sheets

footwall block
the block below a fault

foraminifers
shells from tiny one-celled animals or marine snails

foreset beds
sand rolls down the leading edge, or steep slope, to create this aspect of a dune

foreshore
the beach region upon which the daily tides oscillate

forked lightning
when a bolt of lightning takes on the appearance of a branching network

formation
key unit of measure in rock stratigraphy

fractional crystallization
a process that magma bodies go through as they work toward Earth's surface

fracture
minerals with little difference in the strength of chemical bonds from one part of the mineral to another will break along rough surfaces

free oxygen
oxygen in the O_2 state, or oxygen that is not bound to rocks

front
atmospheric phenomenon created at the boundary between two different air masses

frost wedging
the process of freezing and subsequent thawing of ice that can tear rocks apart

Fujita scale
used to compare the force by which destructive tornadoes are classified

funnel cloud
the air enters the low-pressure column of a tornado, water condenses out, forming a cloudy funnel

gas tail
part of the tail of a comet that is made up of gas molecules; it is straighter than the dust tail

gelifluction
the process of frozen soil moving downslope during the summer

gemstone
any of various minerals highly prized for beauty, durability, and rarity

geostrophic currents
the result of a balance between the wind and the Coriolis force

geostrophic winds
winds that move parallel to straight isobars

glacial moraines
mounds of till

glaciation
a thick mass of ice showing signs of former flow

glaciation process
the freezing, melting, and movement of ice, along with accumulated debris

glaciers
masses of recrystallized snow from which all air has been removed

glaze
frozen precipitation that forms when rain freezes on contact with the ground or with other objects

gneissic banding
high grade metamorphic rock with bands of pyroxene and hornblende

Gondwanaland
the southern continent that separated from Pangaea, including Australia, Africa, South American, India, New Zealand, and Madagascar

grabens
valleys formed by the downward displacement of a fault-bounded rock

graupel
frozen precipitation, with diameters up to 5.0 mm, fall as a soft and mushy ice

gravity waves
waves with periods up to five minutes

Great Red Spot
Jupiter's trademark sign, believed to be a hurricane that has been blowing for at least 350 years; it is larger than Earth

greenhouse effect
process in which solar radiation is trapped within Earth's atmosphere causing global warming

groins
barriers that trap sand on a coastline

Gulf Stream
an ocean current that begins near the equator

guyot
an eroded seamount that is subsurface

gyre
a large oceanic current marked by a circular rotating body of water

Hadley cell
rising air at the equator that moves north and south until it begins to sink at about 30° latitude

hail
irregular to rounded clumps of hard ice larger than 5.0 mm that falls as frozen precipitation

hair hygrometer
common instrument used to measure humidity but less accurate than the psychrometer

halides
gaseous elements (halogens), like chlorine and fluorine

haloclines
oceanic layers having marked changes in salinity

hanging wall block
the block above a fault

hardness
one of the physical properties of minerals

heavy bombardment
a period of intense strikes by meteorites and asteroids during an early epoch of the solar system

hexagonal crystals
crystals with four crystallographic axes of equal length at angles of 120°

high-grade metamorphic rock
rocks produced when temperatures are above 300°C and pressures are high

humidity
amount of water vapor present within the atmosphere

hurricane
a tropical cyclonic storm having winds in excess of 119 km per hour

hydrogen bond
when water molecules are close together, their positive and negative areas are attracted to the oppositely charged areas of nearby molecules

hydrogenetic deposits
minerals that form by precipitation from seawater

hydrothermal deposits
mineral deposits formed in association with underwater vents of mineral-rich hot water

ice cap
a glacier, but one that is formed on an extensive area of relatively level land

ice sheet glaciers
glaciers that cover significant portions of a continent

ice shelve
glaciers that rest on top of seawater

igneous rocks
rocks produced from the crystallization of an assemblage of minerals from magma

impact basin
the largest classification of craters; colossal holes with multiple-ringed mountains exceeding 100 km in diameter

impact cratering
the process by which holes on the surfaces of terrestrial worlds are caused by the fall of meteorites or even asteroids from space

inert argon
a minor gas making up one percent of atmospheric gasses

inosilicates
chains of silica tetrahedra

inshore
an area where waves begin to pile up and break seaward from the foreshore

intercloud lightning
lightning that moves between two oppositely charged clouds

intermediate
a rock composition that falls somewhere between felsic and mafic and is between 55% and 65% silica

intracloud lightning
lightning that moves between oppositely charged areas of the same cloud

intrusive
rock that crystallizes into masses prior to reaching Earth's surface

invertebrates
organisms with no backbone

ionic bond
when two ions of opposite charge are attached

ionosphere
another name for the thermosphere, where atoms experience the loss or gain of electrons and thus have an electrical charge

ions
atoms with an unequal charge because of a gain or loss of electrons

island arc
arc-shaped band of volcanic islands produced by the melting of rock and sediments along a sub-duction zone

isobars
lines of equal pressure on a map or chart

isometric crystals
crystals with faces that are square or triangular

isotope
variations of a given element caused by varying numbers of neutrons.

jetties
pairs of structures that extend into the ocean at the entrance to a harbor or river

jovian planets
the outer, Jupiter-like planets—these include Jupiter, Saturn, Uranus, and Neptune; these are low-density objects with gaseous atmospheres and mostly liquid interiors

Jurassic
period of the Mesozoic era when dinosaurs flourished

Kuiper Belt
icy asteroid belt comprised of hundreds of tiny blocks of ice found in the same orbit around the Sun as Pluto.

lahar
a muddy volcanic flow created by volcanism and melting of mountainous ice or snow

laminar flow
water flowing in parallel layers

laminations
layers of sedimentary rocks of less than 1 cm in thickness

lander
an exploratory type of mission where the space-craft makes a soft landing at a predetermined site, occasionally being equipped with a mobile rover that can venture away from the initial landing base

lapilli
volcanic stones no larger than a walnut

lateral continuity
theory that layered sediments extend in a lateral fashion in all directions from one point

Laurasia
one of the first major continents to separate from Pangaea (North America, Europe, and Asia)

leading edge
top of the steepest slope of a sand dune

levees
the accumulation of sediment that forms banks, confining a river to a channel

lightning
an intense electrical charge released from cumu-lonimbus clouds

linear dunes
sand dunes with the long axis more or less parallel to the prevailing wind direction

lithification
pressure of accumulated layers of sedimentation causes minerals to be cemented between the grains of rock

lithosphere
rigid plates of Earth's crust

lithospheric plates
the rigid outer shell of Earth

longshore current
when waves break at an oblique angle to the shore, current moves parallel to the coast

low-grade metamorphic rock
rocks formed when the temperatures are between 200°C and 300°C and pressures are relatively low

lunar maria
younger terrains on the surface of our Moon composed of dark basaltic lava flows; the lowlands of the surface, within colossal impact basins.

luster
the way a surface of a mineral reflects light

M–type asteroid
asteroids that are composed of metal-rich silicates or perhaps pure metal

mafic
igneous rocks that are gray to black in color and are made up of mostly silicate minerals with magnesium and iron

magma
subsurface molten rock

mantle
the thick intermediate layer between the core and Earth's crust

marine biology
study of the nature and distribution of marine life

marine engineering
the design and construction of structures used in or on the ocean

marine geology
focuses on the study of the Earth's crust and composition covered by water

maritime air mass
an air mass produced over the sea

mass wasting
a surface-modifying process caused by gravity

mercury barometer
a simple instrument consisting of a column of mercury within a pan used to measure atmospheric pressure

mesopause
the upper part or boundary of the mesosphere

mesosphere
atmospheric layer above the stratopause extending upward to 80 km

Mesozoic
the era of time from 245 to 66 million years ago

metallic hydrogen
a region of very dense hydrogen that exists in a liquid state, but because of the high pressure it has the characteristics of some metals

metamorphic rocks
rocks that are changed after being subjected to extreme pressures and temperatures

meteorites
a fragment of a meteor that has fallen to Earth

meteoroids
small debris in interplanetary space

meteorologists
scientists who study weather phenomena

meteorology
the science that deals with the phenomena of the atmosphere

meteors
material that may pass through our atmosphere and appear as a "shooting star"

midoceanic ridges
continuous mountainous ridges on the floor of all the major ocean basins

millibars (mb)
the metric measure for pressure

mineral
naturally occurring, inorganic, solid substance with a specific composition and arrangement of atoms

Mississippian
geologic period of time marked by great coal swamps

Mohs' Hardness Scale
a scale measuring ten variations of hardness in minerals

monocline
a fold that occurs when two limbs are still horizontal and the rock has been pushed upward

monoclinic crystals
prisms, domes, and pyramids with axes of unequal lengths, and only two perpendicular to each other

mountain glaciers
glaciers that blanket the peaks of tall mountains

mudflows
a very fluid type of volcanic flow

native element
when a single type of atom occurs alone or does not bond with other atoms, making a mineral

neap tides
if the Sun and Moon are not aligned exactly with Earth—at the first and third quarter phases of the Moon, when the Sun and Moon are at right angles and each offsets the influence of the other—then there is not such a dramatic difference between high and low tide

Neptunists
people who believed that the great Biblical flood created all sedimentary rocks

nimbostratus
clouds thick enough to block the Sun entirely and usually tied to continuously falling rain or snow that reaches the ground

nonclastic sedimentary rocks
rocks formed by chemical precipitation from water in a process called chemical sedimentation

nonconformity
an unconformity separating igneous and/or metamorphic rocks from overlying sediments

normal fault
the hanging wall is shifted downward on the footwall block and horizontal extensional stress on the rock unit pulls the block apart

nuee ardente
a volcanic eruption of glowing ash and rock fragments

occluded front
occurs when a cold front surpasses or overruns a warm front

oceanic crust
mafic materials and rock like basalt that makes up Earth's surface beneath ocean basins

oceanic trench
a linear trench on the sea floor where dense oceanic crust is sliding into the asthenosphere

oceanography
the study of the chemical, physical, biological, and geological aspects of the oceanic world

offshore
place where sediment can accumulate seaward of breaking waves

ooze
particles of plants, shells, teeth, and bones covering the seafloor

orbital resonance
a phenomena that occurs when two orbiting bodies have periods of revolution that are in a simple integer ratio so that they exert a regular gravitational influence on each other; may serve to destabilize one of the orbits

orbiter
an exploratory type of mission where the spacecraft circles the planet like a satellite in order to acquire information over a longer period of time

Ordovician
a period of the Paleozoic era during which insects and algae got a foothold on land

ore
a metal-bearing mineral or rock

orientation
direction of crystallographic axes

orthorhombic crystals
pyramid-shaped crystals, with angles of unequal lengths intersecting at 90°

osmosis
movement of a solvent through a semipermeable membrane into a solution of higher solute concentration that tends to equalize the two

outgassing
the process by which gases, including water vapor, are released from the mantle and vented out from beneath the Earth's surface through volcanoes

oxbow lakes
isolated lakes forming in a main river channel

oxidation
free particles of oxygen combine with rocks or elements to form oxides

oxides
the combination of one or more metallic elements with an oxygen ion

ozone
a molecule of oxygen containing three oxygen atoms (O_3)

P waves
See compressional waves

pahoehoe lava
volcanic flow with a smooth surface texture

paleo-coasts
terraces or benchlike platforms that marked the position of the original coastline

Paleozoic
the era of time from 570 to 245 million years ago

Pangaea
a single giant landmass comprised of all Earth's continents, estimated to be in existence about 250 million years ago

parabolic dune
similar to the barchan dune, but with crescents oriented upwind

passive continental margin
margin characterized by minimal tectonic activity

pearly luster
minerals with the surface appearance of pearls

pegmatitic
coarse-grained texture in a rock, with mineral grains exceeding 2 cm in diameter

Pennsylvanian
period during which first reptiles appeared

period
the amount of time it takes a wave to pass a specific point

period
key unit of measure in time stratigraphy

periodic table
organization of elements, all composed of similar atoms, on one chart

permafrost
rock or soil that remains at or below 0°C for two or more years

Permian
a period of the Paleozoic Era

phaneritic
rocks with crystals large enough to discern with the naked eye

Phanerozoic
the eon of time from 570 million years ago to the present

photosynthesis
the process by which plants turn carbon dioxide into oxygen

phyllosilicates
when chains of silica tetrahedra are linked in sheets

physical oceanography
study of waves, currents, and climates

phytoplankton
a kind of photosynthetic plant found in saltwater

piedmont glaciers
glaciers that extend from the flanks of the mountain onto the surrounding lowlands

pillow lava
volcanic flow that is smooth, bulbous-looking, and occurs underwater

piloted mission
an exploratory type of mission that is manned; the culmination in planetary exploration happens when humans actually set foot on another world

pixels
picture elements into which digital cameras divide an image; the more pixels included in the image, the greater the detail that can be rendered by the camera

placer mineral deposits
minerals, because of their weight, settle at the bottom of a stream bed

planetary science
the study that applies the principles of Earth science to the study of the solar system

planetesimal
any small body thought to have orbited the Sun during the formation of the planets

plungers
waves that break over a short distance and crash abruptly onto the beach

plutonic
igneous rocks that crystallize before reaching the surface of Earth

Plutonists
scholars who believed that all rocks were of an igneous origin, formed of molten magma

plutons
volcanic materials that solidify underground

point bars
sediment accumulated on the inner portion of a channel, where velocity is low

polar air mass
air masses formed at colder, high latitudes

polar cell
characterized by a high-pressure down flow of air at the poles and a low-pressure up flow of air at 60° latitude

polar easterlies
easterly airflow situated at about 50° to 60° north and south of the equator

polar high
high-latitude regions where dry cold air sinks toward the surface

porphyritic
igneous rock characterized by large crystals in a matrix or groundmass of smaller crystals

Precambrian
the time from the formation of the planet until 570 million years ago

precipitation
any form of water—such as rain, snow, sleet, or hail—that falls to Earth's surface

preferred orientation
the layers of minerals, regardless of type, are all parallel

pressure gradient
a change in pressure over a given distance

prevailing westerlies
a steady set of winds that flow from the west

probes
unmanned spacecraft that are sent into orbit around a specific planet or moon, equipped with scientific instruments that can send back all sorts of specific information

psychrometer
tool consisting of two identical thermometers mounted side by side, which can measure both dew point and relative humidity

pycnocline zone
stable layer of water that resides beneath the surface zone

pyroclastic
igneous rocks formed when volcanic rock fragments and ash are welded together from intense heat

pyroclastic flows
solid debris from a volcanic flow

radioactive age dating
See radiometric age dating

radioactive half-life
the amount of time required for one-half of the parent atoms to be converted to daughter atoms

radiometric age dating
technique for dating rocks based on the proportion of original material to decay products

rain gauge
instrument used to measure the amount of rainfall

reflectance spectrometer
a device that works by measuring the amount of sunlight reflected from a target at different wavelengths to determine the mineralogy of a far celestial object

reflectance spectroscopy
technique used to link some meteorites to specific asteroids, by means of a reflectance spectrometer

regional metamorphism
rock that is shaped by compressional stresses on a large scale

regolith
unconsolidated layer of sediment that blankets a terrestrial planet's surface

relative age dating
placing rock units into a chronological sequence

relative humidity
the moisture content of air; the ratio of the amount of water vapor in the air at a specific temperature to the maximum amount the air could hold at that temperature, expressed as a percent

reservoirs
caverns of melted rock deep inside Earth

retrograde
the planet spins in such a way that it is rotating backwards

reverse fault
the hanging wall block is pushed upward, relative to the footwall, and horizontal compressional stress is applied to the rock unit, squeezing the blocks together

Richter scale
an instrument designed to measure the intensity of an earthquake

rift
the sinking of the rock into the asthenosphere, which forms a central valley

rime
a deposit of ice that freezes out of the air onto a surface that has a temperature below the freezing point of water

rip currents
gaps across an offshore sand bar can form "channels" that funnel water away from the shore; also called rip tides

Roche limit
zone of destructive tidal forces

rock cycle
the process linking igneous, metamorphic, and sedimentary rocks

rock flour
rocks carried by a glacier that are broken into tiny pieces and ground up

rock stratigraphy
strategy for considering or classifying layers of rock by relative age

rotation axis
the time that it takes a planet to complete one spin on its axis

S waves
See shear waves

S-type asteroid
asteroids that are stony to stony-iron in construction

Saffir-Simpson scale
scale used to classify hurricanes based on their potential to inflict damage

salinity
the measure of the saltiness of seawater; it is defined as the amount of material dissolved in 1 kg of seawater

salt marshes
flat coastal wetland ecosystems that are inundated for some period of time, usually at high tide, by seawater

saltation
sediment that is carried in short spurts, in a bouncing manner, across a river bottom or desert surface

sand dunes
wind-formed accumulations of sand

sandbars
areas in a river where sediment is deposited, where water speed decreases

sapping
a process by which the sublimation of permafrost functions as an erosive factor

scarp
a physical boundary that has been called the highland/lowland dichotomy; a line of cliffs that approximately separates the two hemispheres of Mars

schistosity
foliation of high-grade metamorphic rock characterized by the preferred orientation of mica minerals, biotite, and muscovite

scoria
the slag or clinkerlike remains of vesicular volcanic rock

sea arch
two caves, formed by wave erosion, that have merged together

sea stacks
mounds of material created when waves destroy a sea arch

seamount
underwater volcano

seas
smaller bodies of water that are partly closed off by land

seawalls
walls or embankments that help to prevent shoreline erosion

sediment
small pieces of rock

sedimentary rocks
rocks formed from the accumulation of sediment

seiche
a type of wave known as a standing wave

seismic energy
the energy created by an earthquake

seismic sea waves
rapidly moving ocean waves generated by earthquake activity

seismograph
graphs that allow scientists to show the distribution and intensity of seismic waves, energy waves released from a specific point within the earth at the time of an earthquake

seismology
study of the motion and effect of seismic waves

seismometer
a device that measures the distribution and intensity of seismic waves

shales
sedimentary clastic rocks made of very fine grained clay particles

shear waves (S waves)
a body wave that has velocity dependent on rock type and propagates by cutting rock in a direction perpendicular to the motion of the wave itself

sheet lightning
lightning that illuminates the sky and clouds in a flash of light

shepherd moons
small jovian moons that have influence on ring structure

shield volcano
a volcano produced from layers of lava flows

shoals
sandy elevations that form underwater

shoreline
boundary of the water–land interface

silicates
most abundant mineral group, or four oxygen ions surrounding a silicon ion

silicon tetrahedron
primary building block of the silicates with a net charge of -4, allowing it to bond with positive ions (or cations) to make different silicate minerals

silky luster
minerals with a surface that resembles silk

sills
tabular igneous bodies that intrude parallel to the preexisting rock

Silurian
a period of the Paleozoic era during which vertebrates called amphibians took to land

simple craters
craters less than about 5 km across with a bowl-shaped appearance

sinuous rille
a dry channel on the surface of our Moon formed by the collapse of a lava tube once it was drained and its roof could no longer support itself

slatey cleavage
a preferred orientation of minerals at some angle to the original bedding plane

sleet
mushy frozen raindrops between 0.5 and 5.0 millimeters

slip face
the side of a sand dune that is steeply inclined so grains slide down at a rate proportional to that at which they accumulate

SNC (pronounced snick)
an acronym for martian meteorites that fell in Shergotty, Nakhla, and Chassigny

snowline
the altitude at which snow doesn't melt

solar wind
a stream of particles from the Sun

space probes
unmanned spacecraft sent to a specific moon or planet

specific humidity
the ratio of the mass of water vapor to the mass of dry air in a chosen volume of moist air

spectrometer
a device that can determine the chemical composition of rock and soil

spillars
waves that break in a slow and even fashion

spits
elongated ridges of sand

spreading center
the center of a midocean ridge where new crust is created

spring tides
when the Sun and Moon are in line with Earth, either at times of a full or new moon, the added gravitational tug creates very high and alternately very low tides

star dunes
clumps of ridges, or dunes, with the overall look of a starfish

stationary front
occurs when two air masses collide, so that the flow is nearly parallel to the front produced between cold and warm air masses

storm surge
a rise in sea level associated with a storm or hurricane

straight rille
a linear depression believed to have been produced by faulting on the surface of the Moon

strata
individual layers of sedimentary rocks, based on color and texture

stratigraphy
study of layered sedimentary rocks

stratopause
the upper part or boundary of the stratosphere

stratosphere
atmospheric layer above the tropopause extending upward to 50 km

stratus
clouds found at the lowest elevation that completely cover the sky in layers or sheets

streak plate
an unglazed porcelain surface used to test color of minerals

stream channels
the beginning of all rivers, starting out as straight waterways

striations
the effect of a moving ice sheet, polishing and covering rocks with long parallel grooves

strike slip fault
the motion of the two blocks is horizontal due to the vertical orientation of the actual fault plane

subduction zones
the areas where lithospheric plates are pushed into the asthenosphere

sublimation
when ice skips the water phase and changes from a solid to a vapor

submarine canyon
a channel on the seafloor carved by swift currents

submergent coast
an area in which formerly dry land has been recently drowned, either by land subsidence or a rise in sea level

submersibles
vessels capable of operating or remaining underwater

subtropical high
a high pressure center that is formed when upper-level airflow begins to cool and fall toward the surface; located in the equatorial regions and characterized by hot and arid surface conditions

sulfates
minerals constructed of a sulfate anion (SO_4) combined with other elements

sulfides
formed when sulfur bonds to one or more metallic elements

surf zone
area of turbulent water where waves rush onto the shore

surface waves
seismic waves that travel across the surface of the planet away from the epicenter

surface zone
upper 100 meters of the ocean

swell
a group of waves that resemble rolling hills in the open ocean and move away from a storm in all directions

syncline
a fold that occurs when the once-horizontal layered rock has been folded so that it has been pushed downward with two limbs pointing upward

talus
an accumulation of rock debris at the bottom of a cliff

tectonism
fracturing and deformation of the planet's crust

terrace deposits
sediment that forms a flat river floodplain

terrestrial planets
the inner planets, relatively small in size and situated rather close to the Sun; often called the earthlike or rocky planets because of their solid surfaces; they include Mercury, Venus, Earth, and Mars

Tethys
the now-extinct sea that separated Laurasia and Gondwanaland

tetragonal crystals
crystals of a prism shape and two axes of equal length intersecting at 90°

thermoclines
layers of water with steep changes in temperatures

thermohaline currents
salty mass of water that sinks and drives deep-ocean circulation

thermosphere
last atmospheric layer above the mesopause, marked by a rise in temperature

thrust fault
a reverse fault that occurs when the fault space separating the upper and lower block creates an angle of less than 15°

thunder
sound waves generated by lightning

thunderstorms
atmospheric condition characterized by intense winds, hail, heavy rain, lightning, and thunder

tidal currents
the horizontal flow of water accompanying the rise and fall of tides

tidal flat
an area of marshland that is alternately exposed at low tide and submerged at high tide

tides
waves with periods larger than five minutes

till
small particles of unsorted glacial sediment

time stratigraphy
technique for classifying rocks based on the time at which layers of rock were deposited

tombolos
sand bars that connect the mainland to an island

topographic map
a rendering or drawing of a surface created with the precise distances from the surface and elevations that are gathered by an altimeter

topset bed
shallow slope of a dune that faces the wind

tornado
a small, very intense cyclonic storm characterized by high winds, usually produced along cold fronts in conjunction with a severe thunderstorm

trace precipitation
rainfall amounts of less than 0.025 cm

trade winds
movements of air that come from subtropical zones and flow toward the equator where they are deflected by the Coriolis effect

transform faults
two plate boundaries glide past each other, creating linear valleys

transform plate boundary
area between the offset ridges of transform faults

transverse dunes
dunes constructed so that the longest axis is perpendicular to the blowing wind

trellis
stream drainage patterns when tributaries meet the main channel at a 90° angle

Triassic
period at the beginning of the Mesozoic era when the first mammals are recorded

triclinic crystals
pinacoid-form crystal with three unequal crystallographic axes that occur at oblique angles to each other

tropical air mass
air masses formed in warmer, low latitudes

tropical depression
a low-pressure storm with winds that circulate with speeds between 23 and 39 miles per hour

tropopause
the upper edge of the lowest part of the atmosphere

troposphere
the lowest part of the atmosphere

trough
a low atmospheric pressure pocket

trough
the lowest point of a wave

tsunamis
large seismic sea waves

turbidity currents
a downslope movement of dense, sediment-laden water created when sand and mud on the continental shelf and slope are dislodged and thrown into suspension

turbulent flow
water that doesn't flow in parallel layers

twister
colloquial term used to refer to a tornado

typhoon
another name for a hurricane

ultramafic
a rock composed mainly of the minerals pyroxene and olivine

unconformity
period of erosion in rock layers indicating breaks in geologic time

undertow
a current underneath the surface current moving in the opposite direction

uniformitarianism
theory that states that all physical forces change Earth's structure consistently over time

unit cell
a regular pattern repeated throughout a mineral

upwelling
the process by which cold water from deeper layers replaces warmer surface water

valley glaciers
glaciers that can extend over a considerable portion of a mountain

ventifact
rock that is shaped or sculpted by wind

vertebrates
animals with a backbone

vesicular
rocks that are filled with holes, or vesicles

viscosity
resistance to flow

viscous
thick or slow-moving magmas or lava flows

vitreous luster
a mineral that looks like a piece of broken glass

volcanic neck
a column of rock marking the conduit of a volcano

volcanism
the process that occurs whenever molten rock reaches the surface of Earth

vortex
a rotating column of air that can reach from a cloud to the ground

warm front
the boundary where warm air moves in and displaces an area of once-cooler air

water–land interface
the boundary between coast and sea

wave frequency
number of waves passing a specific point each second (or hour)

wave height
the distance from the trough to the crest of a wave

wave-cut cliffs
structures formed by the undermining of the coastal land by the action of waves

wave-cut platforms
benchlike surfaces formed as a cliff erodes and scoops out part of the wall

wavelength
distance between a wave crest and the next crest, or from any point on a wave to the same point on the next wave

waves
disturbances in the sea that move across the ocean surface with distinct periods

weather vane
consists of a needle with a fin that always points into the direction from which wind blows

Wentworth scale
a scale used to determine the size of rocks

Widmanstatten figures
lines or patterns in a distinctive geometry formed by crystals of metal if an iron meteorite is cut open and the inside is polished smooth and treated with nitric acid; named after a Viennese scientist who first described them in 1808

wind vane
device that consists of a needle with a fin that always points into the direction from which wind blows (also called a weather vane)

wrinkle ridges
volcanic and/or tectonic processes creating creases in the surface of the Moon; these ridges might have originated when the mare surface was compressed

yardangs
boat-shaped mounds of consolidated sand

zap pits
microscopic impact craters on the surface of our moon

zones
the light-colored bands that are found in the atmospheres of the jovian planets

INDEX

A

Aa lava, 30-31
Absolute age dating, 45-47
Abyssal hills, 69
Abyssal plains, 66, 68-69
Acadia National Park, 76
Achondrites, 176
Acoustic tomography, 84
Active continental margin, 66
Adaptation, 108-109
Adiabatic temperature, 112
Aeolian processes, 36-39
Aerosols, 104, 106-107
Air. *See also* Atmosphere; Winds
    circulation of, 119
    masses, 128-129
    pressure, 105-106, 119-121
    strength of, 105
Air-surface interface, 59
Albedo, 165
Aleutian Islands, 27, 70
Algae, 77
Alluvial fans, 35
Altimeter, 144
Altitude, 105-106, 112, 114-115, 144
Altocumulus clouds, 113-114
Altostratus clouds, 113-114
Ammonites, 44
Amor asteroids, 171
Amplitude of oceanic wave, 90
Andaman Sea, 56
Aneroid barometers, 120-121
Angular unconformity, 45
Anions, 6
Anticline folds, 27
Anticyclones, 122
Apatite, 11
Aphanitic igneous rock texture, 15
Aquaculture, 61-62
Arabian plate, 22

Archipelago, 77
Arctic Ocean, 56
Argon, inert, 104
Aristotle, 55
Arkose, 19
Arthropods, 44
Asteroids, 170-171, 174
Asthenosphere, 26
Atlantic Ocean, 56, 69
Atmosphere. *See also* Air
    climactic differences and, 108-109
    composition of, 104-105
    creation of early, 101-103
    definition of, 101
    gases in, 59, 101-104
    greenhouse effect and, 106
    of Jupiter, 159-160
    layers of, 106-108
    of Neptune, 165-167
    origins of, 101-104
    pressure in, 105-106, 119-121
    of Saturn, 164
    structure of, 105-109
    summary of, 109
    temperature and, 112
    of Uranus, 165-167
    water in, 105
Atolls, 77-78
Atomic number, 6
Atoms, 5-7
Aurora australis, 107
Aurora borealis, 107

B

Backshore of beach, 75
Ballistic trajectory, 148
Barchan sand dunes, 38
Barite, 11
Barographs, 120-121
Barometers, 119-121

Barometric pressure, 119-121

Barrier islands, 76

Basalt, 14

Basaltic lava flows, 30-31, 74, 151

Basin floor of ocean, 68-69

Batholiths, 34

Bathythermography, 55

Beaches

    backshore, 75

    drift, 73-74

    erosion of, 78-79

    foreshore, 75

    inshore, 75

    nourishment, 79

    offshore, 75

    rocky, 74-75

    sandy, 74

    sediment on, 74

    zones of, 75

Becquerel, Henri, 46

Bed forms, 19-20

Bed load, 34

Belts of Jupiter, 160-161

Benioff, Hugo, 27

Benioff Zones, 27

Biogenic sedimentation, 19

Body oceanic waves, 24

Bottomset bed of sand dunes, 37-38

Boundary oceanic currents, 84-85

Bowen's Reaction Series, 16-17

Brachipods, 44

Brahmaputra River, 71

Brines, 58

Bryozoans, 44

Burial metamorphism, 17-18

C

Calcite, 13, 18

Calcium carbonate, 10, 59-60

Caldera, 32

Callisto (Galilean satellite), 162

Cambrian period, 48

Cameras for space probes, 144

Capillary oceanic waves, 90-91

Carbon-14 dating, 47

Carbonaceous chondrites, 176

Carbonates, 9-10, 59-60, 74

Carbon dioxide, 59, 71, 103-104, 106, 108

Caribbean Sea, 56

Caspian Sea, 57

Cassini division, 163

Cassini, Giovanni, 163

Cataclastic metamorphism, 17

Cations, 6

Celestial bodies

    asteroids, 170-171, 174

    comets, 171-174

    heavy bombardment of, 151

    meteorites and meteors, 173-176

    summary of, 176-177

Cenozoic eon, 48-49, 67

Charon (Pluto's moon), 168

Chemical oceanography, 54

Chemical sedimentation, 19

Chemistry

    elements, 5-7, 9

    rock, 15-17

Chesapeake Bay, 76

Chevron feature, 167

Chondrites, 176

Chondrules, 176

Cinder cone volcanoes, 32-33

Cirque glaciers, 40

Cirrocumulus clouds, 113-114

Cirrostratus clouds, 114

Cirrus clouds, 113

Clastic sedimentation, 19

Cleavage of minerals, 12, 18-19

Climactic differences, 108-109

Clouds

    definition of, 110

    formation of, 112

    humidity and, 110-112

    of Jupiter, 159-161

    precipitation and, 114-117

    summary of, 117-118

    types of, 112-115

    water vapor and, 110-111, 114-115, 117

Cloud-to-ground lightning, 130

Coal, 20, 49

Coasts. *See* Shoreline

Coccolithophores, 71

Cold front, 129

Colombian River Flood Lavas, 31

Color of minerals, 11

Coma (envelope around comet nucleus), 171

Comet nuclei, 171

Comets, 171-174

Complex craters, 143

Composite cone volcanoes, 32

Compressional (P) seismic waves, 24

Condensation, 110, 112

Condensation nuclei, 112

Conference on the Law of the Sea (1974), 56

Conglomerates (clastic sedimentary rocks), 19

Contact metamorphism, 17-18

Continental air mass, 128

Continental break, 67

Continental crust, 22

Continental drift theory, 21

Continental margins, 66-68

Continental rise, 67-68

Continental shelf, 67

Continental slope, 67

Contour lines, 144

Convection cells, 123-124

Convection oceanic currents, 28

Convergent plate boundaries, 26-27

Copernican model of solar system, 161

Copper, 10, 13

Coral reefs, 77

Coriolis effect, 82, 85-86, 119, 122-123, 125-126, 135

Coriolis force, 87, 160

Country rock, 17, 34, 45

Covalent bond, 7

Craters, 143, 148, 151

Crest of oceanic wave, 90-91, 93

Cretaceous period, 49

Crevasses, 39

Crinoids, 44

Crosscutting relationships principle, 45

Crystal habit, 10

Crystals and crystallography 7-9

C-type asteroids, 171

Cumulonimbus clouds, 113-114

Cumulus clouds, 113

Cup anemometer, 125

Curie temperature, 26

Currents, oceanic
    boundary, 84-85
    convection, 28
    Coriolis effect and, 85-86
    deep circulation patterns, 87
    Earth's rotation and, 87
    ebb, 95
    Ekman spiral and, 87
    equatorial, 83
    flood, 95
    Florida, 83
    geostrophic, 86-87
    Labrador, 83
    longshore, 73-74
    measuring, 84
    movement of water and, 82
    North Atlantic, 83-84
    North Pacific, 83-84
    rip, 97
    significance of, 85
    summary of, 88-89
    surface, 84
    surface circulation patterns, 82-87
    thermohaline, 87
    tidal, 95-97
    turbidity, 68
    undertow, 97
    upwelling and, 85-86

Cyanobacteria, 103

Cyclones, 122. See also Tornadoes

Cyclosilicates, 9

D

Darwin, Charles, 43-44, 108

Dead Sea, 57-58

Decay constant, 46

Deep circulation patterns of oceanic currents, 87

Deep zone of ocean, 61

Deimos (moon of Mars), 155-156

Deltas (river), 35, 76

Dendritic streams, 36

Density of water, 87-88

Deposition, 110

Desert pavement, 37

Detritus, 18-19

Devonian period, 48-49

Dew point, 111, 114

Diamonds, 10-11

Differentiation, 102

Dikes, 34

Dinosaur extinction, 49

Disconformity, 45

Distributaries, 76

Distributary channels, 35

Divergent plate boundaries, 25-26

Divides (topical highlands), 36

Doldrums (region of ocean), 82-83

Doppler, Christian, 134

Doppler radar, 133-134

Drift, beach, 73-74

Drumlins, 39

Dunes, sand, 37-39

Dust tail of comet, 172

Du Toit, Alexander, 21

E

Earth. *See also* Geology; Meteorology; Oceanography;
    Planetary science
        age of, 43
        crust of, 7, 22
        faults, 25, 28
        history of, 48
        interior of, 22-23
        lakes of, 57-58
        magnetic field of, 22, 26
        mantle of, 23, 28
        moon of, 150-153
        movement of, 22
        mysteries of, 1
        oceans of, 56-57
        rotation of, 85, 87, 95, 119, 146
        science, 1-2
        seas of, 57-58
        seasons of, 123, 164

Earthquakes, 23-25, 93

Earth science, 1-2. See also Geology; Meteorology;
    Oceanography; Planetary science

Earthy luster of minerals, 12

East Africa rift, 26

East Pacific Rise, 26

Ebb oceanic currents, 95

Ebb tides, 95-97

Echinoderms, 44

Ejecta, 143

Ejecta blanket, 143

Ekman spiral, 87

Electrons, 5-6

Electrostatic attraction, 170

Elements
        chemical, 5-7, 9
        in Earth's crust, 7
        native, 9

Elevation, 105-106, 112, 114-115, 144

Elysium Bulge, 154-155

Emergent coasts, 79-80

Emperor Seamount Chain, 70

Environments
        Mercury's, 149
        shoreline, 75-80

Eons, 48-49, 152

Epicenter of earthquake, 23

Epochs, 48

Equatorial Countercurrent, 82

Equatorial low region, 124

Equatorial oceanic currents, 83

Equilibrium of oceanic crust, 26-27

Eras, 48-49

Erosion
        of beaches, 78-79
        oceanic waves and, 94-95
        sapping and, 154
        shoreline, 78-79
        winds and, 38

Erratics (rocks moved by glaciers), 41

Eskimo mythology, 107

Estuaries, 76, 80, 97

Evaporation, 54, 60, 110-111, 114

Evaporites, 20

Evolution, theory of, 43-44

Extinction of dinosaurs, 49

Eye of hurricane, 134

Eye wall of hurricane, 134

F

Falling stones, 175

Faults, 25, 28, 68, 153

Faunal success principle, 45

Feldspar, 11

Felsic class of igneous rocks, 15-16

Ferrell cell, 124, 126

Fetch (distance wind is blowing), 92

Fire fountain, 31

Fish as resource, 61-62

Fission track dating, 47

Fissures, lava, 31

Fjord glaciers, 40

Flood basalts, 31

Flooding, 91

Flood oceanic currents, 95

Floodplain deposits, 35

Flood tides, 95-97

Florida Current, 83

Fluorite, 11

Fluorocarbons, 106

Fluorspar, 11

Fluvial forces, 34-36, 154

Flyby space mission, 144

Fog, 114

Folds, rock, 27

Foliated rock, 18

Foliation, 18

Fool's gold, 10

Footwall block, 25

Foraminifers, 71

Foreset bed of sand dunes, 37-38

Foreshore of beach, 75

Forked lightning, 130

Formation (rock stratigraphy), 47

Fossils, 44, 47, 49

Fractional crystallization, 17

Fracture of minerals, 12

Frequency of oceanic wave, 90

Fronts and storms, 122, 128-129

Fujita (F) scale, 132-133

Fujita, Theodore, 132

G

Galapagos Islands, 32, 70, 108

Galaxies, 146. *See also* Planetary science

Galileo, 159, 161-162, 173

Ganges River, 71

Ganymede, 162

Gas tail of comet, 172

Gelifluction, 41

Gemstone, 13, 16

Geology. *See also* Minerals; Plate tectonics; Rocks
    of Jupiter, 159

Geology (*continued*)
    marine, 54
    of Mars, 153-154
    of Mercury, 148
    of Moon, Earth's, 150-152
    of Neptune, 165-167
    processes
        aeolian, 36-39
        fluvial or water-modifying, 34-36, 154
        glacial, 39-41
        mass-wasting or gravitational, 41
        summary of, 41-42, 49-50
        volcanic, 30-34, 41
    of Saturn, 163-164
    of space rocks, 170-176
    time
        absolute age dating, 45-47
        age of Earth, 43
        relative age dating, 44-45
        summary of, 49-50
        time scale, 47-48
    of Uranus, 165-167
    of Venus, 150

Geostrophic oceanic currents, 86-87

Geostrophic winds, 122

Glacial moraines, 41

Glacial processes, 39-41

Glaciation process, 40-41

Glaciers, 39-40

Glaze (precipitation), 116

Global circulation and winds, 123-126

Gneissic banding, 18

Gold, 6

Gondwanaland, 21

Grabens, 150

Gradient pressure, 121

Grand Canyon, 39, 68

Granite, 14

Graupel, 116-117

Gravitational processes, 41

Gravity, law of, 148-149

Gravity oceanic waves, 91

Graywacke, 19

Great Lakes, 57-58

Great Red Spot, 159

Great Salt Lake, 57

Greenhouse effect, 106

Greenschist, 18
Groins (sand traps), 78-79
Gulf of Mexico, 56, 58
Gulf Stream, 83, 85
Guyot, 70
Gypsum, 10-11, 20
Gyres (current pattern), 83-84

H
Hadley cell, 124, 126
Hail, 116
Hair hygrometer, 111-112
Half-lives, 45-46
Halides, 10
Halite, 10, 13, 20
Haloclines, 61
Hardness of minerals, 10-11
Hawaiian island chain, 28, 32, 70, 74, 77
Heavy bombardment of celestial bodies, 151
Height of oceanic wave, 90-91
Helium, 102
Hematite, 10
Hermes asteroid, 171
Hexagonal crystals, 8-9
High-grade metamorphic rocks, 17
Himalayan Mountains, 27
HMS Challenger, 55
Hodges, Mrs. Hulitt, 175
Hubble Space Telescope, 153, 173
Hudson Bay, 56, 58
Humidity, 110-112
Hurricane Andrew, 94, 135-136
Hurricane Mitch, 136
Hurricanes, 134-136
Hydrogen, 6-7, 58, 102
Hydrogenetic deposits, 63
Hydrothermal deposits, 63

I
Ice cap, 40
Ice as geologic force, 40
Ice shelves, 40
Igneous rocks, 14-17
Impact basins, 143
Impact cratering, 142-143
Indian Ocean, 56
Inert argon, 104
Inner planets. *See* Terrestrial planets

Inshore of beach, 75
Intermediate class of igneous rocks, 15-16
International Hydrographic Organization, 56
International Ice Patrol commission, 55
Intertropical convergence zone, 83
Intracloud lightning, 130
Intrusive igneous rocks, 15
Invertebrates, 44
Ionic bond, 6-7
Ionosphere, 107
Ions, 6
Iron, 6, 104
Iron meteorites, 176
Island arcs, 27, 70
Isobars, 121-122
Isometric crystals, 8
Isotopes, 6, 46, 88

J
Japan, islands of, 70
Japan Trench, 70
Jetties, 78-79
Jovian planets
    description of, 141-142, 158
    Jupiter, 141-142, 158-162, 173
    Neptune, 141-142, 165-167
    Pluto, 141-142, 146, 167-168
    rings of, 163, 165
    Saturn, 141-142, 158, 162-165
    summary of, 168-169
    Uranus, 141-142, 165-167
Jupiter, 141-142, 158-162, 173
Jurassic period, 49

K
Kilauea, 32
Kuiper Belt, 142

L
Labrador Current, 83
Lahar, 30-31
Lakes, 57-58
Laminar water flows, 34
Lander space mission, 144
Lapilli, 32
Lateral continuity principle, 44
Laurasia, 21
Lavas, 30-34

Lead, 10

Leading edge of sand dune, 37

Length of oceanic wave, 91, 94

Levees, 35

Light

    albedo and, 165

    in seafloor, 65

    ultraviolet, 103

    waves, 104

Lightning, 130

Limestone, 13, 18, 20, 60, 104

Lithification, 19

Lithosphere, 22, 28

Lithospheric plates, 25-26, 154

Longshore oceanic currents, 73-74

Lowell, Percival, 153

Low-grade metamorphic rocks, 17

Lunar maria, 148

Luster of minerals, 12

Lyell, Charles, 43

M

Mafic class of igneous rocks, 15-16

Magma, 7, 14-15, 17, 26, 28, 34

Magnetic field of Earth, 22, 26

Magnetite, 10

Mantle of Earth, 23, 28

Mariana Trench, 56, 70

Marine biology, 54

Marine engineering, 54

Marine geology, 54

Maritime air mass, 128

Mars, 141-142, 153-156

Marshall-Ellis island chain, 28

Mars Rover, 145

Mass-wasting processes, 41

Matterhorn, 39

Mauna Loa, 32

Mediterranean Sea, 56

Mercury (planet), 142, 147-149

Mercury barometer, 120-121

Mesopause, 107

Mesosphere, 107

Mesozoic eon, 48-49

Metallic hydrogen, 159

Metamorphic rocks, 14, 17-18

Metamorphism, 17

Meteorites and meteors, 173-176

Meteorologists, 110-112, 126

Meteorology. *See also* Atmosphere; Clouds; Storms;
   Winds

    definition of, 101

    of Mars, 155

    of Mercury, 149

    precipitation and, 114-117

    of Venus, 150

    weather and, 110, 119, 122-123

Mid-Atlantic Ridge, 26, 69-70

Mid-oceanic ridges, 69-70

Midway Island group, 78

Millibars (mb), 120

Minerals. *See also* specific types

    cleavage of, 12, 18-19

    collecting, 12

    color of, 11

    crystallography and, 7-9

    definition of, 5-9

    economic value of, 12-13

    fracture of, 12

    groups of, 9-10

    hardness of, 10-11

    luster of, 12

    in ocean, 62-63

    placer, 62

    preferred orientation of, 18

    properties of, 10-12

    shape of, 10

    summary of, 13

Mississippian period, 49

Mississippi Delta, 35

Mist, 116

Mohs, Friedrich, 10

Mohs' Hardness Scale, 10-11

Mojave Desert, 37

Mollusks, 44

Monocline folds, 27

Monoclinic crystals, 8-9

Moons

    Earth's, 150-153

    Jupiter's, 161-162

    Mars's, 155-156

    Neptune's, 167

    planetary, 166

    Pluto's, 168

Moons (*continued*)
    Saturn's, 165
    tides and, 95-97
    Uranus's, 167
Moon National Monument, 31
Mountain glaciers, 40
Mount Etna, 32
Mount Fuji, 33
Mount Hood, 33
Mount Kea, 70
Mount Pelee, 31-32
Mount Rainier, 33
Mount Shasta, 33
Mount St. Helens, 33
Mount Vesuvius, 32
Mudflows, 30-31, 41
Mythology
    Eskimo, 107
    Roman, 148, 161-162

N
National Oceanic and Atmospheric Administration, 55
Native element, 9
Natural gas as resource, 62-63, 68
Natural selection, 43, 108
Nazca plate, 22, 26
Neap tides, 95-96
Near-Earth objects (NEOs), 171
Neosilicate, 9
Neptune, 141-142, 165-167
Neptunists, 43
Neutrons, 5-6
New Jersey shoreline, 79
Newton, Isaac, 148-149
Nile Delta, 35
Nimbostratus clouds, 113-114
Nitrogen, 59, 104
Nonclastic sedimentation, 19
Nonconformity, 45
Nonfoliated rock, 18
Normal fault, 25
North Atlantic Current, 83-84
North Pacific Current, 83-84
Nourishment, beach, 79
Nucleus of atom, 5
Nuée ardente, 31

O
Occluded front, 129
Oceanic crust, 22, 26-27
Oceanic trenches, 27, 70
Oceanography. *See also* Currents, oceanic; Oceans;
    Seafloor; Shoreline
    chemical, 54
    definition of, 53
    fields of, 54
    history of, 54-55
    physical, 54
    of Venus, 150
Oceans. *See also* Currents, oceanic; Oceanography;
    Seafloor; Shoreline; Tides; Waves, oceanic
    basin floor of, 68-69
    deep zone of, 61
    descriptions of, 56-57
    layered structure of, 60-61
    minerals in, 62-63
    origins of, 53-54
    pollution of, 63
    resources of, 61-63, 68
    salinity of, 57-60, 82, 88
    summary of, 63-64
    zones of, 60-61, 85
Octahedral mineral fragments, 12
Offshore of beach, 75
Ooze (seafloor sediment), 71
Orbital resonance, 162
Orbiter space mission, 144
Ordovician period, 48
Ore deposits, 10
Orientation of crystallographic axes, 8
Origin of the Species by Means of Natural Selection, The
    (Darwin), 43
Orthorhombic crystals, 8
Oscillatory motion, 90
Osmosis, 59
Outgassing, 53
Oxbow lakes, 35
Oxidation, 103-104
Oxides, 10, 103-104
Oxygen, 59, 102-104, 108
Ozone, 103

P

Pacific Ocean, 56, 69

Pacific Tsunami Warning System, 93

Pahoehoe lava, 30-31

Paleo-coasts, 80

Paleogene period, 49

Paleozoic eon, 48

Pangaea and Pangaea puzzle, 21, 49

Parabolic sand dunes, 38

Passive continental margin, 66

Pearly luster of minerals, 12

Pegmatitic igneous rock texture, 15

Pennsylvanian period, 49

Peridot, 16

Periodic table, 5-6

Period of oceanic wave, 90-91

Permafrost, 154-155

Petroleum as resource, 62-63, 68

Phaneritic igneous rock texture, 15

Phanerozoic eon, 48

Phenocrysts, 15

Philippines plate, 22

Phobos (moon of Mars), 155-156

Photosynthesis, 53, 59, 103

Phyllosilicates, 9

Physical oceanography, 54

Phytoplankton, 62

Piedmont glaciers, 40

Pillow lava, 30-31

Piloted space mission, 144

Pixels (picture elements), 144

Placer minerals, 62

Plagioclase, 11

Planetary science. *See also* Celestial bodies; Jovian
    planets; Terrestrial planets
        definition of, 141
        galaxies, 146
        impact cratering and, 142-143
        moons of planets, 166
        naming of planets' features and, 154
        seasons, 123, 164
        space probes and, 143-145, 165, 167
        summary of, 145
        universe, 146, 161

Planetesimal (small body that orbited Sun), 152

Planets. *See* Jovian planets; specific names;
    Terrestrial planets

Plate boundaries
        convergent, 26-27
        divergent, 25-26
        transform, 28

Plate tectonics
        continental drift theory, 21
        convergent plate boundaries, 26-27
        divergent plate boundaries, 25-26
        earthquakes and seismic energy, 23-25, 93
        Earth's interior, 22-23
        Earth's movement, 22
        summary of, 29
        transform plate boundaries, 28

Plunger oceanic waves, 93

Pluto, 141-142, 146, 167-168

Plutonic igneous rocks, 15

Plutonists, 43

Plutons, 34

Point bars, 35

Polar air mass, 128

Polar cells, 124, 126

Polar easterlies, 125

Polar high regions, 125

Polar molecules, 58

Pollution of ocean, 63

Porphyritic igneous rock texture, 15

Precambrian eon, 48

Precipitation, 7, 114-117

Preferred orientation of minerals, 18

Pressure
        air, 105-106, 119-121
        barometric, 119-121
        gradient, 121

Prevailing westerlies, 125

Primary (P) waves, 24

Principles of Geology (Lyell), 43

Protons, 5-6

Psychrometer, 111-112

Ptolemy, Claudius, 55

Pumice, 32

P waves, 24

Pycnocline zone of ocean, 61, 85

Pyrite, 10

Pyroclastic igneous rock texture, 15

Pyroclastic volcanic flows, 30-34

Q

Quartz, 11, 13, 74

R

Radioactive dating, 45-47
Radioactive half-life, 45-46
Radioactive isotopes, 46
Radiocarbon, 47
Radiometric age dating, 45-47
Rain, 116
Rain gauge, 116
Reefs, coral, 77
Reflectance spectroscopy, 144, 175
Refraction and oceanic waves, 73-74, 94-95
Regional metamorphism, 17-18
Regolith, 41
Relative age dating, 44-45
Relative humidity, 111
Reservoirs of cinder cone volcanoes, 32
Resources of ocean
        fish, 61-62
        natural gas, 62-63, 68
        petroleum, 62-63, 68
Retrograde motion, 149
Reverse fault, 25
Rhyolite, 16
Richter, Charles, 24
Richter scale, 24-25, 93
Rime, 116-117
Rings of jovian planets, 163, 165
Rio Grande rift, 26
Rip current or tide, 97
Rivers and river channels, 35-36, 71, 76
Roche limit, 155
Rock flour, 40
Rocks. *See also* specific types
        age of, 47
        chemistry of, 15-17
        cycle of, 14
        definition of, 14
        deformed, 27
        folds of, 27
        foliated and nonfoliated, 18
        igneous, 14-17
        metamorphic, 14, 17-18
        sedimentary, 14, 18-20
        space, 170-176
        summary of, 20
Rock stratigraphy, 47
Roman mythology, 148, 161-162

Rotation axis, 146
Rutherford, Ernest, 46

S

Saffir, Herbert, 135
Saffir-Simpson Hurricane Scale, 135-136
Salinity of oceans, 57-60, 82, 88
Saltation, 34
Salt marshes, 75-76
Sand. *See* Beaches
Sand bars, 35, 74, 76
Sand dunes, 37-39
Sandstone, 18-19
Sapping, 154
Sargasso Sea, 84
Sargassum seaweed, 84
Saturn, 141-142, 158, 162-165
Scarp, 153-154
Schist, 18
Schistosity, 18
Scoria, 32
SCUBA breathing apparatuses, 65
Sea arch, 78
Seafloor
        basin floor, 68-69
        continental margins, 66-68
        exploring, 65-66
        light in, 65
        mid-oceanic ridges, 69-70
        seamounts, 28, 66, 70
        sediment, 71
        summary of, 71-72
        trenches, 27, 70
Sea of Japan, 70
Seamounts, 28, 66, 70
Seas, 57-58
Seasons
        Earth's, 123, 164
        planetary, 164
Sea stacks, 78
Sea walls, 78-79
Seawater, 57-61, 82, 88
Seaweed, 77, 84
Sediment
        beach, 74
        definition of, 14
        land-based, 71

Sediment (*continued*)
    seafloor, 71
    settling of, 71
Sedimentary rocks, 14, 18-20
Seismology and seismic energy
    plate tectonics and, 23-25, 93
    sea waves, 91, 93-94
Shales, 19
Shape of minerals, 10
Shear (S) seismic waves, 24
Shepherd moons, 163
Shield volcanoes, 32-33
Shklovskii, Iosef, 155-156
Shoals, 77
Shoemaker-Levy 9 comet, 172-173
Shoreline
    emergent coasts, 79-80
    environments of, 75-78
    erosion of, 78-79
    features of, 73-75
    New Jersey, 79
    paleo-coasts, 80
    sand dunes and, 39
    submergent coasts, 79-80
    summary of, 80-81
    tides and, 79
    waves and, oceanic, 94
Silicates, 9
Silicon tetrahedron, 9
Sills, rock, 34
Siltstone, 19
Silurian period, 48-49
Simple craters, 143
Simpson, Bob, 135
Sinuous rille, 151
Sky. *See* Atmosphere
Slate, 18
Slatey cleavage, 18
Sleet, 116-117
Slip face slope of sand dunes, 37-38
Smokers (underwater vents of hot water), 63
SNC, 175
Snowline, 39
Snow and snowflakes, 116-117
Solar radiation, 83, 172
Solar system, 146, 161. *See also* Planetary science
Solar wind, 172

Sorosilicate, 9
South China Sea, 56
Southern Ocean, 56
Space probes, 143-145, 165, 167
Space rocks, 170-176
Specific humidity, 111
Spectrometer, 145
Spectroscope, 104
Spectroscopy, 104, 144, 175
Spillar oceanic waves, 93
Spits (ridges of sand), 74
Spreading center, 69
Spring tides, 95-96
Star sand dunes, 38
Stationary front, 129
Steno, Nicholas, 44
Stony-iron meteorites, 176
Stony meteorites, 176
Storms
    air masses and, 128-129
    fronts and, 122, 128-129
    hurricanes, 134-136
    solar radiation and, 83
    summary of, 136-137
    thunderstorms, 129-130
    tornadoes, 130-133
Straight rille, 151
Stratavolcano, 33
Stratigraphy, 44, 47
Stratocumulus clouds, 113-114
Stratopause, 106
Stratosphere, 106
Stratus clouds, 112-113
Streak plate, 11
Stream channels, 34-35
Striations, 40
Strike slip fault, 25
S-type asteroids, 171
Subduction zones, 27
Sublimation, 110, 154-155
Submarine canyon, 67-68
Submarine, making own, 66
Submergent coasts, 79-80
Subpolar low regions, 125
Subtropical high region, 123-124
Succession, 45
Sulfates, 10

Sulfides, 10

Sun

growing crystals in, 8

plantesimals orbiting, 152

tides and, 95-97

Surface circulation patterns of oceanic currents, 82-87

Surface-modifying processes

aeolian, 36-39

fluvial or water-modifying, 34-36, 154

glacial, 39-41

mass-wasting or gravitational, 41

volcanism, 30-34, 41

Surface oceanic currents, 84

Surface tension, 91

Surface seismic waves, 24

Surface zone, 60-61

Surf zone, 74

S waves, 24

Syncline folds, 27

T

Talc, 10-11

Talus (pile of sediments), 41

Tectonic activity and tectonism, 30, 66. *See also* Plate tectonics

Tectosilicate, 9

Telescopes, 151, 153, 162, 173

Temperature, 26, 110, 112

Terrace deposits, 35

Terrestrial planets

description of, 141-142, 146

Mars, 141-142, 153-156

Mercury, 142, 147-149

Moon of Earth, 150-153

summary of, 156-157

Venus, 141-142, 149-150

Tethys (extinct sea), 21

Tetragonal crystals, 8

Tharsis bulge, 154-155

Thermoclines, 61

Thermohaline oceanic currents, 87

Thermosphere, 107

Thrust fault, 25

Thunder, 130

Thunderstorms, 129-130

Tides

ebb, 95-97

flood, 95-97

Tides (*continued*)

generation of, 95

Moon and, 95-97

neap, 95-96

oceanic currents and, 79, 91, 95-97

rip, 97

shoreline and, 79

significance of, 95-96

spring, 95-96

summary of, 97-98

Sun and, 95-97

Till (unsorted sediment), 41

Time scale, geologic, 47-48

Time stratigraphy, 47

Titan (Saturn's moon), 165

Titanic (sinking of), 55

Tombolos, 74

Tomography, acoustic, 84

Topaz, 11

Topographic map, 144

Topset bed of sand dune, 37

Tornado Alley, 131

Tornadoes, 130-133

Tourmaline, 9

Trace precipitation, 116

Trade winds, 82

Transform faults, 28

Transform plate boundaries, 28

Transverse sand dunes, 38

Trellis (river drainage pattern), 36

Trenches, oceanic, 27, 70

Triassic period, 49

Tributaries of river, 36

Triclinic crystals, 8-9

Triton (Neptune's largest moon), 167

Tropical air mass, 128

Tropical depression, 134

Tropopause, 105

Troposphere, 105-106

Troughs

of isobars, 122

of oceanic waves, 90-91, 93

Tsunamis, 93-94

Turbidity oceanic currents, 68

Turbulent water flows, 34

Typhoons, 134

U

Ultramafic class of igneous rocks, 15-16
Ultraviolet light, 103
Unconformities, 45
Undertow, 97
Uniformitarianism, 43
Universe, 146, 161. *See also* Planetary science
Upwelling, 85-86
Uranus, 141-142, 165-167
U.S. Coast Survey, 55
U.S. Department of Charts and Instruments, 55
Ussher, James, 43
U.S. State Commission of Fish and Fisheries, 55
U.S. Weather Bureau, 55

V

Valles Marineris, 153, 155
Valley glaciers, 40
Vanes, weather, 125
Ventifact, 37
Venus, 141-142, 149-150
Vertebrates, 44
Vesicular igneous rock texture, 15
Vitreous luster of minerals, 12
Volcanic neck, 34
Volcanism and volcanoes, 15, 23, 25, 30-34, 41, 154
Vortex of tornado, 131
Voyager and Voyager 2 space probes, 165, 167

W

Wadati-Benioff Zones, 27
Wadati, Kiyoo, 27
Warm front, 129
Water. *See also* Lakes; Oceans; Rivers; Seas
    age of, 88
    in atmosphere, 105
    atoms in, 7, 58
    condensation and, 110, 112
    density of, 87-88
    deposition and, 110
    evaporation and, 54, 60, 110-111, 114
    on Mars, 154
    modifying force of, 34-36
    precipitation from, 7
    sublimation and, 110, 154-155
    surface tension of, 116
    unique properties of, 58

Water droplets, 111, 112, 115-116
Water-land interface, 73
Water-modifying forces, 34-36
Water vapor, 54, 105-106, 110-111, 114-115, 117
Wave-cut cliffs, 78
Wave-cut platforms, 78
Waves
    light, 104
    oceanic
        amplitude of, 90
        behavior of, 90
        capillary, 90-91
        consequences of, 94-95
        crest of, 90-91, 93
        erosion and, 94-95
        fetch, 92
        frequency of, 90
        gravity, 91
        height of, 90-91
        internal, creating, 92
        length of, 91, 94
        making, 91-92
        observing, 92
        parts of, 90-91
        period of, 90-91
        plunger, 93
        refraction and, 73-74, 94-95
        seismic sea waves, 91, 93-94
        shoreline and, 94
        spillar, 93
        tides and, 79, 91, 95-97
        trough of, 90-91, 93
        tsunamis, 93-94
        types of, 91-94
        wind-generated, 91-93
    seismic
        body, 24
        compressional (P), 24
        plate tectonics and, 23-25
        shear (S), 24
        surface, 24
    summary of, 97-98
Weather, 110, 119, 122-123. *See also* Atmosphere;
    Clouds; Storms; Winds
Wegener, Alfred, 21
Wentworth Scale, 19

Widmanstatten figures, 176
Winds
    air circulation and, 119
    air pressure and, 119-121
    cyclones and anticyclones, 122
    Earth's rotation and, 87
    erosion and, 38
    geostrophic, 122
    global circulation and, 123-126
    measuring, 125
    oceanic waves generated by, 91-93
    solar, 172
    summary of, 126-127
    weather and, 119
Wind tunnel, 38
Wrinkle ridges, 151

Y
Yangtze River, 71
Yardangs, 37
Yellow River, 71

Z
Zap pits, 142
Zinc, 10
Zones
    of beach, 75
    of destructive gravitational tidal forces, 155
    Jupiter, 160-161
    of ocean, 60-61, 85